# WAYS OF RE-THINKING

*Ways of Re-Thinking Literature* creates a unique platform where leading literary thinkers and practitioners provide a multiplicity of views into what literature is today.

The texts gathered in this extraordinary collection range from philosophy to poetry, to theater, to cognitive sciences, to art criticism, to fiction, and their authors rank amongst the most significant figures in their fields, in France, the United States, and the United Kingdom.

Topics covered include an assessment of the role of literary narratives in contemporary writing, new considerations on the novel, a redefinition of the "poetic" factor in poetry and life, and a discussion of how literature engages with contemporary forms of individuality.

Under the auspices of literary luminaries Hélène Cixous and the late John Ashbery, these new pieces of writing bring to light contributions by innovative and well-established authors from the English-speaking sphere, as well as never-before-translated prominent new voices in French theory.

Featuring original work from some of today's most influential authors, *Ways of Re-Thinking Literature* is an indispensable tool for anybody interested in the future and possibilities of literature as an endeavor for life, thought, and creativity.

With special cover artwork by Rita Ackermann, the volume includes contributions from Emily Apter, Philippe Artières, John Ashbery, Paul Audi, Dodie Bellamy, Tom Bishop, Hélène Cixous, Laurent Dubreuil, Tristan Garcia, Stathis Gourgouris, Donatien Grau, Boris Groys, Shelley Jackson, Wayne Koestenbaum, Camille Laurens, Vanessa Place, Maël Renouard, Peter Schjeldahl, Adam Thirlwell, and Camille de Toledo.

**Tom Bishop** is the Florence Lacaze Gould Professor of French, Professor of French and Comparative Literature at New York University (NYU), USA. For fifty years, he served as Chair of the Department of French at NYU and Director of the Center for French Civilization and Culture. Amongst his many publications are, *From the Left Bank: Reflections on the Modern French Theater and Novel* (1997) and *Pirandello and the French Theater* (1960, 1970).

**Donatien Grau** is a Guest Curator at the Getty Museum, Los Angeles, USA. He holds a *doctorat* in French and Comparative Literature from the Sorbonne, France, and a DPhil from the University of Oxford, UK. He was twice a Guest Researcher at the Getty Research Institute, Los Angeles; a Florence Lacaze Gould Lecturer, New York University; a Special Guest of French Studies, Cornell University; a Visiting Scholar, Stevanonich Institute for the Formation of Knowledge, University of Chicago; and a teaching fellow at the Sorbonne and École Normale Supérieure, Paris, France.

# WAYS OF RE-THINKING LITERATURE

*Edited by Tom Bishop and Donatien Grau*

Routledge
Taylor & Francis Group

LONDON AND NEW YORK

First published 2018
by Routledge
2 Park Square, Milton Park, Abingdon, Oxon OX14 4RN

and by Routledge
711 Third Avenue, New York, NY 10017

*Routledge is an imprint of the Taylor & Francis Group, an informa business*

*British Library Cataloguing-in-Publication Data*
A catalogue record for this book is available from the British Library

*Library of Congress Cataloging-in-Publication Data*
A catalog record has been requested for this book

ISBN: 978-1-138-67574-2 (hbk)
ISBN: 978-1-138-67575-9 (pbk)
ISBN: 978-1-315-56048-9 (ebk)

Typeset in Bembo
by Deanta Global Publishing Services, Chennai, India

Printed and bound in Great Britain by
TJ International Ltd, Padstow, Cornwall

# CONTENTS

# CONTRIBUTORS

**Emily Apter** is Professor of French and Comparative Literature and Chair of Comparative Literature at New York University. Her most recent books include: *Against World Literature: On the Politics of Untranslatability* (2013), *Dictionary of Untranslatables: A Philosophical Lexicon* (co-edited with Barbara Cassin, Jacques Lezra and Michael Wood, 2014), *The Translation Zone: A New Comparative Literature* (2006). A French translation of *The Translation Zone: A New Comparative Literature* was published in 2016 by Fayard in the series "Ouvertures", edited by Barbara Cassin and Alain Badiou. Together with Bruno Bosteels she co-edited Alain Badiou's *The Age of the Poets and Other Writings on Poetry and Prose* (Verso, 2014). Her most recent project is *Unexceptional Politics: On Obstruction, Impasse and the Impolitic* (Verso, 2017). She edits the book series *Translation/Transnation* for Princeton University Press.

**Philippe Artières** is a historian and writer. A Research Director at the French CRNS (National Center for Scientific Research), he is the author, co-author, or editor of a dozen books.

**John Ashbery**'s last collection of poems was *Commotion of the Birds* (Ecco/HarperCollins, 2016). A two-volume set of his collected translations from the French (prose and poetry) was published in 2014 (Farrar, Straus and Giroux). Active in various areas of the arts throughout his career, he served as executive editor of *Art News* and as art critic for *New York* magazine and *Newsweek*; he also exhibited his collages at Tibor de Nagy Gallery, New York. He received many honors and awards, including a Pulitzer Prize, two Guggenheim Fellowships, a MacArthur Fellowship, the Medal for Distinguished Contribution to American Letters from the National Book Foundation (2011), and a National Humanities Medal, presented by President Obama at the White House (2012). He died in September 2017 at the age of 90.

**Paul Audi** is a French philosopher living in Paris. For many years, he taught in several French academic institutions, as the University Paris-Val de Marne and the Catholic Institute of Paris (ICP). He is today a statutory member of the Center of Philosophy, Epistemology and Politics (PHILéPOL) at the University Sorbonne Paris Descartes. Author of some thirty books, most of them exploring the relations between ethics and aesthetics in the West during the modern period, he published recently *Le Pas gagné de l'amour* (Galilée, 2016) and *Analyse du sentiment intérieur* (Verdier, 2017).

**Dodie Bellamy** writes genre-bending works that focus on sexuality, politics, and narrative experimentation, challenging the distinctions between fiction, essay, and poetry. Her most recent collection is *When the Sick Rule the World* (Semiotext(e), 2015). Her reflections on the Occupy Oakland movement, "The Beating of Our Hearts," was published as a chapbook in conjunction with the 2014 Whitney Biennial. With Kevin Killian, she edited *Writers Who Love Too Much: New Narrative 1977–1997* (Nightboat Books, 2017).

**Tom Bishop** is the Florence Lacaze Gould Professor of French, Professor of French and Comparative Literature at New York University. Amongst many awards, he has been granted the Grand Prix de l'Académie française and a Fulbright Senior Research Scholarship. He is a Commandeur in France's Ordre de la Légion d'Honneur; Ordre des Arts et des Lettres; and Ordre national du Mérite. For fifty years, he served as chair of the department of French at NYU and Director of the Center for French Civilization and Culture. Amongst his publications are, *From the Left Bank: Reflections on the Modern French Theater and Novel* (New York University Press, 1997), *Le Passeur d'océan: carnets d'un ami américain* (Payot, 1989), and *Pirandello and the French Theater* (New York University Press, 1960, 1970).

**Hélène Cixous** was born in Algeria in 1937 to a Sephardic Algerian father and an Ashkenazi German mother. She moved to France in 1955, where she became Professor of English Literature. She created the experimental Université Paris VIII in 1968, and the first French doctoral program in Women's Studies in 1974. She is now Emeritus Professor and teaches at the Collège International de Philosophie. She has been distinguished with honorary degrees by many universities around the world, and her literary prizes include the Prix Médicis (1969), the Prix des Critiques for best theatrical work (1994), the Prix Marguerite Duras (2014), the Prix de la langue française (2014), and the Prix Marguerite Yourcenar (2016). She has been 'house playwright' at Ariane Mnouchkine's *Théâtre du Soleil* for more than thirty years. Translations of her work into a wide range of languages attest to the international recognition of her oeuvre. A writer who consistently breaks down the boundaries of genre (and of gender), she poses many intellectual challenges with her texts that are rooted in the practices of fiction, theory, and criticism, and yet depart from them.

**Laurent Dubreuil** is a Professor of Comparative Literature, Romance Studies and Cognitive Science at Cornell University in Ithaca, New York, and the IWLC

Senior International Professor of Transcultural Theory at Tsinghua University in Beijing. His books include, in English, *The Intellective Space* (2015), *The Refusal of Politics* (2016), and *Poetry and Mind* (2018), and, in French, *Pures fictions* (2013) and *Génération romantique* (2014).

**Tristan Garcia** is a philosopher and novelist. He is the author of a dozen books, encompassing fiction (*Hate: A Romance*, FSG, 2011), philosophy (*Form and Object: A Treatise on Things*, Edinburgh University Press, 2014) and essays (*We*, Edinburgh University Press, 2018).

**Stathis Gourgouris** is Professor of Classics, English, and Comparative Literature and Society at Columbia University and the author of *Dream Nation* (1996), *Does Literature Think?* (2003), *Lessons in Secular Criticism* (2013), and *Contingent Disorders* (2016, in Greek), as well as the editor of *Freud and Fundamentalism* (2009). His new book, *The Perils of the One: Lessons in Secular Criticism II*, is forthcoming in 2018.

**Donatien Grau** is a Guest Curator at the Getty Museum, Los Angeles. He holds a *doctorat* in French and Comparative Literature from the Sorbonne, and a DPhil from the University of Oxford. A contributing editor of *Flash Art International*, an editor-at-large of *Purple Fashion Magazine*, a member of the editorial boards of *Commentaire* and *La Règle du Jeu*, a co-editor of the book series "figures" with Grasset, he has been twice a guest researcher at the Getty Research Institute, Los Angeles; a Florence Lacaze Gould Lecturer, New York University; a Special Guest of French Studies, Cornell University; a Visiting Scholar, Stevanonich Institute for the Formation of Knowledge, University of Chicago; and a teaching fellow at the Sorbonne and Ecole Normale Supérieure. He is notably the author of *Tout contre Sainte-Beuve* (Grasset, 2013); *The Age of Creation* (Sternberg, 2013); *Néron en Occident* (Gallimard, 2015); *Le Roman romain* (Les Belles Lettres, 2017).

**Boris Groys** is Professor of Russian and Slavic Studies at New York University, Senior Research Fellow, Academy of Design, Karlsruhe, Germany, and Professor of the European Graduate School, Saas Fee, Switzerland. Amongst his many publications are, *Particular Cases* (Sternberg Press, 2016); In the Flow (Verso, 2016); *On the New* (Verso, 2014); *Under Suspicion: A Phenomenology of Media* (Columbia University Press, 2012).

**Shelley Jackson** is the author of the forthcoming novel *Riddance*. Previous works include *Half Life* (2006) and *The Melancholy of Anatomy* (2002); hypertexts such as *Patchwork Girl* (1995) and *My Body* (1997); and several children's books, most recently *Mimi's Dada Catifesto* (2010). Her work has appeared in journals including *Conjunctions, The Paris Review, McSweeney's*, and *Cabinet Magazine*. The recipient of a Howard Foundation Prize and the 2006 James Tiptree Jr Award, she is also known for her projects SNOW and SKIN: a story published in tattoos on 2095 volunteers, one word at a time.

**Wayne Koestenbaum** has published eighteen books of poetry, criticism, and fiction, including *Notes on Glaze* (2016), *The Pink Trance Notebooks* (2015), *My 1980s and Other Essays* (2013), *Hotel Theory* (2007), *Best-Selling Jewish Porn Films* (2006), *Andy Warhol* (2001), *Humiliation* (2011), *Jackie Under My Skin* (1995), and *The Queen's Throat* (1993, a National Book Critics Circle Award finalist). He has had solo exhibitions of his paintings at White Columns, New York, 356 Mission, Los Angeles, and the University of Kentucky Art Museum. His first piano/vocal record, *Lounge Act*, was issued by Ugly Duckling Presse Records in 2017. He is Distinguished Professor of English, Comparative Literature, and French at the CUNY Graduate Center in New York City.

**Camille Laurens** is an award-winning French novelist and essayist living in Paris. In 2000, she received the Prix Femina, one of France's most prestigious literary prizes, for *Dans ces bras-là*, which was published in the United States as *In His Arms* in 2004. In 2017, Other Press released the translation of *Celle que vous croyez* (Gallimard, 2016) as *Who You Think I Am*, and in 2018 it will publish the English translation of the author's most recent non-fiction, *La petite danseuse de quatorze ans*.

**Vanessa Place** is a writer, poet and lawyer. She was the first poet to perform as part of the Whitney Biennial; a content advisory was posted. Her exhibition work has appeared at MAK Center/Schindler House; Denver Museum of Contemporary Art; the Boulder Museum of Contemporary Art; The Power Plant, Toronto; the Broad Museum, East Lansing; Various Small Fires, Los Angeles; and Cage 83 Gallery, New York. Selected recent performance venues include Museum of Modern Art, New York; Museum of Contemporary Art, Los Angeles; Detroit Museum of Contemporary Art; Mestno Musej, Ljubljana; Swiss Institute, New York; the Kitchen, New York; Andre Bely Center, St. Petersburg, Russia; Kunstverein, Cologne; Whitechapel Gallery, London; Frye Art Museum, Seattle; the Sorbonne; and De Young Museum, San Francisco. Her books include *Boycott* (2013); *Statement of Facts* (2010); *La Medusa* (2008); *Dies: A Sentence* (2005); *The Guilt Project: Rape, Morality, and Law* (2010); *Notes on Conceptualisms* (2009, with Robert Fitterman), her translations from the French of *Guantanamo* by Frank Smith (2014) and Image-Material by Dominique Peysson (2016), and her art-audio book, *Last Words* (2015). Place also works as a critic and criminal defense attorney specializing in sex offenses.

**Maël Renouard** is a writer, philosopher, and translator. A laureate of the Prix Décembre in 2013 for *La Réforme de l'opéra de Pékin*, he is also the author of *Fragments of an Infinite Memory* (NYRB, 2018, first edition published in French in 2016).

**Peter Schjeldahl** was born in Fargo, North Dakota, in 1942, and grew up in small towns in Minnesota. He attended Carleton College and the New School. From 1961 to 1964, he worked as a reporter for newspapers in Minnesota, Iowa, and New Jersey. Beginning in 1962, he participated in the New York poetry world. He authored five books of poems. He has been a staff writer at *The New Yorker* since

1998 and is the magazine's art critic. He came to *The New Yorker* from *The Village Voice*, where he was the art critic from 1990 to 1998. Previously, he had written frequently for the *New York Times's* Arts and Leisure section. His writing has also appeared in *Artforum*, *Art in America*, the *New York Times Magazine*, *Vogue*, and *Vanity Fair*. Schjeldahl has received the Clark Prize for Excellence in Arts Writing from the Sterling and Francine Clark Institute; the Frank Jewett Mather Award from the College Art Association, for excellence in art criticism; the Howard Vursell Memorial Award from the American Academy of Arts and Letters, for "recent prose that merits recognition for the quality of its style;" and a Guggenheim Fellowship. He is the author of four books of criticism, including *The Hydrogen Jukebox: Selected Writings* (1991). And *Let's See: Writings on Art from The New Yorker* (2008).

**Adam Thirlwell**, born in London in 1978, is the author of three novels – *Politics* (2003), *The Escape* (2009), and *Lurid & Cute* (2015); a novella, *Kapow!* (2012), and *Multiples* (2013), a project with international novels. His work has been translated into 30 languages. He is the winner of a Somerset Maugham Award; the EM Forster Award from the American Academy of Arts and Letters; and has twice been chosen as one of *Granta*'s Best of Young British Novelists. He is the London editor of the *Paris Review*.

**Camille de Toledo** (CHTO) is a fiction writer, theoretician, and artist of Jewish descent living in Berlin. He studied literature, law, and history in Paris, and continued his studies in London, and then at the Tisch School of the Arts in New York. In 2004, he obtained a grant from the Villa Médicis in Rome. In 2008, he founded the European Society of Authors (www.seua.org), in order to promote the paradigm of "translation-as-language". Since 2012, Toledo has been working on extended forms of writing under the acronym CHTO, which he describes as "spatial narratives" or "material narratives" (www.mitteleuropa.me). Resulting projects include *The Fall of Fukuyama* (2013), an opera with the Orchestre Philharmonique de Radio France, and, in 2015, at Leipzig Contemporary Art Center, Halle 14, the "Potential exhibition", "History Reloaded" and "Europa – Eutopia". Among his books are, *Lives and Death of American Terrorist* and *The Inversion of Hieronymus Bosch* (Gallimard – Verticales, 2004, 2007), his *European Trilogy* (Le Seuil, 2009, 2010, 2014), and his new novel, *The Book of Hunger and Thirst*, (Gallimard, 2017), a world-fiction whose main character is the book itself. His first graphic novel, *Herzl: A European Story*, will be published by Denoël Graphics in 2018. Since 2016, Toledo's research on vertigo (contemporary readings) has been presented in an ongoing seminar at the Maison de la Poésie de Paris.

# ACKNOWLEDGMENTS

Special thanks to Peter Behrman de Sinéty for his contribution to the editorial process.

Philippe Artières' essay was translated from the French by Pedro Rodríguez.

Paul Audi's essay was translated from the French by Dafydd Edward Hughes.

A slightly different version of the first four paragraphs of Dodie Bellamy's essay was published under the title "Ephemeral" in the San Francisco Museum of Modern Art's online journal *Open Space,* November 9, 2015.

Hélène Cixous' text was translated from the French by Eric Prenowitz. *Ayaï* d'Hélène Cixous, copyright © Editions Galilée, 2013.

Camille Laurens' essay was translated from the French by Tom Bishop.

Maël Renouard's essay was translated from the French by Peter Behrman de Sinéty.

A version of Adam Thirlwell's essay was first published in *Letras Libres* in 2015.

John Ashbery's contribution: "Golden Discount", copyright © 2017 by John Ashbery. All rights reserved. Used by arrangement with Georges Borchardt, Inc.

Peter Schjeldahl's essay, Frank O'Hara, "The Day Lady Died", was taken from *Lunch Poems.* Copyright © 1954 by Frank O'Hara. Reprinted with the permission of The Permissions Company, Inc., on behalf of City Lights Books, www.citylights.com.

Heiner Müller's poems are published in Stathis Gourgouris' essay with permission from Suhrkamp Verlag. Copyright © Suhrkamp Verlag Berlin. All rights reserved.

# INTRODUCTION

## Tom Bishop and Donatien Grau

After the age of theory, after the disarray of history, after the end of Communism as a system, in the age of global economy, and of terrorism, how is one to "Re-Think Literature"? Post-colonialism is a methodological given; gender equality, a given as well, or at least it should be. Minorities matter: the Western world has to adapt with our time of "provincialization" (Homi H. Bhabha) of the West, of advanced capitalism, and of the Internet's rhizomatic web.

Such was our premise when organizing the international conference "Re-Thinking Literature", at New York University's Center for French Civilization and Culture (September 18–21, 2013). The purpose of the conference was also rooted in the history of the Center and of NYU's Department of French, which have played a major role in finding new ways of making and thinking literature over the last sixty years. The Center has fostered French-American relations, on topics related to the philosophical and literary worlds, and in connecting them to the world at large of politics, history, geography, and the visual arts. This was a crucial part of our methodology. For three days, over twenty speakers delivered readings, papers, performances, on a wide range of topics. This conference thus connected with the great history of French-American intellectual, artistic, and literary dialogue: much thought produced in the last sixty years has brought together the work of figures on both sides of the Atlantic Ocean. Our goal was to perpetuate this dynamic.

The invitation our contributors had been offered was simple – and yet challenging: they were invited to "re-think literature", to offer some new ground on which the audience could experience new forms of simultaneously thinking and making literature; new ways of engaging with this two-hundred-year-old modern concept of "literature", which accompanied the genesis and the growth of Western modernity from the early nineteenth century until now.

This book stems from that conference, from this imperative to re-think literature in a day and age that is so vastly different from the moment when literature itself was first conceived as a model of thought. In this book we brought together authors coming from worlds that often do not connect to each other. They were to re-think literature, together, to engage with the underlying content of the material to which they devote their work and their lives. Theorists, writers, poets, critics, historians, scholars of cognitive sciences, are gathered in this book to discuss aspects of literature itself, and make a case for aspects they identify as being of high relevance. Most of the authors included have, so to speak, dual citizenship: they are at the same time authors and thinkers. It is an underlying claim of this project that, in our time of late modernity, there is no literature which does not consider its own positioning in the world, and there is no relevant literary thought whose form does not somehow manifest literature itself.

## What is literature?

Literature is commonly considered either a concept or a reality. When a concept, it is the object of theoretical and historical debates, which tend to move away from the experience of the author and of the reader. When a reality, it is straightforwardly an object of experience, and not a matter of thought. Both conceptions have different audiences, the one being scholarly and intellectual, the other being known as "the general reader". The gap between these two conceptions and their audiences is rarely bridged.

The situation in which this gap is bridged is most often a body of work: a singular action, a creation by an individual, which can be a matrix for theory as well as a creative manifestation of its own. This is the stuff of masterpieces. But literature as a material for experience is not perceived according to the same principles as literature as a material for thought. And yet many authors have considered precisely the very nature of literary experience, while placing it in the perspective of thought. They have produced porous forms, which bring together narratives, poetry, the self, into literature, and they find themselves in the laboratory of literature.

For this project, authors were not simply invited to produce literature or to reflect on literature: they were invited to think and produce literature simultaneously. They were re-thinking literature while making it at the same time, formally as well as in terms of content.

The authors had total freedom to define their own way of re-thinking literature: their take could be personal, poetic, methodological, theoretical, critical; they could use a subject, or think freely. They could write a poem, an essay, a philosophical commentary, a historical note of contemporary relevance. The ways literature was to be re-thought are many: and only by acknowledging these many ways was it possible somehow to fulfill that purpose. Pluralism allows to read better the inherent rules that govern the creative structure through times and cultures – as Nelson Goodman reads art in *Ways of Worldmaking*.

In this book, readers will find many ways of re-thinking literature. There is not one definitive way of thinking any topic, let alone such an important one in our culture, and certainly not of thinking and producing it at the same time. This book only provides a starting point for a much wider, ceaseless, enterprise: re-assessing the concept and the reality of literature, and considering this concept and this reality as connected and tied to the present. Literature is re-thought locally and globally at the same time, and this collection bears witness to these attempts.

In line with the mission and history of the Center, and perpetuating the dialogue between the United States and France, contributors come mostly from these two countries. Authors were chosen for the originality of their thinking and of their work, for the importance of their contributions, across a wide range of disciplines. For some French authors, it is their first text published in English. They were also chosen for the hybridity of their work, and the combination of the methodologies of thought and the pragmatics of making, between philosophy, human sciences, poetry, criticism, and literary writing.

## In this book

In this book, readers will hear the voices of contributors ranging from John Ashbery to Hélène Cixous. Over the last sixty years, the expansion of philosophy, history, anthropology, sociology, semiology, psychology has found a particularly rich field of action in literature. Every single consistent thinker and practitioner of the human sciences has somehow engaged with literature, and a literary text of some kind. This book aims to provide a sense of this development. Literature, "the great foreigner" ("la grande étrangère") as Michel Foucault called it, was an enigma for knowledge. This involvement of thinkers in literature is tied to the development of a form of writing that would include philosophical reflection as well as poetic, mythical, theatrical manifestations. Hélène Cixous stands at the forefront of this form of writing.

On the other side of that lineage stands metaphysical poetry, consistently self-reflective, taking in the world of thought while existing in its own sphere, deeply rooted in sensations, while remaining highly intellectual. John Ashbery is widely acknowledged to be the preeminent figure of this form of meditative, philosophical poetry.

The voices the reader will hear in this book relate to both sides: they provide the sense of an "archipelago" (Edouard Glissant) of ways of re-thinking literature: literary initiatives no longer belong to a unified continent, nor are they isolated islands, but they result from the natural association of separate but connected islands which makes a new whole.

The structure of this book is divided in four thematic archipelagos of texts, which account for major issues of the present: the first one brings together assessments and analyses of narratives of literature, where authors discuss situations of literature, from the avant-garde (Tom Bishop), to the conception of life (Emily Apter), to the power of literature (Philippe Artières), ending with an attempt toward a literary definition of literature (Donatien Grau). The second part is devoted to the novel, with contributions by Boris Groys, comparing the art installation and the novel; by Adam Thirlwell, proposing a genealogy of new novels; by Tristan Garcia, engaging with the relation between the novel and religion.

In the third part, authors engage with the relation between literature and the poetic: Peter Schjeldahl examines the "varieties of the literary experience"; Laurent Dubreuil, the cognitive structures of the poetic experience; Stathis Gourgouris, the relationship between the body and the myth; Paul Audi offers an entry into aesth/ethics.

The fourth and last part of the book provides views into the way literature deals with contemporary subjectivity: Camille Laurens analyzes the process of feeling; Dodie Bellamy defines hoarding as a form of writing; Wayne Koestenbaum dissects the personal sensation of asemic literature; Shelley Jackson dramatizes literature as a "vocational school for ghost-speakers and hearing-mouth children"; Maël Renouard describes literary life with the Internet; Camille de Toledo's explains existence in a time of "fictional habitation", and Vanessa Place personal literary destiny.

The formats and themes are varied. Each of them is an island within an archipelago – a part of the book – within a larger archipelago, this book, and the many ways of re-thinking literature. Literature is to be thought and made in a pluralistic perspective, but these many experiments all involve literature in itself. Each of these contributions is a reflection of what literature can be, and how it can be created. We hope that readers will find material to explore all these islands and to sense the great human thread that unites the archipelagos of literature.

# PRELUDE

*John Ashbery*

Golden Discount

Turn the bird over,
let the juice drop.
I caught up with him at I don't know for sure,
the other young ones.

What with the abundance of false leads,
only because it's taken so much time
come look at my feet.

I don't want to do this.
We asked him to give a speech
near the toilet factory
the California governor said.

The American bear decorated their faces
with potato prints.
Possibly it hit you,
videotaping.

What are some of the considerations?
If inmates are not clawed
and still eat the fish.

In white linen
including but not necessarily limited to

but that was last week
twenty years ago.

A common side effect.
They had their own receivership
like Tennyson's Maude.

It's too bad of you!
On the blink
make a million of dollars.
Another manhattan,
another eggroll.
Cereal isn't just for eating in the kitchen
not any more.

It's too late. That's for
an important person:
something to sit on
and teach me not to be so lazy,
sort of.
Make it crumble.

# PART I
# Literary narratives

# 1

# THE DISAPPEARING AVANT-GARDE

*Tom Bishop*

What happened to the avant-garde? Omnipresent not long ago, it is hard to find today. Has the avant-garde, the spirit of avant-garde, disappeared or perhaps it is merely hibernating? For much of the twentieth century, literature was profoundly influenced by the inventions, innovations, and discoveries of avant-garde movements, more at some times than others, more in some countries than others, but always present. And usually greatly influenced by avant-garde thrusts in the art world and at times by music. Much of the most interesting, certainly of the most exciting artistic creations during a significant part of the twentieth century were either part of the avant-garde movements of the time or were directly influenced by them.

Avant-garde movements tend to appear and, when successful, remain for a period of time and then be followed either by a period of absorption into the mainstream, or, when unsuccessful, by a period of reaction against. Both phenomena are cyclic, but the strength and duration of the cycles varies greatly; in the twentieth century, avant-garde movements tended to be strong and to remain active for a relatively long time so that one can reasonably think of it as a century of avant-garde. Or perhaps, to be more precise, that was true for about three-quarters of the century or perhaps even four-fifths of it, but in the final years of the twentieth century and these early ones of the twenty-first, the avant-garde seems, on the whole, remarkably silent.

So, whatever *did* happen to the avant-garde? That is a vast question, and this essay will attempt to deal with it by referring to the avant-garde in the theater today, and principally, though not exclusively, to the French theater. As in all forms of contemporary artistic expression, the avant-garde is all-present in the theater and notably in France—a country which has shown itself particularly hospitable to new forms of theatricality. In fact, since the end of the nineteenth century the French theater has been witness to a striking series of avant-garde movements which provided the principal thrust for the renewal of the establishment theater.

So much has been written about the avant-garde that the very expression has become suspect. It is difficult to pin it down because a universal definition applicable to all art forms and to all eras seems impossible. For some, the idea of the avant-garde is limited to what is daring—even though today "daring" applies only to the work whereas, during the Belle Époque and even afterwards, it applied also (and often principally) to the personal behavior of the artist who tried to shock the middle class, "épater les bourgeois." Ubu's "Merdre" defied acceptable stage discourse but some deliberately outrageous public behavior could be equally shocking and provocative. Perhaps the most celebrated incitement to an entire generation's general avant-garde esthetic was Sergei Diaghilev's quasi-order to Jean Cocteau, "Étonne-moi," "Astonish me" (Never mind that Diaghilev, busy talking with Vaslav Nijinsky while crossing the Place de la Concorde during World War I, was being pestered by the very young but already very demanding-of-attention Cocteau, and threw out his challenge to shut the young man up—at least temporarily). But Cocteau did in fact elevate the injunction to astonish to the cornerstone of his lifelong ambition to be an avant-garde artist; he in fact succeeded in becoming one for more than a decade, but not beyond.

The call to astonish, which also inspired many other writers and plastic artists of the twenties, could, of course, lead to trendiness and the avant-garde *has* been compared to fashion as if the spirit of the avant-garde were somehow linked to the psychology of the high fashion industry. In 1923, the great director Charles Dullin touched on an important aspect of the avant-garde when he stressed the nature of the audience: In the theater, as in all the arts, there are those who can see and those who are born blind. The latter require an entire lifetime to get used to great things and it is only after having heard it said over and over for fifty years that something is beautiful that they yield to the judgment of others.[1]

How can one hope to find a global definition when it is not even easy to say what the avant-garde is at any one time in any one field? It may be more fruitful to approach the problem negatively by considering that the essence of the avant-garde is opposed to the essence of what is currently accepted, to the establishment, to even the best of the establishment, *especially* to the best. Keeping in mind both the past and the present, the avant-garde—in theater, novel, or poetry, in ballet, music or painting—represents above all a reaction against the established forms in each of these fields. These reactions take different shapes in different eras and might have nothing more in common than their opposition to the established order. If for instance the current—and therefore, for the experimentalist, already degenerating—mode of literary expression is realism, then the avant-garde will tend to be anti-realist. If, on the other hand, it is symbolism, which, approaching its zenith, becomes formulaic and arbitrary and begins to lose contact with the artistic aspirations of a younger generation, then the avant-garde will be anti-symbolist.

The avant-garde artist is a revolutionary who wages a continuous minority struggle against the artistic forms generally appreciated by others. But these "others" are not the easily satisfied public of boulevard theater or of pulp fiction; rather the avant-garde writer takes issue with literate writers who attract a large, literate public. For example, the theater of a Samuel Beckett or a Jean Genet does not stand in opposition to the light entertainments of a Marcel Achard but rather to the intellectual plays of Jean Anouilh or Jean Giraudoux. It is only in this manner that the military metaphor inherent in the expression "avant-garde" makes sense. The small advance guard of an army prepares the terrain for the main body of troops; similarly, avant-garde writers, when they are successful, show the way not for mere commercialism but for those serious writers to come who will later command a large public.

But that does not mean that the avant-garde, when it exists, necessarily embodies what is most substantive in an art form. By its very nature, it is an esthetic-in-the-making rather than one already constituted, a "becoming" with which not everyone, even among the most refined critics, feels comfortable. Thus, for example, in 1971, at the height of *Tel Quel* and deconstruction, Roland Barthes was reticent, even demurred vis-à-vis the avant-garde of the absurd; only Bertolt Brecht's political theater could find favor in his eyes. Barthes himself described his theoretical position candidly, perhaps not realizing its surprising weakness: "my own theoretical position is to be in the rear-guard of the avant-garde" he wrote ("ma proposition théorique est d'être à l'arrière-garde de l'avant-garde")."[2] Antoine Compagnon was quite right in including Barthes among his "anti-moderns."

It was Eugène Ionesco who best described the avant-garde phenomenon:

> While most writers, artists, and thinkers believe they belong to their time, the revolutionary playwright feels he is running counter to his time. As a matter of fact, thinkers, artists, and so on, after a certain time only make use of ossified forms; they feel they are becoming more and more firmly established in some ideological, artistic, or social order which to them seems up to date but which in fact is already tottering and yawning with unsuspected cracks. By the very force of circumstances any system, the moment it is established, is already outworn. As soon as a form of expression becomes recognized, it is already out of date. A thing once spoken is already dead, reality lies somewhere beyond it and the thought has become petrified, so to speak. A manner of speaking—and therefore a manner of being—once imposed, or simply accepted, is already unacceptable. An avant-garde man is like an enemy inside a city he is bent on destroying, against which he rebels; for like any system of government, an established form of expression is also a form of oppression. The avant-garde man is the opponent of an existing system. He is a critic of, and not an apologist for, what exists now. It is easy to criticize the past particularly when the prevailing regime is tolerant and encourages you to do it; but this is only to sanctify ossification and kowtow to tyranny or convention.[3]

What then happens to the avant-garde once it exists? It becomes necessarily subject to the laws of artistic evolution. An avant-garde can never long remain an avant-garde since it defines itself in relationship to the current establishment which, itself, changes constantly. Thus, it is either rejected or absorbed. If an avant-garde fails (and that is the fate of most), it generally disappears without leaving any trace. But if it manages to impose itself, it eventually changes the current "establishment" or accepted forms. Its influence varies with circumstances: it might be limited to some new techniques or it might be much more extensive, as was the case for surrealism, for instance, which imposed a new esthetic with far-reaching implications, all the way down to advertising.

The very expression "avant-garde" is necessarily restricted to relatively few writers or artists who, at least at first, have only a limited influence. It is a minority thrust that cannot enter the mainstream without ceasing to be experimental. When an avant-garde movement becomes fashionable, its revolutionary value is already spent. At that point, having attained its goal of reform, the avant-garde becomes part of the establishment; it will ultimately inspire new avant-gardes which will rise to oppose the "tyranny" that it has itself become, in a perpetual cyclical movement.

Not so very long ago, during that extraordinary explosion of creative theatrical innovation in the 1950s, the very notion of the avant-garde, so much a part of the esthetics of French art in all its varied forms since the middle of the nineteenth century, finally triumphed in the theater with Ionesco, Beckett, Genet, and Arthur Adamov. *La Cantatrice chauve (The Bald Soprano)* in 1950, followed immediately by *Les Chaises (The Chairs), En attendant Godot*, and the dazzling theatricality of Genet's plays, and eventually numerous other dramatists writing in French and subsequently in various languages throughout Europe and the Americas, radically changed theater, first in France and soon throughout the Western world. This was an iconoclastic avant-garde, one which sought to change the rules of the game, to radicalize theatricality, to do away with what was left of realistic techniques after half a century of brilliant anti-realist reactions against the successful fourth-wall realist brainwashing initiated and exemplified by André Antoine and his Théâtre Libre in the 1890s—itself an avant-garde in its time—and a wildly successful one!

And this *new theater* was an immensely successful avant-garde. Word went out from the little Left Bank playhouses that new concepts of theatricality were downgrading the mainstays of even the best of the playwrights of the time—of Jean-Paul Sartre, Albert Camus, Henry de Montherlant, Jean Anouilh—namely, plot, character, psychology, coherent stories. The new playwrights did not offer a common vision; what united them to some extent though was their opposition to the status quo. Soon they were being performed in larger, more important theaters, like the Odéon and eventually the Comédie Française, and became *the* playwrights of the fifties and sixties. It is rare for an avant-garde to impose itself so thoroughly and for the experimentalists in revolt quickly to become the established figures of an art form. But that is, astonishingly, what happened with what came to be known, for better or for worse, as the "theater of the absurd."[4]

Serious playwrights could legitimately propose that one could no longer write theater as before. Obviously, some dramatists *did* continue to write theater as before, just as many twentieth century novelists continued to produce good or bad nineteenth century novels as if James Joyce, Franz Kafka, Virginia Woolf, Samuel Beckett, Jorge Luis Borges, and the *nouveau roman* had never existed. But for those who thought seriously about the stage, the Parisian avant-garde of the 1950s had shattered the mold and made it impossible to go back to even the *best* of former models. But it also revealed a new, serious problem.

Ionesco, in his brilliant definition of the avant-garde, had warned that as soon as an avant-garde becomes so successful as to be the new establishment, it necessarily engenders its own reaction, another avant-garde which, in turn, seeks to destroy and replace it. However, following its fifteen or twenty years of undisputed triumph, the avant-garde of the absurd, yielded not to new writing but, in France at least, rather to the reign of the director.

To write as before after Ioneso was difficult, after Beckett, impossible. The towering figures, Beckett, Ionesco, Genet, remained; others faded or disappeared. A few important playwrights, like Fernando Arrabal and Michel Vinaver, continue right to the present time creating absurdist-related yet highly idiosyncratic works. If no powerful group emerged to take their place; some splendid writers did turn to the stage but at no point formed anything resembling an avant-garde movement. Among the best of these, in France, were Nathalie Sarraute, Marguerite Duras, Copi, Hélène Cixous, Valère Novarina, followed by Xavier Durringer, Bernard-Marie Koltès, Philippe Minyana, Yasmina Reza.

The only "movement" to speak of was the brief period of success in the seventies and eighties of the "théâtre du quotidien." It was influenced by several brilliant German and Austrian playwrights, notably Franz Xaver Kroetz, Peter Handke, and Botho Strauss, several French authors, especially Michel Deutsch and Jean-Pierre Wenzel, both working in Strasbourg, and later the very talented Parisian Tilly (no first name, like Copi and Brazilian soccer players). These dramatists refocused attention, however briefly, on the text and with it, on the preeminence of the dramatist. They dealt with the things of everyday life, especially in the lives of simple, inarticulate people, thus implying a social critique while eschewing Brechtian didacticism. Most notably, the *théâtre du quotidien* is the first important movement on the French stage since 1900 to go against the almost continuous, century-long reaction against theatrical realism or, against what one critic has called, the flight from naturalism.[5] If this new movement, late in the century did not revert to truly outmoded, nineteenth century forms of theatricality, it certainly did not either point to a new, experimental direction and it did not herald some new avant-garde.

But, of course, it is doubtful whether, towards the end of the twentieth century, a theatrical avant-garde was still even possible in France. Many important elements conspired against it. Strangely enough, one of these was the accession to the Ministry of Culture in 1981 of Jack Lang, a long-time enthusiast of the avant-garde in all its manifestations and especially in the theater. It had after all been Lang who had created the seminal Nancy Theater Festival of New Theater in the seventies. Lang obtained a commitment from President François Mitterrand for an unheard-of 1 percent of the country's budget for his ministry. Culture and the arts had never had it so good!

Lang gave strong support to the growing list of state supported theaters in Paris and accelerated enormously the process of decentralization that brought important companies to the rest of France. To run these many enterprises, ranging in size and importance from modest provincial cities to the Comédie Française, Lang's Ministry of Culture selected talented, innovative directors like Antoine Vitez, Patrice Chéreau, Jean-Pierre Vincent, Jean Jourdheuil, Jacques Lassalle, Marcel Maréchal, Bernard Sobel, Joël Jouanneau, Georges Lavaudant and others.

Together with directors who had already made their reputation earlier—Roger Planchon, Jean-Louis Barrault, Peter Brook, Ariane Mnouchkine—they brought a lively new spirit to the theaters of France. But institutionalizing innovative creators does not necessarily make for innovative institutions—if such a notion is even conceivable. Meanwhile, important foreign influences had come to play crucial roles in introducing startling theatricality, almost always at the expense of text. Following the initial, extraordinary impact of Jerzy Grotowski and Judith Malina and Julian Beck's Living Theater, the French public was much taken by the startling stage images of Tadeusz Kantor and Robert Wilson. Often there was little or no text and no real author. At its best, in the hands of a Wilson and a Kantor, the sheer visual impact of some of these works was not only stunning, it proved effective dramatically.

But not all directors possess so great a power of imagination nor the same means to express it. The French directors of the eighties, on the whole, followed analogous paths, preferring classics to contemporary authors, little known works by famous authors to the best-known ones, stage adaptations of works not written for the stage to existing dramatic texts. More and more theater—*French* theater, but not only French theater—lost one of its key components: a text, a play. Directors tended to make up for this crucial loss by substituting other stage activity: dance, pantomime, movements of various sorts, organized or not, meaningful or not.

Jean-Pierre Thibaudat wrote in 1994,

> The writer for the theater today is the victim of the revolution that turned over power to the director. It left him in a situation of subjection. And after being put through the mill by the staging, his frequently fragile plays are often adapted, transformed, disfigured. The author is no longer God almighty. He is a worker, the specialized worker of the text.[6]

And, unsurprisingly, Thibaudat concludes that this state of things led to generally devitalized writing for the stage.

If the place of the author has not returned to its former position of primacy, it has improved more recently as French directors seek perhaps a more equitable distribution of attention to the various components of the work on stage, *including* the text. But even a modest return to the role of the playwright, does not necessarily mean a revivified avant-garde. It all depends on what kind of writing, what kind of text, leading to what sort of theatricality. A Luigi Pirandello, a Genet, a Beckett expressed a radical theatricality that invited directors to provide, innovative stagings *required* by the written work, inscribed in it. Today one looks in vain for such a need for experimentation.

During the final years of the last century and in this new one French dramatists and directors have been drawn to political and social content, ranging from French problems of immigration and integration to worldwide concerns with AIDS, terrorism, and American military domination. There is no reason why such matters cannot be expressed in theatrically experimental forms. In the sixties and seventies, the creative strength of the work of the Living Theater, Richard Schechner, Jean-Louis Barrault, notably in *Rabelais* (to name just a few) proved that the two presented no contradictions and made for a particularly dynamic avant-garde. Now, the most theatrically stimulating works based on political and social reflections are undoubtedly those of Ariane Mnouchkine's Théâtre du Soleil yet even their highly original stagings no longer qualify as "avant-garde." They are part of the best, the most inventive of contemporary French theater, hailed around the world. Le Théâtre du Soleil (like others) has come a long way; it can now address massive audiences and be fully understood, despite its use of forms of strikingly antirealist theatricality. But if an avant-garde is, as Ionesco rightly claimed, a frontal attack on what *is* with the intent of destroying it and replacing it with a new, radical vision, not even Le Théâtre du Soleil can be considered to be an avant-garde in the twenty-first century.

That is why one may well wonder whether an avant-garde in the French theater today is even possible. The question came to a head at the 2005 edition of the Avignon Theater Festival, always a showcase for the new and the daring, under the leadership of the "artiste associé"—invited each year to give structure and perhaps meaning to the selection of playwrights, directors, choreographers and others. The Flemish mixed-media artist Jan Fabre was selected by the Festival's directors, Hortense Archambault and Vincent Baudriller, to animate the festival. But 2005 proved to be a catastrophe for the public and for critics alike. The co-directors and their "artiste associé" succeeded in alienating audiences with a polemical, vulgar, ultra-violent program that sought to shock—hardly a novelty in 2005 and not successful at that. After all, after nudity, after incest, after murder, rape, and cannibalism, what is left to try shock a public that is subjected to the worst horrors daily on the evening news? Jan Fabre thought that urinating on stage for instance would be one way. The intellectual and esthetic poverty of this strategy may have escaped the festivals' directors who claimed to want to question the limits of theater, but it did not escape the audiences. They were less shocked than irritated and bored. Theater was elsewhere.

One of the healthy signs pointing to a hope of recovery from the dismal current state is in this new refusal (or at least the beginning of it) of audiences and critics to swallow anything and to endure everything. The emperor's clothes were new, and glamorous, and attractive—but perhaps they have faded and even become invisible. Thus, for instance a comment from a *New York Times* theater critic in reviewing Peter Handke's splendid 40-someyear-old play (thus, no longer avant-garde, but possibly still splendid) *Offending the Audience*. Referring to the actors, the *Times* critic, Jason Zinoman, wrote: As much as I tried to get into the far-out spirit, these cuties just couldn't offend me. It's really not their fault. Times have changed. Mr. Handke remains a provocateur but more for his political views; the Comédie Française removed a play of his from its 2007 season because of his sympathy for Slobodan Milosevic. A drama about this controversy would have been more interesting than a work that congratulates itself on speaking directly to the audience. Downtown artists like Young Jean Lee assault the audience much more aggressively now, and other experiments from the 60s, like *A Day in the Death of Joe Egg* have made it to Broadway. As for audience participation, I've seen performers grope ticket buyers, jump on their laps and even suck their toes. A little eye contact won't offend anyone. With this appealing group, I rather enjoyed it.

Even docile audiences have become fed up being subjected to ridicule by some directors. The generally moderate Michael Feingold bemoaned in *The Village Voice* a production of Wedekind's *Lulu* at BAM, perpetrated (I think that is the word he would use) by the German director Michael Thalheimer: Thalheimer is one of the more intelligent of the anti-artists who currently ruin great plays for the joy of artsy pedants and the misery of German audiences long inured to obedient suffering.... Thalheimer's capable actors kept giving off hints that he and they clearly knew better, but his conceptual rigidity kept stifling the richness that you could hear, when they spoke understandably, in Wedekind's wondrous text.

In their wrap-up for *Le Monde* of that 2005 Avignon Festival, Fabienne Darge and Brigitte Salino wrote: It will undoubtedly take some time to begin to understand what really happened at this Festival.... But one can already analyze certain elements.... this Festival will have been an important moment in the history of Avignon, because it has been so revealing. It is evidence of a loss of ideological landmarks (through a brutal and meaningless reproduction of violence) and of esthetic ones (through a formal research that draws on the avant-garde of the years 1960–1970 without managing to bring it to life again).[7]

The trouble is, in fact, that you can't bring an avant-garde to life again. The very idea is self-contradictory. Earlier in 2008, an interesting conference in Paris examined the major theatrical avant-gardes that succeeded the theater of the absurd, namely the brilliant New York avant-garde of the sixties and seventies, which itself nourished by major non-American seminal figures such as Grotowski, Peter Brook, Tadeusz Kantor, Luca Ronconi, Andrei Serban, and others, earned worldwide acclaim and influenced theater and performance (as a new theatrical field came to be called) in many countries and especially in France. Many of these theatrical avant-gardes emanating from New York relegated text to the background: the Living Theater, Richard Foremans' Ontological Hysteric Theater, Richard Schechner's Performance Group and The Wooster Group which grew out of it, and Robert Wilson (to name but the most famous). Other equally inventive collectives, groups, or directors retained a greater—but still modest—link to text: Joseph Chaikin's Open Theater, the Mabou Mines, working with various directors from its midst, Spalding Gray, Peter Schuman's Bread and Puppet Theater. One might mention, outside New York, California's inventive Teatro Campesino and the San Francisco Mime Troupe.

These various theatrical enterprises not only stunned the downtown scene in New York, they performed all over Europe and left indelible marks in France, Germany, Holland, Belgium, Austria, the Scandinavian countries, and Italy, and to a lesser degree in Britain, Spain, and Poland. The Living Theater, the most politically engaged of all, had its heyday in the sixties, culminating in their disruptive, agit-prop performances (or were they "happenings"?) in Avignon in 1968, that probably hurt their host, Jean Vilar, more than their intended target, the "establishment." Still, artistically speaking this was the very spirit of avant-garde. Efforts to revive the Living Theater's productions twenty, thirty, and more years later were inevitably doomed to failure, precisely because you can't reanimate an avant-garde. Bob Wilson's stunning visual, wordless, ultra-slow-motion early experimental productions such as *Deafman's Glance* introduced an entirely new "vocabulary" to what theater is. Thirty years later, his lavish productions, still visually virtuosic, are firmly part of the best of establishment theater. It's wonderful, it's admired, but it's *déjà vu* (literally); nothing new there.

So what? So nothing. Simply a way to underline that the avant-garde doesn't stay in place. At the recent conference mentioned, Richard Schechner, the head of the Performance Group and a guru of the avant-garde, recognized that the American avant-garde is no longer "avant", that it has now become a tradition. In its heyday, he claimed, it was high in innovation and modest in excellence [that is debatable]; now, in its assimilated days, it is, for him, high in excellence and low in innovation. Twenty to twenty-five years is the life span he feels avant-gardes have in general, and that would seem a reasonable estimate.

The fiasco of the 2005 Avignon may well have marked the high water mark of the irrelevancy of theater that scorns text. Yet if one might therefore predict a gradual revalorization of the dramatic text, such a pendulum swing would not inevitably harbinger some incipient avant-garde, and in fact is not likely to do so. The years of the revolutionary theater of the absurd followed by a period of directorial innovation shook up the establishment, as avant-gardes are intended to do. If an avant-garde has been successful (and these were) it is absorbed, as I have suggested, by dominant forms, bringing on new established models of theater. Eventually, this new establishment (once it becomes, in Ionesco's words, a new tyranny) will be brought down by some new avant-garde. But the French theater is not there yet. It is impossible to guess what such a new avant-garde might be; if it were imaginable it would already exist. But it does not.

What seems to be missing most are playwrights—playwrights who present and have staged significant texts which could, of course, include major innovations in staging. But the French playwrights may have abandoned the stage at the moment for television and have been replaced by directors. Directors have become the new playwrights, and so many productions are not presented BY an author but D'APRÈS, AFTER, and what happens between the text being adapted or renewed is not the work of a playwright but of the DIRECTOR, whose name often replaces that of the original playwright. This phenomenon, so common in France and in Germany right now is not present in the United States nor in England. We will have to wait to see which system generates the next important avant-garde movement.

A similar situation existed in the nineteen thirties. After several decades of radical reactions against the realism institutionalized by Antoine, led by such as Aurélien Lugné-Poë, Jacques Copeau, Charles Dullin, the young Cocteau, the Surrealists, Gaston Baty, and Georges Pitoëff, a period of assimilation led to Giraudoux, Montherlant, Anouilh, and Sartre. Who could have imagined while watching, say, Giraudoux's *Intermezzo* in 1933 that twenty years later, two tramps would wade through endless silences while waiting for Godot and that the Martins and the Smiths, interchangeable, two-dimensional pseudo English couples would hurl phrases, words, and syllables at one another while no soprano, bald or otherwise, made a promised appearance. Beckett, Ionesco, Genet, and all the others had to write, to create, before their attack on the French theater establishment could as much as be envisaged. Only then could their avant-garde be detected, named, analyzed.

It is hardly imaginable that no new avant-garde will eventually take form against the current theater establishment in France, in the US, or elsewhere. But what it will be and whether it will be successful, as was the theater of the absurd, or relatively unsuccessful with no strong long-term traces (as was the case for instance of the expressionist theater of the twenties in France), we will need to be patient in order to find out. Companies are currently experimenting with technology, with visual effects, with focus on body, always in the absence of text. Some of the current work is really interesting, such as that of the Ivo van Hove and TG Stan group working in Flemish, and Romeo Castellucci, working in Italian, though in both cases, the language is strictly incidental and mostly inaudible and incomprehensible.

But somehow, one fails to detect the really new, the radically new, the blow to the solar plexus that forces you to take notice, grudgingly or not, and say WOW. But it will come again, sooner or later, and when it does, it is likely to stem from unexpected sources and take unusual directions. Where it will come from and what it might be, we certainly cannot know now. But it is a safe bet that it won't be a replay of the past, it won't resemble past avant-gardes.

Finally, a few comments concerning other art forms. With respect to the novel, the *nouveau roman* was the last successful real avant-garde movement in France. Since then, individual authors have attempted and at times succeeded in developing experimental forms, but in the absence of any movement. Whereas the only important literary movement to stand out in France since the *nouveau roman*, which has been given several names but is best labeled as "Autofiction" and features numerous outstanding writers such as Serge Doubrovsky, Camille Laurens, Philippe Forest, Catherine Cusset and a number of others, is not an experimental movement. The French perspective is reasonably reproduced in other countries.

The odd man out is the art world. There the perspective has entirely changed and no longer resembles the erstwhile "traditional" format of innovation followed by absorption. Now the market has taken over, and the ever-present need to "sell" an artist has created a permanent avant-garde linked principally to what collectors will spend, what auctions will yield. That has put the art world in a place of its own, a realm certainly beneficial to the artists riding the crest of the wave but not at all reassuring with respect to the innate quality and innovation of the "new" artists and their new work. The link between theater and literature in general on the one hand and the art world on the other—so productive in past years—seems arbitrary and unproductive in the early years of the twenty-first century.

## Notes

1  Charles Dullin, "Le mouvement théâtral moderne," *Revue de l'Amérique Latine*, October 1923, 183.
2  *Tel Quel*, Fall 71, quoted in Antoine Compagnon, *Les antimodernes*, Paris: Gallimard, 2005, 419.
3  Eugène Ionesco, *Notes and Counter Notes*, New York: Grove Press, 1964, 40–41.
4  It is easy to quibble with Martin Esslin's famous title. Obviously, the concept of the absurd fits some authors better than others, and some, like Genet, not at all. Still, Esslin focused on one significant new element in the writings of the new dramatists of the fifties and if "theater of the absurd" is not a wholly satisfactory label, it is still better or more meaning-ful than the others, such as "new theater," "antitheater," "theater of derision."
5  Joseph Chiari, *The Contemporary French Theater: The Flight from Naturalism*, New York: Macmillan, 1959.
6  Jean-Pierre Thibaudat, "Tribulations de l'écriture dramatique en France" in *Le théâtre français*, Paris: Ministère des Affaires étrangères, 1994, 23 (translation mine).
7  Fabienne Darge and Brigitte Salino, "2005, l'année de toutes les polemiques, l'année de tous les paradoxes," *Le Monde*, 28 July 2005, 20 (translation mine).

# 2

# THE CRITICAL LIFE

## Rethinking biography in an experimental mode

*Emily Apter*

A pair of epigraphs from avant-garde choreographer Yvonne Rainer's autobiography *Feelings Are Facts: A Life* capture opposing ways in which the biographical genre – conceived as a mix of conventional reader expectations and a series of formal devices that submit inchoate congeries of fact-feeling to the constraints of formal narrative – constrain the options for writing "the Life":

> The autobiography is a covertly anti-intellectual genre, designed for those who are more interested in what Tolstoy had for breakfast than what he thought about Plato." (Terry Eagleton, review of Eric Hobsbawm's *Interesting Times: A Twentieth Century Life*, in *The Nation*, September 15, 2003).
>
> If you're interested in Plato, you're reading the wrong book. If you're interested in difficult childhoods, sexual misadventures, aesthetics, cultural history and the reasons that club sandwich – including breakfast – have remained in the memory of the present writer, keep reading.[1]

The first citation, of Terry Eagleton, challenges the intellectual legitimacy of the (auto)biographic form, posing it as preclusive of philosophy and practices of philosophizing. The second epigraph, Rainer's rejoinder to Eagleton, tosses aside "history of thought" or "great man" paradigms; and takes the messy, non-hierarchical aspect of the Life as the very pretext for experimentation in self-composition. Rainer will own the flaws attributed to the biographic genre, celebrating troves of minor incident and nonhierarchical information. "A Life" should be a self-regarding yet critical labor of production, *absolutely literary* (on the order of Philippe Lacoue-Labarthe and Jean-Luc Nancy's understanding of literature as an autotelic medium no longer reducible to the role of adjunct to philosophy or thought), and lyrically true in the sense of syncopated with the conditions of its own unpredictability, noncertifiability, and discursive contingency.[2] This lyric vulnerability registers in the choreographer's allusions to moments of painful hesitancy, doubt and self-exposure, each of which open onto gulfs of indeterminacy between thought process and creative decision, as when Rainer notes: "I'm conducting very precarious classes in that I'm not always completely prepared and they can observe my thought processes." (FF 307) Or when, with respect to *Continuous Project-Altered Daily*, she recognizes the "phenomenal accomplishment" of an instance where her performers disregard her instructions: "what happened was both fascinating and painful, and not only for me, as I vacillated between opening up options and closing them down." (FF 325, 322). Threaded with personal, "pedestrian" material, and in this respect of a piece with her dance scores and films, Rainer's exercise in self-archiving arranges letters, manifestos, sexual encounters, collaborations, and critical reflections on performance in an open work. (FF 301) Her Life, in this regard, responds to the critique of conventional biography implicit in Walter Benjamin's essay on Goethe's *Elective Affinities*. Taking aim at Friedrich Gundolf's 1916 biography of *Goethe*, which in his view fell into the trap of a textual immanence derived not from the dialectics of a work's conditions of material historicity and critical incompletion, but from overdrawn projections of Goethe "the man" on textual interpretation, Benjamin provided impetus for rethinking the Life as a genre of critical dialectics.

★★★

Biography has emerged in recent years as the premier genre of mainstream literary criticism; spawning multiple subgenres of personal narrative such as memoir, autobiography, and autofiction, the latter a hybrid of memoir and fiction. Under the present Malthusian conditions of book-publishing, the effect of this popularity has been to diminish the market for other ways of writing about texts and authors, especially those relying on constructs of literary theory, from semiotics to narratology. Like the memoir – whose fortune has been buoyed by the appetite for YouTube, DIY footage, and reality TV – biography succeeds because it best "translates" (the term used loosely here) life-properties into narrative. As a genre devoted to "the Life" it lays special claim to what Harold Bloom calls "Literature as a Way of Life" (in the subtitle of *The Anatomy of Influence*).[3] In the alliance between Belles-Lettres and biography we have a super-genre: crowd-pleasing style married to norms of life-writing that assign new credence to the intentional fallacy or the assumption of a common motivational purpose and structure binding the writer's life to the literary work.

It wasn't always thus. When New Criticism, deconstruction and poststructuralism held sway, biography was ranked second-tier in the academy. If its master-practitioners at the time – Richard Ellman (on James Joyce), Hugh Kenner (on Ezra Pound), Leon Edel (on Henry James) – were appreciated it was because they brought unorthodox critical approaches to the analysis of their celebrity subjects. During the heyday of high theory, in which the autonomy of the work of art was paramount, biography came to be seen as a redoubt for theory's detractors; critics who saw the "humanity" of literature threatened by hermeneutics, literary technics and interdisciplinarity. We might refer by way of example to Rodolphe Gasché's profession of dismay on encountering what he takes to be the rehabilitation of biography by Derrida in his "Otobiographies":

> [W]e heard you, Jacques Derrida, proceed with a revalorization and a reeval-
> uation of biography (a philosopher's; in this case, Nietzsche's) in relation to a
> written corpus. This procedure on your part might at first appear paradoxical,
> not to say disappointing. That is, if one were to listen to it with the wrong ear.

Soon, however, Gasché recovers from the shock, acknowledging that Derridean biography is something special; an "internal border of work and life, a border on which texts are engendered," and which derives "from neither the inside nor the outside" of the text."[4] Gasché's initially adverse reaction to Derrida's reclamation of biography attests to theory's profound resistance to what conventional biography promises to deliver. First and foremost, it makes good on the investment in the Life as something narratable, as something possessable and communicable in beautiful words. Burnishing commonplaces about what it means to be human, biography shores up belletristic humanism.

***

Though I would personally like to see biography, especially in the Anglo-American tradition, become a more critical genre, don't get me wrong. I enjoy sinking into a Life as written by some of the finest biographers as much as the next person and personal favorites include Lytton Strachey's *Eminent Victorians*, George Painter's *Proust*, Michael Holroyd's *Lytton Strachey*, Deirdre Bair's *Simone de Beauvoir*, Joseph Frank's *Dostoevsky*, Victoria Glendinning's *Vita Sackville-West*, Claire Tomalin's *Thomas Hardy*, A.N. Wilson's *Iris Murdoch*, Edmund White's *Jean Genet*, Judith Thurman's *Colette*, Hermione Lee's *Edith Wharton*, Frederick Brown's *Flaubert*, Elisabeth Roudinesco's *Jacques Lacan*, Didier Eribon's *Michel Foucault*, and Wayne Koestenbaum's *Andy Warhol*. First, they offer the promise of sex, or at the very least, some prospect of a prurient glimpse of illicit relationships. Literary biographies in this respect are no different from celebrity bios or pathographies, trading in gos-sip, erotic *frisson*, dirty little secrets, and the transactional currency of brand-names. Second, they invite you back to the world as you once knew it, a precritical (or pre-posthumanist) world in which things are as they seem. Biography props up the reassuring belief in historical reality (and the fact-value distinction), while at the same time infusing the amorphous content of a life with story. Lives, instead of being problematized as collections of self-properties provisionally assembled under a proper name or signature are allowed to flower in the form of individual characters whose trajectories obey familiar narrative laws of causal development, anticipation, *Bildung* and dénouement. The ages of man break down into the ages of style − early, middle, late − and the pitfalls of psychological interpretation, or what Theodor Adorno called the "deceptive crown of its metaphysics" are ignored.

Though Adorno argued persuasively that "Death is imposed only on created beings, not on works of art, and thus it has appeared in art only in a refracted mode, as allegory." This caveat against biographical essentialism tends to have minimal traction.[5] When it comes to writing biography, childhood routinely and reliably presages adulthood; traumas return in the form of visible symptoms; class and economic determinants are rarely questioned as conditioners of personality. In this Eden of the precritical, whole systems of social explanation are deemed trustworthy instruments for unlocking secrets of the psyche. There is no unsettling filter of classed, raced, or gendered "sociality" of the kind flagged by Judith Butler, which might come between a biographical subject and her biographic narration. For Butler, discursive sociality foils any attempt at self-accounting:

> The account of myself that I give in discourse never fully expresses or carries this living self. My words are taken away as I give them, interrupted by the time of a discourse that is not the same as the time of my life. This 'interruption' contests the sense of the account's being grounded in myself alone, since the indifferent structures that enable my living belong to a sociality that exceeds me.[6]

This excessive sociality runs interference with the positing of a gendered self, and by extension, of an author-self whose life and work dovetail in a narrative arc. Butler's formulation not only questions the possibility of an "owned" gendered ontology, it activates "undone gender" to disbar the possibility of an "authorized" free-standing identity:

> What I call my 'own' gender appears perhaps at times as something that I author or, indeed, own. But the terms that make up one's own gender are, from the start, outside oneself, beyond oneself in a sociality that has no single author (and that radically contests the notion of authorship itself.[7]

Sociality, a category more diffuse than "the social," implying an infinity of other selves, other genders, other discourses and other material substances, defies containment in a genre of the Life, presented by an "authorized" stand-alone narrator. So, in light of this, a number of questions impose themselves: how would one set about writing the biography of subjective socialities? How could one "biographify" abstract alterity in endless multiples?

★★★

Resolutely practical in its methods, and materialist in orientation, biography treats memorabilia like so many mouse-droppings that lead to the "true" subject. Jeffrey Meyers, introducing an essay collection on *The Craft of Literary Biography* indicates how the very idea of biography is conflated with materialist sleuthing. The book, he states,

[C]onsiders how the biographer chooses a subject, uses biographical models, does archival research, conducts interviews, interprets evidence, establishes chronology, organizes material into a meaningful pattern and illuminates an author's work through a discussion of his life. The ideal circumstances for selecting a modern literary subject are the existence of significant unpublished material, of family and friends who can be interviewed as well as the absence of an obstructive executor or a recently completed life.[8]

Excavated, archived, accounted for, the tangible traces of a life come to resemble items of a person's estate. As the procedures of a self's disposal are followed there is a comforting illusion that life and death can be controlled.

Biography is built to ensure notation of the material manifestations of persons; it protects the material conditions of writers' lives; turning their homes into museums where visitors can check out the implements of craft (plumes, pens, typewriters, computers), the placement of the desk, the library, the outdoor writing shed, the local countryside and vestigial folkways. Biography tries to inoculate "reality" against critical intrusion, something that is especially hard to do in the case of literary biography which must grapple with an author's critical reception as part of their history. Nigel Hamilton, a biographer of the Mann brothers notes for example, that there is "something incestuous… by definition, a writer writing about a writer."[9] Hamilton deems it a great mistake when biographers become "super-articulators" of the work of their subject, leading to a willful confusion with the tasks of literary criticism."[10] He raises an interesting point: most prize-winning literary biographers receive praise as long as they keep their own literary-critical impulses in check.

Critics who play fast and loose with the protocols often run into trouble, as Jacqueline Rose discovered in the fracas that ensued when she published *The Haunting of Sylvia Plath* (1991) in a series edited by Edward Said with the heuristically framed title: "Convergences: Inventories of the Present." Rose was explicit about her treatment of Plath as an epistemological unknowable whose bounds exceed historical certitude. But she ran afoul of the Plath estate when she insisted that,

> [P]sychic life in itself will not be relegated to the private, it will not stay in its proper place. It shows up on the side of the historical reality to which it is often opposed. Nowhere is this clearer than in Plath's own use of historical reference, where it is always the implication of psyche in history, and history in psyche, that is involved.[11]

Though Ted Hughes's plaintive status as Plath's former husband and executor, and his implication in the narrative of her life-story made his policing of the border between biography and interpretation particularly partial, I think it is no accident that it was Rose who aroused his ire to the extreme. For Jacqueline Rose, known as a feminist theorist whose early work engaged deeply with Lacanian psychoanalysis, proposed a mixed genre: a biography of psychic life. It was not that she overstepped the bounds of privacy – the usual complaint – but that she wrote "the Life" of Plath's reality from fantasy's point of view.

Rose's case prompts a look at other incursions by philosophers and critical thinkers into biography. In the early 1990s, Jean-François Lyotard contracted with Grasset and Fasquelle to write a popular biography of André Malraux (*Signé Malraux*, 1996). Would theory have to take a holiday? The answer seems to have been yes. Though Lyotard occasionally lapsed into theory-speak (using the word "differend" for example to describe the bad sex between Malraux's parents), his voice as a biographer was profoundly at odds with the one found in theoretical works like *The Differend* and *The Postmodern Condition*. In a chapter titled "Writing or Life?" for example, Lyotard displayed all the stock devices of biographical art, as in this "you are there" setting of a scene:

> So here he is, at the beginning of 1922, back living on the first floor of Villa des Chalets, once again a prisoner in the house of women. Silk-lined prison: Clara's fortune affords the couple a life in high style. But financial ease or not, wasn't this a dead end following the escapade into Europe and love? There was no question of allowing his resolve to weaken. But what would be his new escape route? Works of course. But what kind? And by what means? The oeuvre of his life or that of his pen? Or would it be uncovering works by others, editing them, dealing in them? Or, again, would it be some great global quarrel in which to take sides, or an action to sign?[12]

Lyotard's *Malraux* never reached mass circulation, and its English edition was taken in hand not by a commercial press, but by a University of Minnesota series already specialized in publishing translations of Lyotard's works of theory.

Some have argued that the French simply do not excel in the art of biography. There might be something to this facile, nationalist explanation – this is the nation, after all, that gave us the theory of the "death of the author." Despite notable exceptions, it would seem that the "great" French biographers practice a more theoretical form of the genre that would be discounted by the Anglo-Saxons. The prototype is Jean Delay's magisterial 1956 psychobiography of André Gide. Trained as a psychiatrist by Pierre Janet and employed at the famous Salpêtrière hospital, Delay plumbed the Gide archive with finesse, but he felt equally free to probe Gide's textual psyche, treating his tropes on virile insufficiency as the stuff of material research. His biography beats a path, in this respect, to Julia Kristeva's trilogy on Hannah Arendt, Colette and Melanie Klein published in the 1990s. Kristeva, like Delay, borrows techniques from traditional biography, but her approach is at a far remove from belletrist precedent. Consider her theory-centric opening to the volume on Arendt, which uses Arendt's philosophical ascription of the narrative life (sent in a letter to Jaspers in 1930) as the watchword of her own approach: "It seems as if certain people are so exposed in their own lives (and only in their lives, not as persons!) that they become, as it were, junction points and concrete objectifications of 'life.'"[13] Contrast this beginning with that of Linda Lear's conventional biography, *Beatrix Potter: A Life in Nature*:

> It was a cold, wet November day in 1918. The frosty air had settled just above the lake… Through the gloom the figure of a woman could just be made out… Her somewhat rounded frame was mostly hidden by several layers of outerwear. She wore a long, coarse wool jacket, wool stockings, and serviceable clogs as defence against the chill.[14]

Lear borrows scene-setting techniques from cinema and the novel-form to quite literally ground her subject in nature. Andrew Delbanco, for his part, in his prize-winning *Melville: His World and Work* achieves an equivalent effect in a historicist vein; projecting the reader into a recreation of the "time and place" of his subject:

> When Melville was born in 1819 in New York City, it was a town of about a hundred thousand people with streets lit dimly by oil lamps as if by so many lightning bugs. The best way of sending a message was via a wax-sealed letter carried by a messenger on a horse. Such giants of the revolutionary generation as Thomas Jefferson and John Adams were still alive, while the political institutions they had invented remained fragile and, according to many putatively sage observers, unlikely to endure.[15]

An earlier generation of Anglophone biographers – best represented by Richard Ellmann – avoided these kinds of belletristic hooks. The opening of his 1959 life of James Joyce typifies the best of the literary critic turned biographer: "We are still learning to be James Joyce's contemporaries, to understand our interpreter. This book enters Joyce's life to reflect his complex, incessant joining of event and composition."[16]

Kristeva's interest in Arendt's biography stems from fascination with the "event" of Arendt's feminist *vita contemplativa*, in fluid sequence with the "event" of her own *vita contemplativa*. (HA 42) "The young philosopher, she writes, focused much of her thinking on *life*." Kristeva attaches the Life, as a genre, to Arendt's concept of "the life of the mind," following it all the way back in the history of philosophy to Socrates, who in her estimation "left to the historian an example of thinking in motion, of a *bios theoretikos* whose permanent questioning should always challenge 'public affairs' themselves." (HA 94) Starting with Arendt's thesis on Saint Augustine, under the supervision of Karl Jaspers (in which according to Kristeva she articulated "Life-questioning from the standpoint of the interval between birth and death"), Kristeva moves to Arendt's 1938 study of a romantic *saloniste* in the orbit of Goethe, *Rahel Varnhagen: The Life of a Jewess*. She emphasizes the anomaly – especially at the time of its writing – of biography cast as a philosophical medium. With this generic hybrid Arendt challenged what it meant to do philosophy in ways that would only come to be significant for theorists like Kristeva herself years later. (HA 37, 48)

Kristeva credits Arendt with understanding that "narrative is the first dimension in which man lives, through *bios* and not through *zoe*, a political life and/or an action recounted to other people." (HA 86) This distinction is important because Kristeva, like Arendt, finds something in the category of "the narratable life" that fills out political philosophy, supplying it with the "who" or agent who connects action and events to thought. (HA 73) According to this paradigm, the conventions of formal narrative coherence in biography hardly matter; it is the exemplarity of *bios*, that is, the ability to "*live* the weightiest problems through the body and the mind" that are crucial. (HA 99) Kristeva's biographical practice encourages by example experimentation in the making of narratable lifeworlds.

***

Literature exists, only really exists, when there is a questioning of its methods of exposition coincident with an incontestable formal achievement and an authorial presence (…) the exposition, to wit, exhibition of self – does not necessarily lend itself to reinventing the rules of the game – if truth be told, this is rarely the case.

– *Donatien Grau, Tout Contre Sainte-Beuve. L'inspiration retrouvée*[17]

The challenge of composing a literary biography that would "inspire" in Grau's sense, which is to say, experiment with critical formalisms and methods of exposition the better to convey the "live" aspect of a writer's *bios*, was taken up by Tiphaine Samoyault in her *Life of Roland Barthes* (which appeared in French in 2015). Like Rose, Lyotard and Kristeva, Samoyault was trained as a theorist rather than as a professional biographer. In undertaking the commission of Barthes's biography with unrestricted access to new source material, she faced the daunting task of, at once, answering to the constraints of the genre (bolstered by the marketing expectations of the publishing house), and to the character of the subject – Roland Barthes – who was himself a master of the detourned biography. Barthes took pleasure in subverting the *l'homme et l'oeuvre* didactic format popular in France even as he showed that he could excel at it in his *Michelet*. In *Roland Barthes par Roland Barthes* he famously wrote the "par lui-même" series monograph dedicated to his own life and work, thereby expropriating the biographer's labor of collating representative citations, photographs, and canonical *bons mots*. It was a mischievous gesture to be sure, but it was also an act of resistance; a prophylactic against the "biographeme," a literary mytheme that shored up patrimonial self-congratulation by claiming "the great writer" as national symbolic capital. Even if the biographeme could be used critically as a structure for examining the chiasmatic exchanges between life-writing ("l'écriture de vie") and life-as-writing ("la vie comme écriture"), it tended to be ranged by Barthes on the side of the "readerly text," (*le lisible*) which located the reader as the receiver of predetermined reading practices that rendered him/her a reproducer of dominant literary modes under capitalism. Its counterfoil was the "writerly text," (*le scriptible*), which occupied a perpetual present and captured "*ourselves writing*, before the infinite play of the world (the world as function) is traversed, intersected, stopped, plasticized by some singular system (Ideology, Genus, Criticism) which reduces the plurality of entrances, the opening of networks, the infinity of languages."[18] The former involved a dead letter, (writing *with* style, the essay *with* the dissertation), the latter an alive one.

Barthes was famous for announcing the "death of the Author," but he should have been equally credited for announcing the "death of the Biographer" because as a critic he preempted the biographer's exclusive hold on the Life, drawing on a lovely hypothetical – "were I a writer, and dead..." – to propel himself into the role of Life-programmer, who treats the biographer as a proxy warden:

> [W]ere I a writer, and dead, how I would love it if my life, through the pains of some friendly and detached biographer, were to reduce itself to a few details, a few preferences, a few inflections, let us say: to "biographemes" whose distinction and mobility might go beyond any fate and come to touch, like Epicurean atoms, some future body, destined to the same dispersion, a marked life, in sum, as Proust succeeded in writing his in his work, or even a film, in the old style, in which there is no dialogue and the flow of images... is intercut, like the relief of hiccoughs, by the barely written darkness of the intertitles, the casual eruption of *another* signifier: Sade's white muff, Fourier's flowerpots, Ignatius's Spanish eyes.[19]

Barthes' conjuration of some atomized "future body" destined to dispersion encourages us to read the Barthes oeuvre as, quite literally, a *body* of work vitally connected to affect, queer temporality, surface reading, psychic states of vulnerability, risk, insecurity, anhedonia, depression, and what Lauren Berlant, in *Cruel Optimism* characterizes as "living trauma as whiplash: a "sense of treading water, being stuck, drifting among symptoms, ... a sense of the present that makes no sense with the rest of it."[20]

In transgressing the values of "fideism" and "realism" identified by Grau as guarantors of autobiographical coherence and credibility, Barthes forged an experimental mode of composing the Life that detached the subject from the first-person "I."[21] Released from fidelity to the belief in self-possession, he discovered inspiration for the Life in *haiku*, in the impersonal technics of semiosis, and in the depersonalization of proper names as they become historicized. And yet, paradoxically, much of his writing solicited personal, affective attachments from its readers. Websites devoted to Barthes typically include "Barthes best-ofs;" quotes that people hold on to like personal talismans, cathected passages they read over and over again and enjoy sharing with others. Barthes was eminently quotable because he himself was expert in finding the perfect quote. He was a past master of what is now being called the "bibliomemoir," (typified by Rebecca Mead's recent bestseller *My Life in Middlemarch*). He left us with documents and jettisoned fragments from his writings that invite new practices of critical archiving. And his citations act as emotional anchors, they create a holding environment that temporarily stanches the panics of existential impermanence and solitude. There may be something morbid and fetishistic about such hoarded likes and dislikes, but this only adds to the interest of trying to figure out why we are attracted to certain texts, people or things, and why we keep on wanting to sort through this affective conundrum by rereading Barthes.

A sophisticated literary critic and literary author, cognizant at every turn of Barthes' allergy to the caricatural stylistics of the Life, Samoyault was faced with a schizophrenic prospect: her mandate was to write the biography of a subject who scorned biography as consumerist literary product and questioned the very premise of a narratable life. She would have to negotiate the complexity of Barthes' notoriously slippery pronouns: the "I" that signified "we;" the "he" that stood in for "I;" the "they" of the Gidean/Proustian transference; or the tertiary term of the Neuter/Neutral. More difficult still, she would have to reconcile the dictates of biography-writing – with its empirical data, historical timelines, family information, transcripts of lectures and interviews of students, friends and colleagues – with Barthes' refusal of positivist histories of the self. Samoyault also had to somehow perform a "straight" reading of her own archival research culled from the work of a writer who constantly plundered his personalized archival material for ironically self-distancing (auto)biographic projects. The notes for his books, lectures, and seminars, his accounts of the "daily grind" of faculty meetings and class preparation, all were harvested as preparatory material for a Life that was also a teaching, and that might or might not become a novel. Barthes had already flummoxed the would-be biographer, leaving Samoyault to devise methods for reckoning with a thoroughly baffled genre.

Several of her strategies would be unthinkable in a conventional biography. She acknowledges "Writing" as a kind of persona that figures into the narrative construction, coming between biographer and biographical subject. After rehearsing the tragic, and by now familiar story of Barthes' fatal traffic accident on the Rue des Ecoles, she takes an unexpected metaphysical turn, hailing Death as the author of the biographic *raison d'être*:

> Death indeed, is the only event that resists autobiography. It justifies the activity of biography, as it is someone else who writes it.
>
> ...Death leads to writing and it justifies the narrative of a life. It begins the past over again, it summons new forms and figures into being. It is because someone dies that we can undertake to relate their life. Death recapitulates and reassembles. This is why I have begun this Life with the story of a death. While it breaks away from life, and in a certain way is life's opposite, death is at the same time identical with life as story. Both are the remainder of a person, the remainder that is at the same time a supplement that does not replace anything.[22]

*14–16*

Death leads Samoyault to a form of critical biography that resembles a glossary of the lost yet present subject. She gleans from Barthes' posthumously published *Le Lexique de l'auteur* (a collection of teaching notes for a class on the author, unpublished entries for *Roland Barthes par Roland Barthes*, a timeline of significant episodes entitled "Biographie," and notes for an atelier devoted to the "Biographematic" [*la Biographématique*]), the form of a Life that could mirror the morcellated body as well as the incohering structure of experience:

> Lost in a box of biographical and administrative documents from the Roland Barthes archives in the Bibliothèque Nationale are seven sheets of manuscript, torn in half then roughly sellotaped back together: the tranquil written attempt at autobiography, or the still living remembrances of a memory full of holes, a 'fragmentary memory' as the sub-title indicates. They may represent, as Anne Herschberg Pierrot suggested when she published them in *Le Lexique de l'auteur*, a first version of the 'Anamneses' we find in *Roland Barthes by Roland Barthes*. But we can also see them as the opposite and antagonistic form of these 'Anamneses,' the only time the author ever tried to set out a continuous biographical account of himself. The anamnesis, which is defined as an operation that tears you apart, marking the division within the subject, does, after all, imply a violent discontinuity. It is excerpted from the narrative, cut out of it, so to speak, and displaced from the chronology of a life.

The glossary, referred to by Barthes as an "anti-dictionary," emerges as the biographic form that allows the reader to surf a collection of discordant moods and subjectivity effects: "*Abgrund, Ablutionnisme, Abstraction, Absurde, Accepabilité, Accomdoation, Acratique, Acrocolia, Acte, Acteur, Actif-Passif, Acting out, Activité structuraliste, Adamique* (Fernando Barros*), Ad'dâd* (Florence Blanc*) Adiaphorie, Adjectif, Adolescence* (Colette Fellous), *Adresse postale, Adultère, Adventure, Adverbe, Aérien, Affectivité…*". and so on, from A to C, in tropic shorthand.[23] Barthes made the glossary his signature, his trademarked medium for an "I" whose presence was perpetually displaced and disseminated. The glossary, he insisted, is infinite and registers as an *après-coup*. The word proliferates inside him as soon as it is indexed; the Seminar is the virtual field of the index. The author consists of someone trying to describe textual production rather than express subjectivity. The author is unhampered by the requisite of consistency, he can reverse position, say what he likes, self-contradict. The "je" or privileged "I" will be reserved for what isn't yet written. The project will be a body, a corpus, the list will be an *oeuvre*.[24] The glossary becomes biography's new form, albeit stripped-down to its essentials, cut into pieces, and fetishized like a living corpse or zombie. This biographic form spills over into the scholarly works and critical essays. Barthes as we know adopted the glossary as the organizing system for his major works: *S/Z, Sade, Fourier, Loyola, Roland Barthes par Roland Barthes, Fragments d'un discours amoureux, La chambre claire*). In this sense, virtually every work Barthes wrote was a kind of autofiction, comparable to Annie Ernaux's *L'Atelier noir,* alternately characterized a "roman total," an "autobiographie vide," a "vie palimpseste." As Michael Sheringham observes, this diary "enables us to observe whole stretches of Ernaux's life, and swathes of her writing career, teaming like microbes under a microscope, initially regarded as constituents of the major work seeking its form, then splitting away to become fully fledged works in their own right."[25]

When Samoyault reassembles the dispersed pieces of the Barthesian corpus, she discovers the originary body of Barthes' mother, embalmed after her death as a maternal memory. If Barthes harbored the dream of writing a novel on the order of Proust's *In Search of Lost Time* or Tolstoy's *War and Peace* it was not, in her view, because he thought himself capable of emulating the scale and quality of these classic works, but rather because these novels "described the incandescence of the spiritual love expressed at the moment of death and constituting the truth of its subject." (p. 677) Behind the desire to write a novel was a longing for *Liebestod* that would allow the biography of oneself to tamper with what Avital Ronell called "finitude's score:"

> ...to lose oneself in the predicament of the other implies no mystical ascension toward the value of infinity; it is rather to abandon oneself to abandonment, which is a 'level equal to death.'...
> ...Sometimes you experience the suspensive nothing. You feel your need for interruption — the hiatus that marks you. There is interruption by the other, or by the presentiment of death.
> ... There is no finitude in or of itself. Finitude can make itself known only through the other's mortality. ... the call of Being... Finitude's score is another tracing or inscription of a thought of mortality.[26]

Ronell pushes us towards narrative surrendered to existential interruption rather than constrained by finitude. Pictured here is a subject who, by opening to the other, and coming to know suspensive nothing, travels, via a wormhole, to transfinite possible worlds.

★★★

Death, always a biographical control, reframes biography in relation to the before-time and the after-time of a lifespan. François Dosse, in *Le pari biographique: Ecrire une vie* [The Biographical Pact: Writing a Life] notes the meeting of two-force fields in the biographical form: the life of the subject before birth (the terrain of psychoanalysis and sociology, fields that emphasize formative social conditions), and the idea that remains of a person in the wake of their physical disappearance. The "*après-mort* of the biographed subject" becomes, according to Dosse, "as significant as the period in which they were alive, through the traces that they leave and by their manifold fluctuations in collective consciousness, in every form of expression."[27] Here we are dealing with an anti-correlationist life of the subject; a subject who exists beyond the confines of human remembrance. As Benjamin would write in "The Task of the Translator:" "One might, for example, speak of an unforgettable life or moment even if all men had forgotten it." (p. 16) [So dürfte von einem unvergesslichen Leben oder Augenblick gesprochen werden, auch wenn alle Menschen sie vergessen hätten."][28]

Technologies of social media yield biographical experiments tailored to the post-mortem biographic subject. In her discussion of what she calls "posthumous automediality" Béatrice Jongy perceives the outlines of "a new ontology" no longer bound to the transcendental "I" as subjects "die" on the Internet. Whether it is the resuscitation of dead links, the apparition in 2005 of a site called MyDeathSpace.com for deceased teenagers, the drawing up of testaments for your avatar ("In your will," one Second Life clause stipulates, "you must include the legal (real-life) name of the person who you want to inherit your Second Life account and assets, in the event of unfortunate circumstances"), or Facebook cases involving petitions to turn the dead person's account into a memorial wall, the late twentieth and early twenty-first century biographeme has assumed new forms consonant with online business models that support its production and dissemination.[29]

Christopher Bartlett's Gay History Wiki operated within this system but turned Facebook against commercial ends by endeavoring to generate online presence for persons who died of AIDS in the 80s and 90s. Described as "a social network-ing space for the dead," the Wiki sourced archival material and "technology that most of those it commemorates did not live to experience," to allow the Life to, as it were, go live; thereby outmaneuvering the temporal closure and *gravitas* of its obituary structure. *NY Times* reporter Guy Trebay noted: "Unlike the AIDS quilt, an intensely elegiac but largely static artifact, the Gay History Wiki, is a sprightly free space open to posts and tags, to biographical data added and amended by sur-vivors for their vanished friends."[30] We become privy to modes of living-on (*sur-vie*) that, instead of being solitary and virtual, are gregarious and vicarious. In this technologically mediated recasting of biography traditional oppositions between the readerly and the writerly, or between belletrisme and theory are seemingly left far behind. We enter the territory of experimentation with auto-bios as a critical practice, one that may be incorporative (as in Derrida's partially ingested "dead object" which "remains like a living dead abscessed in a specific spot in the ego"), or one that may aspire to become a transtemporal live/lived work that questions the conditions of its own mediality and treats the Life as a site of hybrid non-closure.[31] Such a practice comes to the fore in a fragment of Yvonne Rainer's *auteur* statement of 1990: "My films can be described as autobiographical fiction, untrue confessions, undetermined narratives, mined documentaries, unscholarly dissertations, dialogic entertainments." (FF 432)

## Notes

1  Yvonne Rainer, *Feelings Are Facts: A Life* (Cambridge, MA: MIT Press, 2006), np. Further references to this work appear in the text abbreviated FF.

2  Philippe Lacoue-Labarthe and Jean-Luc Nancy, *The Literary Absolute: The Theory of Literature in German Romanticism*, trans. Philip Barnard and Cheryl Lester (Binghamton. NY: SUNY Press, 1988). Second reference, Jonathan Culler, *Theory of the Lyric* (Cambridge, MA: 2015), p. 348.

3  Harold Bloom, *The Anatomy of Influence: Literature as a Way of Life* (New Haven, CT: Yale University Press, 2011).

4 Rodolphe Gasché, "Roundtable on Autobiography," trans. Peggy Kamuf in *The Ear of the Other: Otobiography, Transference, Translation* (New York: Schocken Books, 1985), p. 41.
5 Theodor W. Adorno, "Late Style in Beethoven," *Essays in Music*, ed. Richard Leppert, trans. Susan H. Gillespie (Berkeley, CA: University of California Press, 2002), p. 566.
6 Judith Butler, *Giving an Account of Oneself* (New York: Fordham University Press, 2005), p. 36.
7 Judith Butler, *Undoing Gender* (New York: Routledge, 2004), p. 1.
8 Jeffrey Meyers, ed. *The Craft of Literary Biography*, (New York: Schocken Books, 1985), p. 1.
9 Nigel Hamilton, "Thomas Mann," in *The Craft of Literary Biography*, ed. Jeffrey Meyers, op. cit. p. 115.
10 Ibid.
11 Jacqueline Rose, *The Haunting of Sylvia Plath* (Cambridge, MA: Harvard University Press, 1991), p. 7.
12 Jean-François Lyotard, *Signed, Malraux*, trans. Robert Harvey (Minneapolis, MN: University of Minnesota Press, 1999), p. 75.
13 Julia Kristeva, *Le Génie féminin. La vie, la folie, les mots. Hannah Arendt, Melanie Klein, Colette* (Paris: Fayard, 1999). Vol. 1. *La vie. Hannah Arendt ou l'action comme naissance et comme étrangeté*, translation from Kristeva, *Hannah Arendt*, trans. Ross Guberman (New York: Columbia University Press, 2001), p. 3. Further references to this work will appear in the text abbreviated HA.
14 Linda Lear, *Beatrix Potter: A Life in Nature* (New York: Saint Martin's Press, 2007), p. 3.
15 Andrew Delbanco, *Melville: His World and Work* (New York: Knopf, 2005), p. 3.
16 Richard Ellmann, *James Joyce* (Oxford: Oxford University Press, 1959, 1983), p. 3.
17 Donatien Grau, *Tout Contre Sainte-Beuve. L'inspiration retrouvée* (Paris: Grasset, 2013), p. 14.
18 Roland Barthes, *S/Z*, trans. Richard Miller (London: Blackwell, 1990), p. 5.
19 Roland Barthes, *Sade, Fourier, Loyola*, trans. Richard Miller (New York: Hill and Wang, 1976), p. 9.
20 Lauren Berlant, *Cruel Optimism* (Durham, NC: Duke University Press, 2011).
21 Donatien Grau, *Tout Contre Sainte-Beuve* op. cit. p. 31.
22 Tiphaine Samoyault, *Barthes: A Biography*, trans. Andrew Brown (London: Polity, 2016).
23 Roland Barthes et al., *Le lexique de l'auteur: Séminaire à l'Ecole pratique des hautes etudes 1973–1974 suivi de Fragments inédits du Roland Barthes par Roland Barthes* (Paris: Seuil, 2010), pp. 132–133.
24 Paraphrase of notes from "Le Glossaire," in Roland Barthes, *Le lexique de l'auteur* op.cit. pp. 142–143.
25 Michael Sheringham, "'La Connaissance par corps:' Writing and Self-Exposure in Annie Ernaux," in *Being Contemporary. French Literature, Culture and Politics Today* eds. Lia Brozgal and Sara Kippur (Liverpool: Liverpool University Press, 2016), p. 261.
26 Avital Ronell, *Finitude's Score: Essays for the End of the Millennium* (Lincoln, NE: University of Nebraska Press, 1994), p. 3.
27 François Dosse, *Le pari biographique: Ecrire une vie* (Paris: Editions La Découverte, 2005), p. 447. (Translation my own.)
28 Walter Benjamin, "Die Aufgabe des Ubersetzers," in *Illuminationen: Ausgewählte Schriften* (Frankfurt: Suhrkamp Verlag, 1961), p. 57.
29 Béatrice Jongy, "L'automédialite posthume: Les fantômes du cyberspace" (unpublished paper).
30 Guy Trebay, "Lost to AIDS, but Still Friended," *The New York Times* December 13, 2009, p. 13.
31 Jacques Derrida, "Roundtable on Autobiography," in *The Ear of the Other: Otobiography, Transference, Translation* (New York: Schocken Books, 1985), p. 57.

# 3

# WHAT LITERATURE CAN DO

*Philippe Artières*

We might arrive, first, at a question: "What can literature do?" And to begin our reply we will happily borrow the title of historian Patrick Boucheron's inaugural lecture at the Collège de France, delivered in December 2015.[1] Of course, Boucheron was speaking of history, laying out its *possibles*, as well as its power, and, indeed, its urging of resistance. This same impulse should prompt us to ask what present-day literature can do. What power to disturb does it possess? Where does its subversion lie?

In his celebrated essay "The Life of Infamous Men," first published in *Cahiers du chemin* in 1977, Michel Foucault showed that in the eighteenth-century literature had become a receptacle for all that until then had been the prerogative of the police: the intelligence of daily life, the banalities that had long provided material for lettres de cachet and police blotters: the *nocturnal part* of our existence. For Foucault literature had become since the end of the Ancien Régime a singular place where one was duty-bound to disclose the most commonplace of secrets. "Hence its double rapport to truth and power," he wrote. "Whereas the fabulous can function only where there is indecision between the true and the false, literature is founded on a decision of non-truth: it presents itself explicitly as artifice, but promises effects of truth that are recognizable as such."[2] Foucault went on to consider that the space of literature was the space of the unspeakable, of the most abject and shameless discourse. Literature was indeed just that, undeniably, and quite often still is. Certain writers contemporary with Foucault and whom he esteemed, like Malcolm Lowry and Pierre Guyotat, most certainly figure within that genealogy.

Here we would like to submit the hypothesis that in the early 1980s—the point in history when the idea of revolution faded—literature ceased to serve that function and established a new relationship to truth. It was still a blurring, still an instance of non-truth, but its purpose had changed; rather than mine the secrets of individuals alone, it had now turned to the singular experience of the commonplace event. Literature undertook the new function of recording what has happened. Let us make no mistake. This is no return to an epic literature; it is discourse: specifically, discourse that provides a novel way to write history. The work of Jean Genet, with its departure from autobiography, might mark the shift from reprobate to witness. The den of iniquity is still present in *The Thief's Journal*, but Genet takes the step into new territory with "Four Hours in Shatila," an essay first published in January 1983 in the French edition of the *Journal of Palestinian Studies*. What does Genet do? He fashions a grave for the corpses of the men and women massacred in the camps; he covers the shattered bodies with words, as one covers the dead with earth—not to hide them from sight but to honor them.

> I had spent four hours in Shatila. About forty bodies remains in my mem-
> ory [...] I was probably alone, I mean the only European (with a few old
> Palestinian women clinging to a torn white cloth; with a few young unarmed
> (Fedayeen), but if these five or six human beings had not been there and I
> had discovered this butchered city, black and swollen Palestinians lying there,
> I would have gone crazy. Or did I? That city lying in smithereens which I
> saw or thought I saw, which I walked through, felt, and whose death stench I
> wore, had all that taken place?[3]

Genet slips past Foucault as he had previously slipped past Jean-Paul Sartre; his last book, which he also called his sole novel, *Prisoner of Love,* exists to serve this new task: *bearing witness.*

Let us specify that the act of "bearing witness" that pervades literature today has nothing to do with the huge, encroaching mountain of testimonials. It is alien to the social injunction that victims write autobiographies. This is not to reject the usefulness of such writing as material for history or to ignore its undeniable memo-rial function. The era of the witness, to cite the title of Annette Wieviorka's book,[4] is an essential moment in the memory of the Holocaust, but that is not where literature resides. The perils of confusing the one with the other are well known. Literature and testimony do not rely on the same pact with the reader. In testimony the relationship with truth is primordial: the reader does not question the veracity of statements, because of the form in which they are presented. To reject this differ-ence is to open the door to denialism. The polemic inspired by Elie Wiesel's book *Night* (published first in French in 1957, by Minuit, then in English, in 1960) is a sobering example of those perils.[5] In conveying the experience of imprisonment in the Soviet gulag, the writings of Varlam Shalamov, we should immediately note, take a different, absolutely singular, and antinovelistic but also anti-testimonial path. He composed his *Kolyma Tales* from 1954 to 1972, at which point he wrote in his notebooks: "There is no way to keep tabs on memory anymore. I quit bothering ages ago to keep order in this storehouse, this arsenal, of memories."[6] But Shalamov would have no disciples.

Nor does the literature of "bearing witness" correspond to the mountain of writ-ing in the grand tradition of reportage, with its empathetic stance. Albert Londres, in the penal colonies of French Guyana, was among the most effective exemplars of this tradition, along with many writers in the English-speaking world, where reportage flourished. Consider, for instance, John Hersey's dispatches on Hiroshima, published in *The New Yorker* after the war. Equally worthy of consideration are the writings of Ryszard Kapuściński, correspondent from Communist Poland and author of what for this study are two essential books: *The Emperor* and *Shah of Shahs*. In the former, a few hours after the fall of the emperor of Ethiopia, Kapuściński wanders the corridors of power, observes the spaces, and collects the words of the court's least eminent personages. From these multiple elements Kapuściński assembles a portrait of the emperor, sketching the deposed figure of a sovereign in majesty. In *Shah of Shahs* he takes us into in the Tehran hotel room to which all the journalists have been confined. There he observes his work table, covered with fragments of information about what has just happened in 1978–1979, so many shards that come to compose the despot's portrait. Writing an account of a fall, narrating the crumbling of power oneself: in short, reporting in the sense of recording.

"Bearing witness" has a different relation to the real. In the reality that literature deals with there is another presence: the subject's relation to his past. In an interview with Michel Eltchaninoff for the November 2014 issue of France's *Philosophie Magazine* Svetlana Alexievich delivered a remarkable formulation:

> So I am not a journalist. I do not confine myself to the level of information; I explore people's lives, what they've understood of existence. I am not a historian, because for me everything starts where the historian's work leaves off. What goes on in people's minds after the Battle of Stalingrad or the meltdown at Chernobyl? I write the history not of facts but of souls.

These souls inhabit what we might call "the archive." *Archive* in the singular, so as not to confuse it with *the archives*, an institution that is at once a building and the documents preserved within it. The literature of "bearing witness" does not venture into the vastness of the public archives. It remains warily outside. Most of all, it knows that historians alone appeal to the archives and write with that institution's aid when recording an event. Writers who "bear witness" draw from another source, from less identifiable, less laid-out, less catalogued material. They draw from the archive as utterance sampled from the geyser of contemporary discourses. The resulting fragment might be text, image, or simple sign. This object, whatever its form, is what enters into literature and is reworked by a series of authors. Three of these authors, and not the least of them, in French, German, and Russian, have experimented with singular ways of *using the archive*, as we will demonstrate with specific examples.

## Blurring the past through the archive

Among literature's "bearers of witness," Patrick Modiano plays an undeniably important role. For one thing, an archive that in his first novels served strictly as background has gradually come to the fore, becoming the subject, the core, and, indeed, the title of his work. His novel *Livret de famille* (1977), a case in point, offers for an epigraph a verse by René Char: "To live is to persist in finishing off a memory." In his stories Modiano introduces written objects that form part of police inquiries and owe much to what Carlo Ginzburg calls the evidential paradigm.[7] The narrator introduces the reader to a collection of tiny and often graphical bits of information, and through them the reader feels he can grasp some tangible fragment in the fog of the past: not a piece of reality redeemed from the passage of time but, rather, a potential key to some measure of understanding of what has happened.

The reason to construct an enigma that is gradually unraveled through the discernment of traces left behind is not to resolve a mystery—we are not "historians" here—but to create an atmosphere. And to create this atmosphere, it should be noted, administrative documents (identity cards, identity booklets, membership cards of every stripe) play the most remarkable role. The omnipresence of objects that signal membership, establish identity, or enable surveillance is, of course, not incidental. The German occupation of France figures in many of Modiano's novels, and for his readers these objects embody the period. It hardly bears mentioning that the emergence of what we now call document forgery coincides with this same period: falsity as the paradigm of an era.

We thus have a veritable unfolding of administrative archives: from the birth certificate to the family register and on to other documents that establish the subject within the social institution. In his schema of postwar graphical culture Modiano leaves plenty of room for personal papers, which serve to mirror administrative documents. A jotted word or a laconic business card are set against the specificity of an official document, often to blurring effect.

Letters and personal papers abound, but writing in the public sphere is even more prominent, though not accorded the same development. The street and place names of the city are an undoubted hallmark of Modiano's style. There is a whole cartography superposing métro stations, streets, and squares. "Place de l'Étoile" is an inscription on a plaque at a particular spot in the city, but also a sign, and a neighborhood on a map. Modiano carefully details each of these inscriptions in the urban space, and thereby sets up a precise typology with which to distinguish those objects by medium—paper, cardboard, wooden plank, marble plaque, wall, window—and especially by letter and type of inscription. The materiality of the sign—effaced over here, in bright-red or brownish characters over there, in an arc elsewhere—is precisely described in the manner of American artist Ed Ruscha during his classic period, when Ruscha was interested in certain written objects (the colors of signs, the techniques used, etc.) and made a photographic inventory of them.

Urban writing (from the signs in a building's stairwell to the signs on a highway) preserves a memory that Modiano restores by describing the way it was forged and the way it appears today: what it provokes when one encounters it. With this typology Modiano elucidates a scale of things-that-bear-witness: from writing that escapes all forms of apprehension to writing that leaps to the eye, and on to writing that blinks as if to indicate presence/absence. The author of *Dora Bruder* (1997) is forever blurring, but the blurring is never effacement. Rather, it is an act of inscription. The last lines of the novel read as follows:

> I still didn't know how she spent her days, where she spent her days, where she lay her head, whose company she kept during those months when she first ran away [...] That is my secret. A meagre, precious secret that the executioners, the batmen, the so-called occupation authorities, the army depot, the barracks, the camps, History, time, – all that sullies and destroys us – will have failed to get from her.[8]

From book to book Modiano has revealed a veritable art of inscription that returns time and again to the erosion of signs and thus makes memory into the very locus of literature. The Austrian writer W.G. Sebald inverts this method: he compounds the archive, puts it in series, and constructs exhibitions not of things forgotten but of traces.

## Staging traces

Though he too "bears witness," Sebald's is a wholly different kind of writing from Modiano's. He composed each of his works in the form of an exhibition, with formats, heights, distances, rooms... He produced, in short, a veritable scenography. The account as document that he offers us is nevertheless not a parallel account. Nor, on the contrary, is he absorbed in the textual account, like Modiano. Each image operates on multiple levels: within the immediacy of the page itself, within a chapter and its particular sequence, within the totality of a book, within the whole body of work. We cannot consider the documents presented in Sebald's books as simple commentary. They are to Sebald what they are to his character Vera, in *Austerlitz*:

> I heard Vera again, speaking of the mysterious quality peculiar to such photographs when they surface from oblivion. One has the impression, she said, of something stirring in them, as if one caught small sighs of despair, *gémissements de désespoir* was her expression, said Austerlitz, as if the pictures had a memory of their own and remembered us, remembered the roles that we, the survivors, and those no longer among us had played in our former lives.[9]

Sebald's selection and placement of images produce not a dramatic but a memorial tension. In arranging detail and setting out his larger scheme over the course of the pages he constructs a veritable sensorial system that shifts us suddenly into memorial space. By accumulation of images, and through the use of large-scale tryptic, he suspends time while the reader reads. It is a singular experience; Sebald stems the flow not with a blank page to be turned but with images that gradually slow the reading, eventually to a halt, and jolt the reader into something akin to another experience: vision. Through his arrangement and the way the arrangement lies in the textual space Sebald lets us "see the past."[10]

This does not mean that we are projected into the past (as if by some time machine called literature) but that we take stock of what separates us from what was, from what has happened. In "hanging his pictures" W.G. Sebald prompts us— through the senses, not the intellect—to perceive memory: invisible memory forever at work.

## Deconstructing memories

It has been said: the work of Svetlana Alexievich is where the function we have attributed to literature since late Genet, the function of "bearing witness," most vividly appears. More specifically, it is with her that the relation with the archive is most frontal. Modiano suggests it through blurring omissions, and Sebald stages an exhibition. Alexievich, a Belorussian writer born in Ukraine in 1948, has put together a singular body of work with the collection of memories at its core. For her to write is to set down dispersed, silenced, squelched memories. Need we recall that her work does not constitute what we call "oral history"? Alexievich's work lies precisely in the remnant of history—in its folds, we ought to say. She appeals to memory when memory is not taken into consideration, when by the criteria of history it is in some way not credible. Into this fragile sediment Alexievich digs, not with the psychoanalyst's tools but as a geologist. She explores it with sensitive core drilling, and reports on each sample in a book. We are far from epic, far from the grand Russian novel. We are far from the psychological as well. Of traditional Russian literature she preserves only the infinite list of characters that make up the story. She preserves only the singular, the singularity of the archive. But the protagonists come onstage only once, and speak only once, in words of absolute singularity. One can read *War's Unwomanly Face* (1985), *The Last Witnesses* (1985), *Zinky Boys* (1990), *Chernobyl Prayer* (1997), or *Secondhand Time: The Last of the Soviets* (2014) by reading only the words of Valia Iuorkevitch, seven years old in 1941, now retired; or of Sofia Konstantinovna Doubniakova, stretcher-bearer during the war; or of the Red Army soldier fighting the war in Afghanistan; or of Nadjda Petrovna Vygovskaïa, evacuated from the city of Pripyat after the Chernobyl disaster, in 1986. These blocks of text nonetheless do not amount to a patchwork; they are not merely sewn together. Alexievich has developed a montage technique, naturally, but she does not arrange her fragments of collected memory in any old order. Rather, they sketch out a series of parallel collective stories. Her medium is indeed the codex, not the scroll, but the linearity of her technique allows for discontinuities. This is no doubt why every one of her works has caused a scandal when published. "Bearing witness" means breaking not only with the narrative line but also with the idea of having a beginning and an end. There is no exterior with Svetlana Alexievich. There is no way out. Like Modiano, like Sebald, in certain regards she leaves the reader no choice. He will henceforth live within the interiority, and the uncertainty, of fragile memory.

*The Last Witnesses* is in this sense exemplary. Alexievich mounts an attack from behind on a constructed, often official, and sacred memory: that of Soviet combatants in the Second World War. She does this by digging into a buried stratum whose existence is all but denied: the memory of children from the Soviet entry into the war until the German capitulation. Boys and girls aged three to twelve—become in adult life a milkmaid, a painter, a worker, a seamstress—recount not the war but their memory of the war. One after another, as if taking turns, as if needing to listen to their predecessor before dredging up the remnants of that terrible period, as if each memory owed its potency to the previous one. Alexievich decides to entrust the account to the memory of children—children who supposedly would not remember. One of the children, Valia, says: "Things stick in a child's memory like photos in an album. In isolated snapshots..." Vassia insists: "Nobody believes me... My mother didn't either. When we spoke of it again, after the war, she was astonished: 'You can't remember that. You were too young. Someone must've told you.' But no. I remember everything. [...] Yes, I remember. [And, four lines below:] Everything... I remember everything." Leonida continues: "Does a three-year-old child remember anything? Let me tell you. There are three or four images I remember very clearly." Alexievich's material consists of these scattered mental images, but also of everything her speakers say about their memories. "Memory has a color," says Galia Spannovskaïa, seven years old in 1941 and now a technician at an R&D firm. "I don't want to remember... I never want to remember," mutters Valia Zmitrovitch, eleven at the time and now a worker. It recalls the opening of the book, the Dostoyevsky quote that Alexievich selected for her epigraph: "The single tear [of a child] can justify no progress, no revolution. No Revolution. The tear will always carry more weight."

Alexievich collects these little tears and fashions them into a collective account. Each individual account bears a title that tells its own little tale. Thus *The Last Witnesses* can be read as a text of brief fragments: "I picked them up with my own hands. They were white, all white" / "I want to live! To live!" / "So all I heard were my mom's cries." / "We played, and the soldiers cried." / "Don't burn, my dear little house." / "I saw them with my little-girl eyes." The reader can delve into the thick of the sediment, and lose himself within. Chronology has no meaning; it is the hour of "bearing witness." Suddenly, in the middle of the book, the present surges forth. Until then all the accounts had been in the past. Zina Prikhodsko, four years old, worker, cries: "Bombs dropped... The earth trembled... Our house too... [...] I don't know why, but it seems to me if I fall asleep they'll kill me."

This literature's power to disturb is evident, especially when it occasionally draws from the remembered dreams of children, when the bedrock on which it lays its foundations is so unsettled. But in Alexievich, Modiano, and Sebald literature is venturing no longer into the imagination but into the uncertainty of our memories. These writers stir our memory; in fact, they embody it. I am reminded of Mathieu Riboulet's great book *Entre les deux, il n'y a rien*, published in 2015 by Verdier. This was followed, after the terrorist attacks of January 2015, by a brief text written in collaboration with Patrick Boucheron and titled *Prendre date*. In these two texts—the first of which deals with what Western Europe has called its *années de plomb* (literally "leaden years"): years of protest, and of armed struggle against the powers of Germany and Italy—Riboulet "bears witness." The memories of others and the memory of the scribe become superimposed, and a common "we" emerges. He is twelve years old and remembers our memories. It is undoubtedly not incidental that the vehicle of common memory in this enterprise is Mathieu Riboulet's own body. In Alexievich we find the body's presence hinted at when she supplies the speakers' names and ages during the war, followed by their professions at the time of her writing. Sebald conveys the body in images of fragmentary manuscript documents, whereas Modiano is always cataloguing the clothes, dresses, and suits of his characters. This once again calls to mind Genet, when he enters the camp of Shatila and steps over the corpses. Literature is no longer the locus of secrets, of our iniquities; it is now the receptacle of what remains. To write is now to list the bones and the ruins.

## Notes

1  Patrick Boucheron, "*Ce que peut l'histoire*," 17 December 2015, available at: www.college-de-france.fr/site/patrick-boucheron/inaugural-lecture-2015-12-17-18h00.htm.
2  Michel Foucault, "La Vie des hommes infâmes," *Les Cahiers du chemin*, no. 29, 15 January 1977, pp. 12–29, in *Dits et écrits*, Daniel Defert et al. (eds.), vol. III, no. 198, Paris: Gallimard, 1994.
3  Jean Genet, "Four Hours in Shatila," *Journal of Palestinian Studies*, vol. 12, no. 3, Spring 1983: pp. 3–22.
4  Annette Wieviorka, *The Era of the Witness*, Ithaca, NY: Cornell University Press, 2006.
5  See notably the 1996 article published in *Jewish Social Studies* by Naomi Seidman, Professor of Jewish Culture at the University of California at Berkeley.
6  Cited by Hélène Chatelain in her preface (p. 12) to Varlam Chalamov, *Vichéra*, Lagrasse, France: Éditions Verdier, 2000.
7  See Carlo Ginzburg: "Spie. Radici di un paradigma indiziario," in A. Gargani, *Crisi della ragione. Nuovi modelli nel rapporto tra sapere e attività umane*, Torino: Einaudi, 1979, pp. 56–106; English translation: "Clues: Roots of an Evidential Paradigm," in *Clues, Myths and the Historical Method*, Baltimore, MD: Johns Hopkins University Press, 1989, pp. 87–113.
8  Patrick Modiano, *Romans*, Paris: Gallimard, Collection Quarto, 2013, p. 735.
9  See notably his final book: W.G. Sebald, *Austerlitz*, Anthea Bell (trans.), New York: The Modern Library, 2001: pp. 182–183.
10  See Lynne Sharon Schwartz et al., *Emergence of Memory: Conversations with W.G. Sebald*, New York: Seven Stories Press, 2007.

# 4

# SOME NOTES TOWARDS A LITERARY CONCEPTION OF LITERATURE

*Donatien Grau*

What do we say when we use the word 'literature'? What do we refer to? Has the meaning shifted, over centuries and especially in recent years? And while we are using this signifier, are we covering all the meaning it induces? Do we all agree on its content? Or to phrase in other words: is literature *literature*?

I will start by focusing on the seemingly traditional question "what is litera-ture?": we often consider "literature" to be a given notion, or a given reality, when-ever we use that word, and we often forget about its very charged and ideological meaning. And those who take on the fact that the word is indeed charged, either do so as historians – thereby not addressing its contemporary potency – or do so as ideologists, eventually not encompassing the Aristotelian proliferation that builds our world and our creativity, today. I will therefore aim to emphasize its highly problematic ambiguity, and, from there, try to see how we can formulate the terms of the literary equation now, and how we could solve it for the present.

## A problematic definition

This question "what is literature?" might seem straightforward, which, as we will see, it definitely is not. Of course, it was famously asked by Jean–Paul Sartre in his 1947 book, continuing a lineage that starts at the origins of modern thinking, with Madame de Staël's *De la littérature* (1800). Let us look briefly at the structure of *Qu'est-ce que la littérature?*, as it may indicate how the problem was paradigmatically raised by Sartre – who was equally a philosopher and a writer.

*Qu'est-ce que la littérature?* is structured in four chapters: "Qu'est-ce qu'écrire"?", "Pourquoi écrire?", "Pour qui écrit-on?", and "Situation de l'écrivain en 1947". "What is writing?", "Why do we write?", "For whom do we write?" and "Situation of the writer in 1947". The chapters' titles all feature the verb "to write" or the noun "writer". It seems that literature is what writers do – in the same way Duchamp would say that art is what artists do.

What appears vividly, when we take some distance from Sartre's conception of literature, is that his definition is not descriptive: it is normative. By defining literature he does not seem to seek to delimitate the term from the point of view of its content, which would be structured according to rules that would be historical, architectural, in a sense, and would be articulated from the perspective of the object. His point of view is a late modernist's, and its very counter-intuitive nature incites us to understand that what seems in Sartre's world perfectly legitimate and coherent is actually a coup de force: it is not obvious historically to define literature as what writers do. We can find ten other definitions, which introduce plurality in the conception of this word. I will simply name seven fundamental other forms this definition has taken in the construction of Western traditions.

## Seven definitions of literature

The word "literature" comes from Latin, and from the "litterae", which firstly simply meant "letters", in an alphabetical sense, and, from there, anything made of those. Literature would be, in that regard, anything involving the alphabet. Anything and everything could be, at this point, literature. And thus we are, at this point, quite far from Sartre's idea.

The second one was wonderfully analyzed by Marc Fumaroli in his 2002 book *L'âge de l'éloquence* (The Age of Eloquence). It is the neo-Latin concept of "res literaria" – literally, "the literary thing", which is the closest etymological ancestor of the word "literature". The "res literaria" is the form eloquence takes while re-using and re-arranging resources from the past. In a sense, it is the activation of rhetoric. And it does not relate to anyone specifically who would gain dignity from dealing with it. The concept of "writing", as an autonomous activity, such as phrased by Sartre, and the idea of a symbolically predominant "writer" make absolutely no sense in the framework of rhetoric.

Let us move from the early 17th century to the early 19th century, and to Madame de Staël's rephrasing of the word in French. *De la littérature* chronologically and intellectually paved the way to the 19th century and romanticism. Before Madame de Staël, as in the *Encyclopedia*, the word was used to describe what is now general known as the Belles-Lettres – that is: the production of texts in various situations, for various purposes, and without any dignity attached to it. Madame de Staël, who had been highly influenced by Herder, completely changed the meaning of the word. "Literature", as defined in *De la littérature*, is the textual, often poetic expression through the work of an individual of the spirit of a nation. Madame de Staël, from that definition, retraces a narrative of literary history, going from Homer and the Ancient Greeks to modern 18th century works. That narrative leads to the present, as it does in the galleria of *Corinne*, where all the history of Italian art is only designed to lead to the figure. The articulation of individuality, poetry, and the idea of a nation is equally disconnected from the rhetoric concept of "res literaria".

Then, 27 years after Madame de Staël's *De la littérature*, in his conversation with Johann Peter Eckermann held on January 31st, 1827, Goethe used the word

"Weltliteratur", "world-literature", thereby meaning the objective community between authors – specifically poets – from the East and the West. He opposes to Madame de Staël's idea of specific national literary forms the notion of "allgemeine Weltliteratur", "general world-literature", engaging within a process of identifying the human similarities that we sensed through literature.

Fifty years later, the extremely famous and enigmatic last line of Verlaine's 1874 poem *L'Art Poétique* goes "Et tout le reste n'est que littérature", as opposed to the vibrant movement of the line as transcription of the world's musicality. In that sense, Verlaine, in his use of the word, emphasizes the fixity, and the vacuity of literature as text. Literature would be the death of that of which poetry is the life.

At the same time as Verlaine used the word with that meaning, German philologists, around Theodor Mommsen, developed the historiographical concepts of *Primärliteratur* and *Sekundärliteratur*, primary and secondary literature, the first being the totality of texts that can be used as sources for historical research, the second being the studies on this primary literature.

In 1919, André Breton, Philippe Soupault and Louis Aragon created a Dadaist journal called "Littérature", in which they aimed to destroy the institution this word signified for them. They stood for poetry against "literature", for inspiration against institution, for disorder against structure.

In 1924, Leon Trotsky felt compelled to bring out a Marxist reading of the role of literature in the communist world, and he wrote the book *Literature and the Revolution*. At the same time as he engaged with a Marxist reading of the literature of his time, and of the recent past, he ascribed to the transformation of this bourgeois institution a crucial role in the evolution of society, culture, and mankind. Famously his text ended on the rather optimistic note:

> Man will become immeasurably stronger, wiser and subtler; his body will become more harmonized, his movements more rhythmic, his voice more musical. The forms of life will become dynamically dramatic. The average human type will rise to the heights of an Aristotle, a Goethe, or a Marx. And above this ridge new peaks will rise.

Ultimately, and this will be the end of our brief journey into the various meanings of the word "literature", in his 1953 book *Le degré zéro de l'écriture* (Writing Degree Zero), Roland Barthes developed the idea according to which writing as an activity would be obliterated by literature as an institution, and that it was in regaining the innocence of the pure gesture of writing that literature could reach a new momentum. In a sense, it would be in its own negation as an institution that literature could perpetuate its own existence, specifically as institution.

## Impossible unity

Between the Latin alphabet, Jesuit rhetoric, Madame de Staël, Goethe, Theodor Mommsen, André Breton, Philippe Soupault, Louis Aragon, Trotsky, Sartre, and

Barthes, there seems to be very little in common. And yet, every time, the same word is used, in different languages, pertaining extremely dissimilar realities. What is most important here is that every iteration of the word is ideological: at every given moment "literature" is a word used in the framework of a certain structure of power in order to serve or to question that very structure of power. Every time, it is situational, and therefore does not have the possibility of being universal in time and place.

Such a diversity – to use a polite word – and such a localization, have critical consequences. The fact that the word "literature" would mean such different things in such different contexts makes it extremely difficult to use. When we use this word now, are we talking about national identity? Are we talking about the alphabet? Are we talking about rhetoric? About philology? About a social, and even bourgeois institution? What is it we are talking about? Who is speaking and from what point of view? How could we save literature either from naivety or from annihilation?

When a word becomes so difficult to use, the easiest way might be either to accept that it means everything and nothing, or to give up on it. Both options do not seem very enticing: let us start with the latter. The "death of literature", as the "death of art", has become a well-known phrase: and yet, more people write and publish texts than ever; they publish books online, on print, they do not even need to write books anymore, and can feed the internet with their production. There is more desire for literature than ever – and that desire is wider-spread than ever. We would not want to get rid at a concept when it is reaching its own democratic significance.

The former – accepting that it means everything and nothing – might appear less unacceptable: there are so many words we use without even knowing their content, why wouldn't we do the same with literature? The problem, however, is that literature is not just any other phrase. It is a belief in the transcendence and sublimation of the world through the word – it is as such that many people practice it, both as readers and as writers. Very much has been, and is today at stake in its meaning. Because of the role of literature today, in an age where our individuality is being questioned, and therefore constantly needs to be asserted, we somehow feel we cannot give up on defining it.

## A contemporary question

The number of books published today on this topic signifies how unable we are to give up defining literature. To name simply a few: Antoine Compagnon's *Literature, Theory, and Common Sense*; Jacques Rancière's *Politics of Literature* and *Mute Speech: Literature, Critical Theory and Politics*; Terry Eagleton's *The Event of Literature* and *How to Read Literature*. All are recent books, with quite strong political agendas – standing for a certain notion of literature, a certain view on the world, both being closely linked to each other.

Even with a word whose meaning we do not really know, we as a culture tend to analyze situations in which it culturally did not exist – let us think for instance of Richard Hunter's seminal book *Plato and the Traditions of Ancient Literature*. Plato did not know "literature", a Latin word, he did not know it in the sense used by any of the previously mentioned authors. And yet, one of the world's leading classicists uses it in his investigation of the textual traditions of Platonism. It is a necessary tool for us to keep inhabiting symbolically the world we live in.

So there seems to be at the same time a considerable interest in literature and a crucial disarray in defining it. Even these three critics – Compagnon, Rancière, Eagleton – in books dating from the same years, do not use it with the same meaning – from a political institution (Rancière) to the result of writing (Compagnon) to a cultural experience (Eagleton); and yet all three share that ideological embedding.

And yet, we can learn from all these experimentations with a single word. Indeed, these three critics, as all their numerous predecessors in raising that issue, adopt a normative approach, and not a descriptive one. They too strive to produce rules in order to define what is literature and what is not – often in the idea of defending a certain conception of literature they feel is threatened.

This normativity is not the only problem raised by this tradition of defining literature. All these definitions somehow stand the one against the other: they are not only normative, but they also tend to be mutually exclusive. A conversation between a German philologist from Theodor Mommsen's circle and a Dadaist might have been quite a performance. Or even between Verlaine and Breton, with a forty-year time difference; not to mention between a Jesuit and Madame de Staël. Each time, either the definitions are totally foreign, the one to the other, or they are constructed against each other. It is not easy to produce a synthesis and try to bring out a comprehensive conception of what literature is – a conception that, even though itself ideologically rooted, in an ideology of non-ideology, would embrace rather than divide, and therefore, from the distance of "intelligence" (the concept used by the great literary historian Sainte-Beuve), allow for a greater understanding.

## Analyzing a question

We sensed that the question "what is literature" was normative, and led to a mutually exclusive set of answers. But we need to ask ourselves an even more fundamental question: what do we say grammatically, syntactically, when we ask the phrase "What is literature?".

In that question, every word carries highly problematic suggestive content: "what" signifies that literature is actually something, and from there, can we add, something univocal and coherent. Literature might seem, from the use of "what", to be an identifiable and even solid reality.

In the same way, "is" lies to the idea that such a thing as literature exists as a reality: from the transitive notion that literature is something, we can conclude that it is "something", and, again, something stable, as the use of the interrogative pronoun "what" equally signifies.

Ultimately, the most problematic part of the question is the use of the word "literature" itself. What does literature mean in "what is literature"? Is it the concept itself? The reality related to the concept? And if so, which of the realities does it refer to?

"What is a literature?" as a question is actually filled with pre-conceived ideas, with definitions that are being made in the phrasing, in the enunciation of it. Therefore, it might appear an extremely difficult one to ask, for several reasons:

- it presupposes that there is a fixed objective identity of literature;
- it is implicitly based on a decision as of the ideal/material conception of it;
- it relates to the idea that literature is not only identifiable, but monolithic.

In a nutshell: the question presupposes an objectification and an essentialization of literature, which raises considerable issues as of the relation between the conception of the word as a concept, the multiple paradigms that have been historically developed to define it, and the proliferating realities of which it is supposed to provide an account.

While we use the word "literature", in that phrase, we actually construct our object as much as we take it and analyze it. "What is literature?" is fundamentally a constructive, hence highly problematic question. Its very relevance is conditioned to the acceptance that it does not lead to an attempt to produce an accurate definition of what it is, but actually makes its object, at the same moment as it makes it visible.

There might be a sense of uneasiness in discovering that, in the very process of pretending to ask what literature is, we actually already present half of the answer, all terms of which can be challenged. Literature is not necessarily objective; it certainly is not monolithic; and we cannot pretend to describe it while we are constructing its notion.

Another element makes this question problematic: the present tense of "is". Asking what literature is, now, is not the same as asking what it has been, what it was, and what it will be. It presupposes the existence of literature essentially in the present, as an element of our time, which can be defined specifically then – or, on the other hand, which has been existing forever, *sub specie aeterni*. The very idea that literature exists in the present, let this present be eternal, or let it be immediate: in both cases, this emphasis creates a sense of disconnect from other temporalities, and dramatizes the "here and now" of literature, and of its very definition.

We have understood so far how incredibly charged this common attempt to define literature actually is, as Sartre enacted it. It is difficult to pretend to define an object while you are making it up; to consider the possibility of producing a straightforward univocal definition, while others exist simultaneously. You may have something more to bring to the table, something others have not thought about yet, but undoubtedly you need to acknowledge the fact that there has been some serious thinking going on in other brains. But from the moment that one is putting together yet another conception of anything, and specifically literature, why acknowledge the possibility for others to be right? If one thought they were right, why add anything to the table?

This is one of the utmost issues of literature today: redefining the definition; not theoretically; not only critically; not in an ivory tower of any kind; but in the middle of the messy world, of the rhizomatic world in which we live; the world where literature is part of culture, once a part of the dominating West, and now of the weak "global"; when we deal with "literature", we deal with what is now, because of history, because of Western imperialism, and yet it is, the potential of mankind.

We need to put together another methodology in order to define literature, one that would take its roots in reality itself and, while emanating from the present, discussing exclusively the present, would encompass the variety included in the palimpsest that constitutes our very situation.

## Aristotle versus Plato, once again

In some sense, we need to engage anew with the debate between Aristotle and his master Plato.

The core element of Platonism is that it produces a coherent – or let's say relatively coherent – vision of the world, the universe, and the human being. We all know of "Platonic love", being disconnected from the body; we all know of the characterization of the body as a tomb; we all know of the refusal to integrate poets in the city, for grounds of immorality. We all know, eventually, of the hierarchical structuration of the ideal city. All that makes for a pretty solid coherent anti-worldly philosophical and intellectual construction.

The crux is that, while Plato strongly defends this conception – his conception – of the world, he also knows that it does not resist reality. The Republic is not a city he would like to implement in the world – it is a "polis en tois logois", "a city in discourse"; it is a poetic – we would today say: fictional – creative process, making something up from the world and for the world, both in stylistic terms – this is poetry – and in terms of content.

Aristotle is an extremely different animal, fascinated with the observation of reality. The series of books his students wrote on the Constitutions of the different cities, some of which have been transmitted to us, stand for that: he wanted to know everything on actual situations, in order to be able to build up from these actual situations intellectual patterns.

Plato builds a system, which he knows to be a construct; Aristotle identifies patterns, and organizes them around an overall schema of the sublunary world. So on the one hand we have a thrift to present to the world, another world; on the other, the desire to excavate from the world the meaning that is inherent to it.

The Plato/Aristotle debate is very much alive in the field of contemporary Continental philosophy. The names have changed, since we are not dealing with the masters themselves, but with their epigones: with Alain Badiou and Bruno Latour, and now with the new transformative generation of Emanuele Coccia and Tristan Garcia. Most literary thinkers, in the continuity of Plato and in the way Alain Badiou does it now, construct a univocal perspective, while still keeping open the possibility for others to utter a statement they eventually seek to overrule.

The much more comprehensive Aristotelian perspective might be of use in reconsidering the issue of redefining the process of defining literature. In the same straightforward way as Aristotle did, why wouldn't we identify and name all the forms literature takes, and start an inquiry into modes of literature – as Bruno Latour began an "inquiry into modes of existence"?

This experience might prove extremely rewarding, as it would enable us to know actually, and also slightly basically, what we are talking about when we use the word "literature". We would not limit ourselves to one definition, but actually engage with the fact that the great fortune of literature today lies in the coexistence of a plurality of meanings into one word.

Literature might well be, indeed, as a term, hence as a linguistic reality, wealthier and more complex than it has ever been. As a starting point, for us to understand the extraordinary possibilities of opening this new field, let us name the contents of the word as it exists now – so all these definitions are strictly contemporary:

- literature is a textual corpus of authors and masterpieces, which emanates from the past and goes until now (what we could call: retrospective literature);
- literature is a belief that words can transcend the world;
- literature is a series of critical scholarly inquiries;
- literature is a political institution which is related to bourgeois culture;
- literature is a mode of production of books and texts (in the form of "contemporary literature", specifically);
- literature is an accomplishment (in the form of the phrase "this is literature");
- literature is an economic system.

These are simply seven characterizations, rather than definitions, of the meaning covered by the word today. They provide a limited, but relevant insight on the complexity of the world, a complexity that exists very much in the present and carries the legacy of the past; seven characterizations that all exist in the online as well as in the offline world.

It is difficult, if not irrelevant, while pretending to discuss literature in one of those seven meanings, to accept the fact that we would lose six-sevenths of the actual overall content of the word.

Therefore, we need to accept the fact that literature can only be defined in its plurality, which does not mean that we should surrender to vagueness or indecisiveness – but rather the opposite. As we know how complex and pluralistic the literary field is, the greatest aim would be to analyze the coalescences between these definitions, to see how the most energy gets created from the dialogue, the conversation, the interaction, the friction, between these definitions of literature.

## Making a world/digging into the world

Francis Wolff, in a *Dire le Monde* (Saying the World), analyzed how we constitute our world with language: the world exists as much as it is a combination of the different worlds different individuals construct individually. This point on which different worlds coincide and coexist, this is the world, as existing for humans, shaped by humans, from reality.

What Wolff says of the world could be said of literature: as we argued, literature is many things, which, in a Latourian fashion, can be numbered, and whose number remains open. At the same time as we acknowledge the absolute necessity to number the forms of literature, to accept all of them, and to judge them, in the same way as Aristotle would have done, by their "telos", their achievement, it is essential to understand that their other meaning lies in the point where they coincide. And the coincidence of these paradigms of literature can be identified with one single phrase: human knowledge. From human knowledge and from its limits come fiction; come creation, in all its forms; come inquiry; come sublimation. The human thirst for knowledge and the meaning that emanates from it is embodied in science; in art; in literature. Literature is the consequence of an awareness to this human process of world-making. This awareness leads to a thrift for sublimation. And that is literature, in all its forms. Literature, as art in any kind, is the constant digging in of one's research; it is, equally, the constant blending of forms; when at its most fulfilled in any definition, it ends up potentially being the other six at the same time.

One of the great contributions of neurology lies in the understanding of the structure of the brain. The brain constructs a narrative. It takes elements from the senses, from memory, every piece of information it has at hand, and from that it builds a narrative. This narrative as narrative is not wrong, is not right, it might be accurate or not. Let us use the word: it is a fiction. We as brains, as spirits, are fiction-producing machines, we try to make an account of the world that surrounds us − as Wolff would say − and as we do so we take into account and we produce, simultaneously; what we perceive is always a construct; it is never a transcription of the outside world − it is always a translation, and a transformation.

Once we take into consideration the terrifying and sublime consequences of this discovery, once we feel that the world around us might well vanish, then, in one gesture, we seize it again. We understand the fiction in which we are living, and, while taking it for granted, we construct a world, we build our life. What we considered to be a historical construct of some time is actually the enactment of human activity, and its stakes in the present are human stakes at their highest: all these discussions have a ground, of which they constantly need to be aware, and as such open a gap for literature to exist within a framework of possibilities, of endeavors, of thought, of labor, of genius.

The gesture with which we regain the world is often instinctive, but it carries the energy of so many thoughts. It carries so much knowledge. These thoughts, this knowledge, come at least partly from literature. The solution to our fictional existence is literary fiction, in all its forms. We cannot live without it, so we'd better accept it all, from the transcendence of masterpieces to the proliferation of diaries, from scholarly literature to the belief in the subliming power of fiction as literature. All of literature, from the structure to the concept, from the texts to the people, is an expression of the ideal. Acknowledging it paves the way to literary humanism. If we are deeply aware of it, either we will live a happier life or we will at least have experienced the fulfillment of ecstasy. In both cases, we will have loved life more. All that thanks to literature, whatever it is; and if we are geniuses, so be it, for the best, or for the worse.

# PART II

# Literature and the novel

# 5
# THE INSTALLATION AS NOVEL

*Boris Groys*

The history of modern art was often described as history of the struggle for an autonomous image purified of everything narrative, illustrative. However, a visitor of contemporary art exhibitions is time and again confronted with narrative art forms. Usually, these exhibitions contain extensive written documentations, sound tracks, lengthy videos and films telling different kinds of stories. These can be personal stories of some real or fictional protagonists. Or they can be descriptions of certain historical events, past artistic performances or interventions, political engagements, participatory projects etc. Thus, the art exhibition becomes a specific mode of staging a story. This staging creates a public event and attracts the public attention in a way in which a book is incapable of doing. Being put in a context of an art exhibition a story gets an additional validation – comparable to its theatralization in the 19th Century. And in many cases the exhibited story cannot be told by a book because this story cannot be understood without the use of music, film or video.

However, if we speak about different narratives being presented to the viewer inside an art exhibition space we still interpret this space as something given and neutral. Of course, the behavior of the visitors changes if they begin to be confronted not by an image that can be grasped at a glance but by a text, video, film or sound track that needs some time to be seen in its entirety. That often leads to a fragmentary perception of these texts or videos because of the short time of a usual exhibition visit. Thus, if the contemporary exhibitions include time-based, narrative art forms the perception of art and behavior of the visitors change. But, as I have already said, the exhibition space remains in this case the same neutral, non-narrative, modernist art space. However, I would like to speak today about the narrativization of the exhibition space itself. Here the art space ceases to be simply a neutral stage on which a certain story is staged – but becomes a story.

In other words, I would like to speak about a shift from the traditional exhibition space presenting individual, disconnected art objects, be they narrative or not, to a holistic understanding of space, in which the relations between these objects become more important than the objects themselves. The space of the art installation is by definition such a holistic space because the art installation is an artwork. Here the exhibition space is not any more external and neutral in relationship to the artworks that are exhibited inside it. Rather, the exhibition space comes to be included inside the artwork – becomes a part of it. The visitors leave their own territory – and find themselves on a different territory shaped and controlled by the artist.

Already some avant-garde artists like Marcel Duchamp or El Lissitsky tried to turn exhibitions into installations. But, in a systematic way, the art installation began to be developed since the 1960s and, especially, 1970s. Conceptual artists of that time began to use the syntax of the installational space in a way analogous to the linguistic syntax. One can say that they organized objects and events in the installation's space like individual words and verbs are organized by a sentence. We all know a crucial role that the famous "linguistic turn" played in the emergence and development of conceptual art. The influence of Wittgenstein and French Structuralism on conceptual art practice was decisive – to mention only some relevant names among many others. Art began to make theoretical statements again, to communicate empirical experiences, to formulate ethical and political attitudes and to tell stories.

The installation is frequently denied the status of a specific art form, because the question arises what is the medium of an installation. Traditional art media are all defined by a specific material support: canvas, stone, or film. Now, the material support of the medium installation is the space. Every exhibition space presupposes a certain kind of temporalization and narrativization. The visitors are always instructed how they are supposed to move through the exhibition space from one exhibition item to another. The standard art exhibitions tell "objective", scientifically and institutionally legitimized histories: art history with its standard periodization, biographies of the artists, histories of artistic groups and movements. But an installation tells – almost by definition – a particular, in many cases fictional story from a "subjective", artistic, authorial point of view. The installation is an art form that can include all other art forms. In this respect, the space of the art installation reminds one of the space of the novel. Already Friedrich Schlegel has said that the novel includes all the other literary forms[1] – and that, accordingly, the theory of literature is ultimately the theory of the novel. So, it can be also said that the theory of art is ultimately the theory of art installation.

Indeed, there is a similarity – even a homology – between the installational space and the space of the novel. The installational space always suggests an invisible, ghostly presence of a subject somehow connecting all these texts, things, or videos that are displayed inside the installational space. Every installation looks like an abandoned, haunted house in which the specific arrangement of things, texts and images refers to an absent individual inhabitant – or several inhabitants – of this house. And the visitor is always a detective who comes to this abandoned house to understand who lived and maybe still lives there. In other words, by creating an art installation the artist implicitly or even explicitly builds it around a figure of a protagonist (or a group of protagonists) – like an author of a narrative builds it around a hero. The figure of the protagonist is suggested by an installation – and at the same time is absent from the installational space. This hero (or a group of heroes) is a doppelganger of the author – and at the same does not coincide with the author.

The relationship between the author and the hero of the installation strongly reminds me of the Mikhail Bakhtin's treatise about "The Author and Hero in the Aesthetic Practice" (1920s).[2] In this treatise Bakhtin speaks about the "architectonics" and the "spatial form" of the literary hero – meaning that every literary, narrative text defines the horizon of the hero's experience, builds his or her world and draws the borders of this world. Bakhtin calls the spatial and temporal parameters of the hero existence "chronotops". The individual spaces of a novel's heroes remain separate but at the same time the novel creates a common space in which the particular heroes' spaces can intersect – and the heroes can interact. Often enough Bakhtin is interpreted as a theoretician of the dialogue. But the dialogue has such a central position in Bakhtin's theory precisely because he never expects the protagonists of a dialogue to find a consensus, an agreement, a compromise. The Bakhtinian dialogue is a potentially infinite dialogue, or, rather, polylogue (Bakhtin speaks about the polyphonic novel) because the heroes of the novel are not only connected but also separated by their respective chronotops. And because the heroes' chronotops do not coincide their life positions, "ideologies" also cannot coincide – so that the dialogue between them cannot lead to any common conclusion. Thus, for Bakhtin every literary hero has a certain independence from the author because the hero is never really invented by the author but, rather, defined by his or her own specific chronotop. Of course, Bakhtin's theory of the novel is fascinating in its own right but I mentioned this theory here primarily because it is, I would say, the installational theory of the novel par excellence: the architectonic, spatial form of a hero is what the installation as an art form actually is all about.

Now I would like to present to you some works of Ilya Kabakov – a Russian artist who became famous in the art world primarily because of his installations. In these installations, he explicitly thematizes the figure of a hero, or a protagonist that remains implicit in the installations of many other artists. And he does so partially because he was influenced by Bakhtin and his theory concerning the relation – and the tension – between the heroes' voices and their chronotops, that means the architectonics, the spatial form of their subjectivities. Already in the early period of his work Kabakov localizes the voices – in form of textual replicas – of different invented persons on the surface of his paintings and drawings. Every person gets a fragment of the pictorial space that remains external to all other similar fragments. At the same time the author, in this case Kabakov himself, only marks the topology of the pictorial space – but remains outside this topology, has no place inside it. That corresponds to the role of the author of the novel as it was described by Bakhtin: the author remains always outside the novel, has no voice and no chronotop inside the novel's space. In a certain sense for Bakhtin there is no difference between author and reader because both are able to relate to the topology of the novel but remain external to it.

Kabakov's installations were built according to the same principle. The author seems to be simply one of the accidental visitors of these installations – their inner space being divided among different protagonists. Kabakov's first major installation in the West was called "Ten Characters". The individual art objects that were used in his New York installation, were mainly created by Kabakov in Russia, and then distributed among ten different fictitious authors – whereby each figure was given an imaginary biography, presenting this figure as an artist who practiced his art in the seclusion of a small room. This almost baroque installation offered a programmatic contrast to the "white cubes" of minimalist and conceptual installations. It played a game of light and shadow with the viewer's gaze prying into other people's private lives and contemplating the traces of their earthly existence (all the ten artists were presumed to be dead or, rather, disappeared). Here art is seen as the disclosure of the private things and rubbish of everyday life, which in fact ought to be protected from the public gaze. This communal apartment can, of course, be seen as a metaphor of a life marked by the fear of self-exposure or, rather, self-betrayal. While the persons living in each of the rooms are cocooned within their own private dreams, they all live together in one apartment. We have here a case of communication without communication, of a closely knit daily life led in total inner isolation. For Kabakov the Soviet communal apartment is a paradigm for the place where the individual is exhibited, exposed and disclosed to the gaze of others. Furthermore, this gaze belongs to largely hostile strangers who consistently exploit their advantages of observation in order to gain advantage in the power struggle within the communal apartment. In the extreme intimacy of the shared apartment the entire visual realm becomes a battlefield in the struggle to dominate the gaze. Being able to observe the others is just as important as concealing and shielding from the scrutiny of others. However, others always have a surplus of gaze and power over us, a supremacy we wish to protect ourselves from – but one which we can also enjoy. Since the death of God as a confidential and omniscient observer, the community is the only remaining observer interested in the intimate aspects of our lives. After the collapse of Communism, it became clear that many people missed the pleasure and excitement derived from being watched, from being the object of someone else's constant attention – even when this interest was hostile.

In a certain sense the communal mode of existence turns everyone into an artist – as well as a work of art. Hence, in a dystopic manner, the Soviet communal apartment managed to achieve the utopian vision of Joseph Beuys: here everyone had to become an artist! So, it is no accident that all the residents in Kabakov's communal apartment are artists – and by the same token, his communal apartment also acts as a metaphor for the "art community", the communal life shared by artists in our society. Indeed, what else is a museum or a major exhibition if not a communal apartment in which various artists, who may never have heard of one another before and who each aspire to very different goals and interests in their art, are herded together at the will of a curator appointed by society? In this manner, artists are forever encountering each other within the imposed intimacy of a shared context – together with often unknown, even hostile, neighbors. Thus, the artistic community is very similar to the community of the literary heroes in a novel as it was described by Bakhtin – especially, in relation to the novels of Dostoevsky.[3] Here again the everyday control by the gaze of the others (Jean-Paul Sartre: hell is the others) permanently leads to scandals, confrontations, awkward social events.

Now, Kabakov does not only narrate the lives of the heroes of his installations but also presents them as authors of the artworks that are places inside these installations. Here Kabakov uses the pseudonym in most consequential way – to a degree to which it was used only by few authors like Soren Kierkegaard or Fernando Pessoa but which is quite exceptional in the visual art context. Thus, Kabakov presents himself as merely a curator of the exhibitions in which all the works are created by other (of course, fictitious) authors. And every time the rooms of the installations are presented as being abandoned by their artist-inhabitants. In many of these installations we find the written notice informing us that these inhabitants disappeared leaving no traces other than their works. Even their corpses were never found. Here the reference to the Christian tradition according to which Christ was taken out of his grave into the corporeal immortality cannot be overlooked. In case of Christ the fact that his corpse was not found was taken as the proof of his resurrection – and immortality. In these senses, the heroes of Kabakov's installations can also be thought as being immortal.

Paradigmatic in this respect is an earlier installation by Kabakov, *The Man Who Flew into Space from his Apartment*. The hero of the installation built an apparatus that was capable of catapulting him straight from his bed into outer space. And the experiment evidently worked – because all we see is the room the man used to occupy. The walls of the room are plastered with Soviet posters designed to communicate a sense of historical optimism. Inside the room we see the bed and the remains of the apparatus, along with some technical drawings showing how the apparatus functioned. A section of the ceiling – directly above the bed – has been destroyed. It was through this hole that the man shot out into space. As a new Christ, he propelled himself to the heaven. But the contemporary heaven is not the paradise but the dark cosmic space. The hero of the installation is Christ in the era of globalisation: instead of dwelling in paradise he eternally encircles the Earth. Visitors of the installation cannot enter the abandoned room, but they can look into it from outside – from a small vestibule. On the walls of the vestibule there are texts describing this event from the point of view of the man's neighbours and acquaintances. The apparatus itself doesn't look particularly impressive. What's left of it doesn't give the impression that this could have been the same type of rocket used for "real" voyages into outer space. On the other hand, there was no need for this apparatus to be particularly powerful because its maker had discovered that "immense vertical currents of energy" pervade the whole of the cosmos. In his view, all that was needed was to identify the topology of these currents and calculate the precise moment when a person could take advantage of these currents and get to the cosmic utopia without any very great effort. The real scandal is the pseudo-documentary character of Kabakov's installation. For this is not just some nocturnal dream, in other words it is not just some mental construct, something abstract, spiritual or immaterial. On the contrary, the hero of the installation was brought up on radical Soviet atheism, dialectic materialism and scientific Communism. Dreams and spirits are not enough for him. He only believes in the material, the physical, the real world. He doesn't pray. And he doesn't dream. Instead he constructs a device that he has designed himself on the basis of specific scientific principles, and uses it to launch himself into outer space, body and soul. The only thing that distinguishes this undertaking from a strictly scientific experiment is the supreme importance of the right moment. The positive sciences regard time as homogenous, which by definition means that any experiment is capable of being repeated. The hero of the installation, on the other hand, has to identify the exact moment when certain otherwise dormant cosmic energies enter a period of activity. This is the type of science pursued by revolutionaries and artists – it's a matter of not missing that right moment, of allowing it to propel one into the unknown. And it's a matter of recognising and making specific use of nameless energies that have a cosmic and a collective effect but which generally go unrecognised.

This stress on the unique "here and now" reminds one of Walter Benjamin's essay "The Work of Art in the Age of Mechanical Reproduction". This essay became famous primarily thanks to its use of the concept of aura. Aura is, for Benjamin, the relationship of the artwork to the site in which it is found – the relationship to its external context. Benjamin's formulations are well known: "Even the most perfect reproduction of a work of art is lacking in one element: its here and now, its unique existence at the place where it happens to be."[4] He continues: "These 'here' and 'now' of the original constitute the concept of its authenticity, and lay basis for the notion of a tradition that has up to the present day passed this object along as something having a self and an identity."[5] The copy lacks authenticity, therefore, not because it differs from the original but because it has no location and consequently is not inscribed in history.

One can say that Benjamin practices here a reversal of the usual topology of the relationship between body and soul. The soul of the artwork is not in its body; rather, the body of the artwork is found inside its aura, in its soul. This other topology of the relationship between the soul and the body has its origin in gnosis, in theosophy, and anthroposophy. The body is inscribed into its soul, is surrounded and covered by the soul. The loss of aura is the loss of this inscription in the history, in the here and now – of one's own chronotop, to use the Bakhtinian notion. So, one can say that the installation – at least the installation as it is understood by Kabakov – is the lost aura, the lost soul that remains after the body abandoned it – or propelled itself out of it. The aura is the "architectonics of the hero's space", spatial form of the subjectivity – but uninhabited any more by the hero's body. This is how the aura becomes an installation. The installation is a copy of the aura – in which the aura does not get lost but begins to be reproduced.

Benjamin's interpretation of the distinction between original and copy thus opens up the possibility not only of making a copy out of an original but also of making an original out of a copy. Indeed, when the distinction between original and copy is merely a topological, contextual one, then it not only becomes possible to remove an original from its site and deterritorialize it, but also to reterritorialize the copy. Benjamin himself calls attention to this possibility when he writes about the figure of profane illumination and refers to the forms of life that can lead to such a profane illumination: "The reader, the thinker, the loiterer, the *flâneur,* are types of illuminati just as much as the opium eater, the dreamer, the ecstatic."[6] One is struck by the fact that these figures of profane illumination are also figures of motion – especially the *flâneur.* The *flâneur* does not demand of things that they come to him; he goes to things. In this sense, the *flâneur* does not destroy the auras of things; he respects them. Or rather, only through him do the auras emerge again. The figure of profane illumination is the reversal of the "loss of aura" that comes from siting the copy in a topology of undetermined circulation though the modern mass media. Now, however, it is clear that the installation can also be counted among the figures of profane illumination, because it transforms the viewer into a *flâneur.*

The visitor of an installation is a *flâneur* who substitutes the circulating body of the protagonist with his or her own body – appropriating the aura for the period of the visit. That means: The fate of modern and contemporary art can by no means be reduced to the "loss of aura." Rather, the (post)modernity enacts a complex play of deterritorialization and reterritorialization, of removing aura and restoring aura. What distinguishes the modern age from earlier periods is simply the fact that the originality of a modern work is not determined by its material but by its aura, by its context, by its historical site. In the modern age, the aura of originality has not simply been lost – it has become variable. Otherwise, the eternal value of originality would simply have been replaced by the eternal (non)value of unoriginality – as indeed happens in some art theories. All the same, eternal copies can no more exist than eternal originals. To be an original and possess an aura means the same thing as to be alive. But life is not something that the living being has "in itself". Rather, life is the inscription of a body into a life context – into a chronotop, into the aura, into the novel, into the installation.

The novel can be read and re-read – even if the interpretation of a novel is subjected to the historical change – its textual body remains self-identical through time. The installation can be also visited and re-visited. Every time one enters the installation its space remains also the same. It is this analogy between re-reading a text and re-visiting an installation, between a private church and an artificially constructed nightmare that was thematized by many authors. One can mention here Raymond Roussel (*Impressions d'Afrique*) and Alain Robbe-Grillet (especially, *Les Jalousies*). However, the recent novel *The Remainder* by Tom McCarthy is the more interesting example of the thematization of the installation within the literary text.

The hero of the novel builds the huge installations in which he tries to materialize his visions, dreams but also real contexts and events that left an indelible

**62**  Boris Groys

impression on his brain. He tries to reconstruct these impressions in the most precise way, in the most miniscule details. Thus, he becomes able to reenter and reenact the past situations freely and at every moment. However, as the hero lives further new situations emerge that he wants to objectify and eternalize – so he begins to build one installation after another like one writes one book after another. Every installation allows to repeat, reenter and reenact an auratic event. But this repetition cannot prevent the emergence of the "original" auratic moment that remains unpredictable. Thus, the installations begin to proliferate – and the only possibility to stop this proliferation is to die. At the end of the novel the hero commits a suicide that finally turns his whole life into the installation. Here the death functions as an ultimate possibility to equate time and space – or, in other terms, to equate novel and installation.

## Notes

1  "Athenaeumsfragment 116" in Friedrich Schlegel's *Lucinde and the Fragments*, translated and with an introduction by Peter Firchow, Minneapolis, MN: University of Minnesota Press, 1971, p. 175.
2  *Art and Answerability, Early Philosophical Essays by M.M. Bakhtin*, edited by Michael Holquist and Vadim Liapunov, Austin, TX: University of Texas Press, 1990.
3  Mikhail Bakhtin, *Problems of Dostoevsky's Poetics*, Minneapolis, MN: University of Minnesota Press, 1984.
4  Walter Benjamin, "The Work of Art in the Age of Mechanical Reproduction", in *Illuminations*, London: Fontana, 1992, pp. 214–215.
5  Ibid., p. 214.
6  Walter Benjamin, *Reflections: Essays, Aphorisms, Autobiographical Writings*, New York: Schocken, 1986, p. 190.

# 6

# HISTORY OF NEW NOVELS

## Adam Thirlwell

## The new novel

Of course it's true that every day, in every city on this globe, the junior novelist is imagining how the art of the novel is changing forever. I do this too. Every day from my observation post called London I am trying to imagine my future revolution, the moment when the art of the novel is dazzled and renewed by my experiments. Right now, this future object of mine seems to be some kind of idealised and wild adventure: voyages in space! voyages in the South Seas! I want to write the *universe novel*. Yes, here I am, with the history of my art spread out before me, and the side-step that seems to me to be necessary in this self-conscious era is to enlarge the usual perspective. I want to write a *cosmology*. That seems the appropriate ambition.

Every era believes that it is in the middle of total aesthetic change. Every novelist does too. If you want to try imagining a literary history of the present moment, and this essay will attempt a high-speed genealogy and manifesto, I think it's important to keep these two timeframes visible at once. And to each time-frame, I would offer two corresponding warnings.

## Two warnings about novelty

Because I have to admit: in general I distrust this kind of thinking – the thinking in terms of eras, in terms of a *before* and *after*. To believe that one's own era constitutes a radical difference to previous eras seems, historically, to be so often untrue. And even if it does turn out that one has been living through an era of absolute change, one's definitions of that change will so often seem wilfully premature and sad, the way sci-fi is sad in its outmoded predictions. And yet still, I admit it: for a while now I have at least had a sense that whatever it is I am living is not something that is entirely resolved by the usual categories I have inherited: philosophically, or aesthetically. Vast craziness seems to be afoot in the opaque neon atmosphere. I guess I had felt that from the moment when, as I was finishing my first novel – this bonanza of the private life, ironically titled *Politics* – I watched the World Trade Centre collapse on television. The ironies of my novel seemed suddenly a little old-fashioned… That feeling only increased throughout the subsequent decade, as I watched the various revolutions, and their subsequent counter-revolutions. But then I discovered a sentence by that grandiose reactionary, Joseph de Maistre, a sentence written at the end of the eighteenth century: 'For a long time we didn't understand the revolution of which we were the witnesses; for a long time we took it for an *event*. We were wrong: it was an *epoch*, and woe to those generations who are present at the epochs of the world.'[1] I love that sentence very much – not so much for its melancholy, although that melancholy may well be a useful technique in our current era – but for the precision of its terms and the admission of confusion. Because the problem, of course, at every present moment, is knowing what is just an *event* and what is in fact an *epoch*.

We should be wary of an era that believes too much in its novelty, therefore, and in the same way we should also be wary of a novelist who believes too much in her novelty. For every novelist is belated. It is inherent in the nature of writing itself. And here my authority is the Russian critic Boris Groys, who wrote an essay called 'The Loneliness of the Project' which I love for its way of describing how the artist and society will never obey the same tempo. Every project, argues Groys, must end in isolation.

> Each project is above all the declaration of another, new future that is supposed to come about once the project has been executed. But in order to induce such a new future one first has to take a period of leave or absence for oneself, with which the project has transferred its agent into a parallel state of heterogeneous time. This other time frame, in turn, is undocked from time as experienced by society: it is de-synchronized. Society's life carries on regardless thereof; the usual run of things remains unimpinged.[2]

What a sad fate! To be working on works that will revolutionise one's era, but which require so much time that the era will in fact not notice. And this second truth, perhaps, is the explanation for the first: the true revolutions may go on unnoticed; all society will notice are coincidental and superficial trends.

## Kafka's novelty is infinity

It was the high era of modernism when this idea of the radically new became so addictive and persuasive: the grand era of Proust, James, Stein, Kafka, Joyce, Musil; then Borges and Gombrowicz just behind… That era believed in novelty as an ontological essence, and its greatest theorist was the futurist Viktor Shklovsky, in the craziness of Bolshevik revolution: 'The new form makes its appearance… to replace an old form that has already outlived its artistic usefulness.'[3] But what kind of generalised revolution do these writers represent? So many of them are mutually exclusive. The style of Franz Kafka, after all, was a private revolution: a different form of universe construction. In Kafka, infinity is lurking inside appearances, just as he recounts in his miniature story 'The Next Village':

> My grandfather used to say: "Life is astonishingly short. When I look back now it is all so condensed in my memory that I can hardly understand, for example, how a young man can decide to ride over to the next village, without his being afraid – quite apart from unfortunate accidents – that the whole span of a normal happy life is far from being adequate for such a ride."[4]

In Kafka's fiction, wild elongations of scale are hidden inside classically elegant sentences, and so in this story it can simultaneously be true that an entire life-span can be condensed into a single memory, and that also the smallest action can contain an infinite length. His work is an investigation of the way the mind tries to reason through impossibly contradictory appearances; and so this story is the condensed version of his larger, more garish propositions – where a person, say, is transformed into a beetle – and which is why Theodor Adorno was right to observe the similarity between Kafka's texts and the films which Kafka adored: his novels, wrote Adorno in a letter to Walter Benjamin, 'represent the last and disappearing connecting texts of silent film…'[5]

In Kafka, the infinite irresolvable aspects of a mute universe are subjected to meticulous syntax.

## The hipster idea of the new

Every revolution in the art of the novel is individual, not generational. Every great writer represents their own private epoch. So really there should be no talk of generational change. Who now is more new than Kafka? And yet it's true that, in the Anglophonic world, there is a kind of hipster idea of novelty that is currently *chic*. This idea roughly goes: we are bored with the fictional, we crave only what we persist in calling *reality*. As critics, we want to read sociologically, for information; and as readers, we crave the confessional – and to that end we therefore have a strangely hybrid taste, for the realist fiction of Jonathan Franzen or Elena Ferrante; or the literal micro-descriptions of Lydia Davis; or the memoir-novels of Karl Ove Knausgaard. The realist novel and the *Künstlerroman*: these are the basic hipster forms in New York or London. 'Just the thought of writing fiction, just the thought of fabricated character in a fabricated plot made me feel nauseous', wrote Knausgaard in *My Struggle*.[6] While in a recent Lydia Davis story, she writes, with calm disapproval: 'Writing is often not about real things, and then, when it is about real things, it is often at the same time taking the place of some real things.'[7]

Now, immediately we have some problems. The first problem is historical. There's a basic denial of history in the hipster sense of aesthetics – for this move is just a repeat of previous moves. So many avant-garde revolutions have involved a rhetoric of the real, ever since Cervantes offered his account of the mind's deceptions. Just as so many avant-garde revolutions have involved a rhetoric of formlessness, ever since Laurence Sterne and Proust and Musil contaminated their novels with the dissolving agents of their essayistic thinking. It was Georges Bataille, long ago in the twentieth century, who invented the category of the *informe* to describe this kind of debased art; and it was Clarice Lispector, in *The Passion According to G.H.*, who gave the definitive record of this aesthetic drive to the non-aesthetic, with her prayer to 'have the great courage to resist the temptation to invent a form.'[8]

And also, folks, consider the wildness of Lispector. In that novel, there's a wonderful moment where she writes:

> I wrote "billows of muteness", which I never would have said before because I've always respected beauty and its intrinsic moderation. I said "billows of muteness", my heart bows humbly, and I accept it. Have I finally lost a whole system of good taste? But is that all I've gained? I must have lived so imprisoned to feel freer now just because I no longer fear the lack of aesthetics...[9]

There's a savage wisdom here which distinguishes Lispector's love of the exposed subject from the current hipster mode. She is wise to the philosophical complexity, an attitude whose absence is visible in Knausgaard's melodramatic word *nauseous*, or Davis's idea of the grandeur of *real things*. Their true objection, it turns out, is ethical, not aesthetic. Now, you can call that attitude Puritan, or Protestant, or Philistine, or just *norteamericano*: depending on your location, you can choose your favorite pejorative adjective... The error remains the same: a) to think that the fictive is immoral; and b) to think that the world can be so easily available to our intelligences.

To be bored with the usual novels, absolutely! To be bored is a noble and correct position. But the way out of such conventions is not to believe so bluntly in the real, as if the history of philosophy had never happened. In the hipster suburbs of New York, the confession-novel is often seen as the avant-garde route away from the realist novel. Whereas the confession-novel is realism of the purest kind. And always what the novel needs is the opposite of realism: it needs the *irreal*. (Not, of course, that this is in any way news. 'I do Odalisques in order to do the nude,' observed Matisse, the emperor of appearances. 'And how to do the nude without it being factitious?'[10])

I understand that it seems like an epoch of the naked self: this world of Instagram and SnapChat. It is the era of reality television, not telenovela. But that doesn't mean we're in an era of the real. It means, in fact, the opposite. We are in the grand era of fiction. Everyone is in the business of narrative construction. While at the same time, there is terror everywhere. And well, if the real is marked by such violent discontinuities – political, philosophical, aesthetic – I don't see why the novel can't restage and engross them. In such an era, true novelty in the art of fiction is going to lurk in much more complicated guises.

## New moves

There's a little exchange the composer Morton Feldman once had in conversation with the painter Philip Guston, where Feldman observed how 'there were periods of history where everybody felt that the old systems were dying out and there were no new systems to take their place. And so the work was running every which way... But the great guy was a guy that made moves in this ambivalence between periods.'[11] Feldman's example of that kind of hero was Anton Webern, and his *Six Pieces for Orchestra*: 'He was looking ahead, he was looking backwards,' said Feldman, 'but still he moved. He still moved.'[12]

I love Feldman's groovy sixties slang; but I also love the basic lesson. Whether in an epoch or an era, the problem is how to make moves. Always novelty will be this unique and lonely process. It will be haphazard and private. And the moves that seem most original to me, as I survey the world from London, are not the anti-fictional moves of hipster chic, but the more tropicália moves which play with the process of fiction more artfully: writers, to choose only the old or recently dead, like Bolaño, Krasznahorkai, Vila-Matas – with Calvino and Perec in the background.

I think I'm trying to argue for two particular modes. At the most general level, it seems to me that there's a knowledge particular to the *fictive*, a kind of practical epistemology that can only develop via the notebook-thinking with felt-tip pens, the keyboard time: a trust that if you keep writing, rewriting, cutting and pasting, an improvised knowledge will emerge that you could never have predicted, that could only be produced through this process of the work.

So OK, sure: why make something up? Why not just write history? Or philosophy? This is a question every novelist needs to ask herself every day, but I don't think the obvious answer is to reject the category of *representation*. You make up imaginary models because in that process you can create profounder, richer problems than the ones you might happen to discover by chance, in the course of your everyday life. Or, as Roland Barthes once observed in an essay on Stendhal, noting the transformation of Stendhal's journals into the richness of his novels: 'What happened between the Travel Journal and *The Charterhouse of Parma*, is writing.'[13] And this process of *writing* marks a basic ontological difference. It represents a transformation.

There's a video by the South African artist William Kentridge where a scattering of a few torn sheets of black paper are arranged and rearranged to create the uncannily lifelike image of a horse. That video, *Making a Horse*, is a piece of pure artistic exuberance, but it also proves a complicated truth, which Kentridge went on to explore in some recent lectures: *Drawing Lessons*. Because what is happening, when we see these pieces of paper as a horse? It isn't that we generously pretend to accept their horseness. Instead, writes Kentridge, 'We cannot help ourselves from seeing the horse. It takes an effort, a wilful blindness, to keep the images as black torn sheets of paper.' Or, he corrects himself: 'to see them only as torn sheets of paper. We see them as both, we are not fooled. The horse and the paper are both here. This is an unwilling suspension of disbelief.'[14]

*The unwilling suspension of disbelief!* It's true of art, and it's also true of writing. Which is why I've always loved the fictions of Italo Calvino for their frank description of their own processes, the way he felt – as he put it in 1967 – 'a moral obligation while writing to warn: "Watch out, I am writing"...'[15] It was ethical, true, but it was also the only way of being truthful to the way reality was infinitely receding – and in a note that he wrote towards the end of his life he defined this structure as dependent on the *frame*:

> Both in art and in literature, the function of the frame is fundamental. It is the frame that marks the boundary between the picture and what is outside. It allows the picture to exist, isolating it from the rest; but at the same time, it recalls – and somehow stands for – everything that remains out of the picture. I might venture a definition: we consider poetic a production in which each individual experience acquires prominence through its detachment from the general continuum, while it retains a kind of glint of that unlimited vastness.[16]

It's the frame, I think, that is the route to novelty in fiction in any era: it allows a work that is neither true nor false, neither falsely real nor falsely encoded: a multi-layering of meanings, where each meaning persists simultaneously. With this idea of the frame, you can go inwards, to the literal, and metafictional; and you can go outwards, to the infinite universe. With the frame, you can make new inventions...

## History of new works

I mean, let's just think of the hipster ideal of the real, or Lispector's attack on the *whole system of good taste*. I love the commitment to formlessness, to an object as literal and comprehensive as possible, but I'm not sure it's enough, if you want that kind of ideal, to just increase one's confessional range. The true invention would be to increase the range of permitted aesthetic *tones* – the Gruesome, Tender, Needy, Sleazy, Boring, the Lurid and the Cute... After all, these are the new tones abroad in our general Technicolor atmosphere, and they're dependent on the smudged mixture of distance and intimacy that is now the everyday digital norm – which makes me also think that the way to examine these is to enforce this kind of smudged structure on the reader. You need, I just mean, to exaggerate the presence of a novel's frame. Because if the ideal is to produce a claustrophobia and corruption in the reader, it'll only be possible if the narrator is aware of her own existence.

Like: one version of this kind of experiment in closeness is the hyper-novel of Marcel Proust – who in his novel *In Search of Lost Time* invented the greatest novelist–narrator, in a novel which created such blurring between the real and the unreal that it was possible for Proust to invent not just his famous ambiguity as to whether his narrator was or wasn't called Marcel, but a weird dream-landscape, where real names co-exist with made-up ones; and fictional characters are inserted into real paintings. And the reason Proust could invent such a slippery, strange atmosphere was because he exposes and then exploits so playfully and strangely the construction of his novel. His novel is premised on the exposure of its frame. That visible frame is what allows him to perform his careful, melancholy tricks with time.

Some of the wildest refusals of the novel are still investigations in the fictional mode. They *flaunt* their fictional playfulness. That's one lesson you can learn from a brief history of previous novels. But there's another lesson, too – about the category of history itself. Because sure, Marcel's experiment in interiors – like Lispector's as well – occurred in a previous century. But it also exists ahead of us, in the infinitely receding future.

## New universes

As for me, I also used to want that artistry of an infinite interior. But more and more, I'm wondering about the infinite outside us. Or, to put this another way, I always thought of novelty as a new invention in technique. That has been the manner of my investigations for the decade in which I've written my early novels. But now, I'm not so sure.

Every novel is a mini replica of the universe, and its novelty will depend on the particular exaggeration forced on it by its miniature size. This may be an exaggeration of technique: a novelty of *how*. But it may also – and perhaps more interestingly – be an exaggeration of subject matter: a novelty of *what*. That's why I keep thinking about Calvino and his idea of the frame. You can use the frame to go inside, and to make the novel a literal game between the reader and the writer. But you can also move in the opposite direction, and use the frame to demonstrate the infinity outside: *a kind of glint of that unlimited vastness.*

It's an ideal that Calvino once described as *multiplicity*: 'a work conceived from outside the *self*, a work that would let us escape the limited perspective of the individual ego, not only to enter into selves like our own but to give speech to that which has no language, to the bird perching on the edge of the gutter, to the tree in spring and the tree in fall, to stone, to cement, to plastic…'[17] His own version of this was *Cosmicomics*, his collection of universe-stories, each of which begins with a scientific proposition or hypothesis, and is then followed by a first-person account by his impossible narrator, Qfwfq, who has witnessed every moment in the universe's history. And I think: but what is this ideal multiple novel, if not a cosmogony – a game that also establishes a universe? Or, in other words, not just the twentieth century *Cosmicomics* but also Cyrano de Bergerac's *Estates and Empires of the Moon* in the sixteenth century, or Ovid's *Metamorphoses*, or –

You get the idea. To be modern is no guarantee of novelty. And once a work is new, it is new forever.

## Notes

1  Joseph de Maistre, 'Discours de consolation à la marquise de Costa', Paris, 1846 [1794], p. 273 (my translation).
2  Boris Groys, 'The Loneliness of the Project', New York Magazine of Contemporary Art / MuHKA, 2000, p 3.

3   Viktor Shklovsky, *Theory of Prose*, translated by Benjamin Sher, Champaign and London: Dalkey Archive, 1991, p 20.

4   Franz Kafka, 'The Next Village', translated by Malcolm Pasley, in *Metamorphosis and Other Stories*, London: Penguin, 1992, p 174.

5   Theodor Adorno to Walter Benjamin, 17 December 1934, in *Theodor W. Adorno / Walter Benjamin: Broefwechsel, 1928–1940*, Frankfurt: Suhrkamp Verlag, 1994, p 95 (my translation).

6   Karl Ove Knausgaard, *A Man in Love: My Struggle Book 2*, translated by Don Bartlett, London: Vintage, 2013.

7   Lydia Davis, 'Writing', in *Can't and Won't*, New York: Farrar, Straus and Giroux, 2014.

8   Clarice Lispector, *The Passion According to G.H.*, translated by Idra Novey, London: Penguin, 2012, p 7.

9   Ibid, p 12.

10   Quoted in TJ Clark, *Farewell to an Idea*, New Haven, CT: Yale University Press, 2001, p 110.

11   Philip Guston, 'Conversation with Morton Feldman', 1968, in *Collected Writings, Lectures and Conversations*, Berkeley, CA: University of California Press, p 93.

12   Ibid.

13   Roland Barthes, 'On échoue toujours à parler de ce qu'on aime', in *Oeuvres complètes, V*, Paris : Éditions du Seuil, 2002, p 914 (my translation).

14   William Kentridge, *Six Drawing Lessons*, Cambridge, MA: Harvard University Press, 2014, pp 16–18.

15   Italo Calvino, *Letters*, translated by Martin McLaughlin, Princeton, NJ: Princeton University Press, 2013, p 337.

16   Italo Calvino, 'Note' in *Under the Jaguar Sun*, translated by William Weaver, London: Penguin, 1988, pp 85–6.

17   Italo Calvino, *Six Memos for the Next Millennium*, translated by Patrick Creagh, New York: Vintage, 1996, p 124.

# 7

# WHAT BECOMES OF THE NOVEL WHEN THE GODS ARE COMING BACK

## A secular form of literature facing the return of religion

*Tristan Garcia*

### "The Epic of a world that has been abandoned by God"

I'm an atheist, but every time I have written a novel, I have found myself dealing with some religious concepts – against my will. Here, I am going to try to figure out *why*.

I would like to return to a simple, old idea which deeply influenced my conception of the novel (not of the whole of literature, but only of the novel); the fifth chapter of George Lukács' *Theory of the Novel*, which was discussed in the field of critical theories (from Adorno to Jameson) but also was a work of reference at the time of Structuralist and Poststructuralist literary theories (the Roland Barthes vs Lucien Goldmann debates). And yet, that book has lost much of its appeal since then.

However, it seems to me that some of its intuitions should help us to get an accurate concept of the novel in its relation to religion.

★

Lukàcs's perhaps most famous sentence is the following: "The novel is the epic of a world that has been abandoned by God."[1] I should probably remind you about many other philosophical, sociological and esthetical subtheses, all through Lukàcs's work, to do him justice: the idea of a transcendental place of modern subjectivity, the loss of a sense of wholeness, the loss of the immanence of life and the loss of a sense of destiny that once characterized the Greek world... But for us to go straight to the point that may be of some interest here and now, I will summarize one of many Lukàcs ideas as follows: when the immanence of the meaning of life evaporates, the epic isn't the proper literary form to the human world anymore. As a result of an historical process, gods are withdrawing and becoming demons.

Such is the reason why the psychology of the novel is "demonic", from Lermontov to Dostoyevsky, from Conrad to Highsmith: the life of heroes depend on the demonic irony of the writer, since it cannot have a significance by itself. "Then, suddenly the God-forsakenness of the world reveals itself as a lack of substance."[2]

Thus, the novel is clearly related to the secularization of our world. That idea seems to be simple: the gods retire, as the world is becoming secular, and the novel appears to be the only form – dissonant and ironic – that could fit to comprehend a disjuncted world. Modern novelists are trying to recreate a hidden totality of life, which is not at all sustained by any kind of god.

★

However, since I was a teenager and since I read that text of Lukàcs, an unusual objection has been on my mind, a bizarre question. Assuming that the novel should be the literary form of a world from which the gods have slipped away, throughout the eighteenth, nineteenth and twentieth centuries, what would happen if ever the gods were to come back? What could become of the novel if absent gods were to be present again to the human mind? Should we think that the novel would have no purpose anymore, in a world where the gods would be re-included into society?

Would a possible – and maybe absurd – return of the gods mean the historical decline of the novel?

## The return of the gods

It turns out that, since the 1990s, the "return of religion" seems to be one of the very recurring assertions of contemporary philosophy and sociology.

The first serious example that comes to my mind is the book of Gilles Kepel, *The Revenge of God*,[3] which was a very early analysis of the renewed influence of fundamentalism, as a result of an eclipse of Marxist movements. The reading of Kepel, interested in evangelical churches, Teshuva and Islamism, might have suggested to some of his readers that Max Weber's conception of the "disenchantment of the world",[4] one of the major influences of Lukàcs, was no longer self-evident. Modern industrialism and depersonalized relations, secularization and alienation were supposed to necessarily undermine all of the forces which had underpinned the medieval cosmos. And the novel was considered an expression, as a form of art, of that new world of modernity.

Along with Gilles Kepel, Samuel Huntington pretended, on the contrary, that "the late 20th century had seen the global resurgence of religion around the world".[5] Huntington took into account a much broader geographical area than Kepel: Africa and Asia were included in his geopolitical diagnosis. But, as we all know, Huntington's interpretation of this religious backlash in terms of "Us and Them" was largely questionable, and we should remain cautious with such large political and sociological observations.

I would simply like to get to a right formulation of the intuition of a *possible* desecularization, which would clash with Lukàcs's definition of the novel. It would also be an occasion to disprove our very familiar theoretical background of the novel, which can be found in Milan Kundera's *The Art of the Novel*, for example. Because of our education, we are used to thinking that the novel is not only a genre, but also a specific way of conceiving the human world, expressing the withdrawal of gods, religions and beliefs.

I believe that this modernist conception of the novel is grounded in some philosophical and sociological considerations on modern history seen as secularization, by Auguste Comte, Max Weber or Georg Simmel. But if we read carefully some contemporary works about secularization, we will find that the closing decades of the 20th century may "provide a massive falsification of the idea"[6] that modernization and secularization will lead to a decline in religion. Instead, we are witnessing a massive upsurge in religion around the world: that is what Peter Berger, for example, describes in *The Desecularization of the World: Resurgent Religion and World Politics*.

Secular intellectuals and elites have been shocked by this development, because it is proving that their fundamental assumptions about human beings and human society could be wrong. The modern secular notion that religion is archaic and irrelevant has caused many to overlook the importance of religion in human affairs.

As a result, they have may been taken by surprise by the return of religion. As Peter Berger wrote: "Those who have neglected religion in their analysis of contemporary affairs do so at great peril."[7]

Let's try not to do so.

*

Huntington, or even Berger, could be accused of being reactionary thinkers. And one might think that the idea of the return of religion does not apply to the critical and Marxist tradition, to which Lukàcs was connected. Thus it would be a mistake to oppose some reactionary or conservative thinking to a modern and progressive conception of the novel.

But in the critical and Marxist tradition, the very idea of desecularization seems to be rising as well. I would like to quote Alberto Toscano, a great contemporary Marxist theoretician, who wonders whether: "Marx's thinking on religion can survive the challenge posed by what appears to be the dramatic reversals in the secularizing tendencies of revolutionary opportunities all of which he identified in the European nineteenth century ?"[8]

*

Let us remain cautious in our interpretation, not take side, nor claim that there is really such a thing as a return of religion; we just have to admit that, even for the philosophical tradition on which Lukàcs relied to define the novel as a result of secularization, secularization is no longer self-evident. It should at least lead us to review our basic intuitive concept of the novel. In some celebrated contemporary works, like Orhan Pamuk's most recent novels, we can already witness something like a tension between faith and fiction, secularization and desecularization, religion and the novel. This is obviously one of Pamuk's most central themes. But I would like to point to a less-expected manifestation of a possible return of religion, not in world literature, but in fantasy books.

*

In a way, George R. R. Martin's *Game of Thrones* tells the return of such beliefs and gods in a seemingly secular political world – unlike *The Lord of the Rings*, which told the departure of mythical creatures and gods.

While Tolkien's trilogy showed the gradual disenchantment of the world, the withdrawal of the Gods and the bitter triumph of man, *Game of Throne* begins in an almost secular world, dominated by political conflicts and where religious values no longer matter. But the series becomes more or less a chronical of the return of religion in this world: R'hllor the God is rising, as well as the Red priests, Melissandre or the drowned Gods of the Iron Islands… As Daenerys' dragons grow up, the Wall hardly contains the outside civilization and old beliefs. There are signs in the sky, everybody is waiting for the winter to come and we all have the impression that different plots are leading to the destruction of the Seven Kingdoms. The series plays on the feeling of resurgence of religion in a secular political world we thought would be forever.

*

Contemporary fantasy might be the epic of desecularization… But if the novel is – as Lukàcs thought – the epic of a world without God, what does it become in this desecularized world? Is it an illusory representation of European or Western upper class atheists? Will the novel turn into a singular form of secular resistance for people who do not believe in gods? However, novels are published all over the world, in many religious contexts; most of the time, they are written by people expressing secular opinions, but there seems to be a secret tension between religion and irreligion in the art of the novel itself, whatever a writer's or a reader's opinions may be.

*

The question I would like to raise is: if we do not pay any attention to the content of novels, but to its form, as Lukàcs did, if we take this kind of modernism at face value, would it be possible to think what is – or is not – religious in the art of the novel? It would be the only way to know the exact part of the novel in a possibly desecularized contemporary world.

We can make several assumptions. First hypothesis: the novel is in itself an irreligious or secular resistance, a commitment to the disenchantment of the world.

This would mean that the novel is now running against the course of history, while it was supposed to run all along the course of history. It would be a major change in our historical conception of the novel.

Second hypothesis: the novel has always been religious or non-secular without knowing it. It is not what we thought it was after the 19th century.

Either way, we need to revise our beliefs about the so-called "spirit" of the novel, and maybe we should read Lukàcs, Kundera, and others, in a different light.

*

If we are talking about religion and the novel, we should first admit there has always been some militant religious novels – let's remember C.S. Lewis or G.K. Chesterton. Today, there is an "Urban Christian fiction" – only to mention Christian fiction.

There are novels written by true believers: Graham Greene, Georges Bernanos, which reflect internal tensions to their faith.

There are also many novels with controversial issues: Salman Rushdie, Taslima Nasreen..., which were condemned as blasphemous by fanatical believers.

And there are novels written by notorious infidels, or anticlerical authors: Diderot, Sade, Ayn Rand, or written by authors who have very irreligious opinions – let's say Philip Roth.

To cut a long story short, I won't speak about religious or irreligious novels; I am not interested in the opinion expressed by the writer, the narrator or some of the characters.

I just want to know how, if the novel in its form (not in its content) shares something with religious thought or not – not with any religion in particular, but with certain categories of religious human thinking.

*

May certain categories of the novel be the object of a clash between the religious and the irreligious way of thinking?

We should remember the famous intervention of Sartre against Mauriac on the freedom of his characters. This is a good example of a use of the novel as a symbolic stage for religious and irreligious *Weltanschauungen*. The idea is that the point of view, seen as an esthetic category of the novel, could be the object of a struggle between religious concepts and existential, humanistic and irreligious concepts.

Sartre compares Mauriac the novelist to God, because there is a "God who sees the inside and the outside, the depths of the soul and the body, the whole universe at once. Similarly, Mr. Mauriac is omniscient on everything related to his small world".[9] Sartre concludes: "He chose the all-knowing and all-mighty power of God... God is not an artist, neither is Mr. Mauriac."[10]

Later, Sartre confessed in an interview that he should have been be less affirmative:

"This is because I realized that all methods are trickery, including American methods. It always manages to say what one thinks to the reader and the author is always present."[11]

In my opinion, the problem faced by Sartre is that he thought that blowing the omniscient point of view, for the very Catholic Mauriac, would eliminate any religious point of view in the novel. But religion is not bound only to the omniscient point of view of the Christian God. I would argue, for example, that creating a character, while writing, or admitting its existence, while reading, is close to an animist way of seeing things, because one cannot but assign to manifold manifestations something like an inner nature.

## Character and soul

On the contrary, behaviorism in the modernist novel – Claude-Edmonde Magny wrote on that topic very early on – could be understood as a reaction to the religious and idealistic categories of mind. Of course, we all remember Dashiell Hammett or Horace McCoy, and their influence on Albert Camus. One should only describe what appears from the outside. Gestures, movements. Behavior. We are not supposed to infer the existence of any soul, any spirit, any interiority anymore. This was the literary vague equivalent of the black box in Comportementalist theories.

But, it seems to me there has always been a confusion. The question should not be whether the character *has* a spirit or not, but whether he or she *is* a spirit or not. And spiritism, to my opinion, has a lot to do with the novel. Diderot once described the theatrical character as a "wicker mannequin",[12] a hollow man awaiting on his soul, waiting to be animated. But this character seen as a puppet or as a mask, waiting to be incarnated, this picture waiting for life, is the character on the stage, not in the novel.

Because the character of a novel does not need any actor. It is not an empty thing in search for an incarnation.

First, the character of the novel is strictly invisible, unlike the character on the stage or the one in a painting; it is a whole person inaccessible to view in his physical appearance. Obviously, all the task of writing is, as Conrad once said, "to make you hear, to make you feel, and, above all, to make you see"[13] on the basis of this absolute invisibility of the character.

The character, as a result, is connected with *characterization*, as a process. The character can be *characterized* in its interiority or its externality, by his or her actions, by his or her stream of consciousness, etc.; for he or she has to become particular. He is a non-universal invisibility. He cannot stay absolutely undetermined, being "whoever" or "whatever". He or she is a determined someone. First, he or she gets an identity – even a minimal one. Then, he or she must *endure:* he or she has got to be re-identified.

★

What really interests me is this question: what is the cognitive impulse taking place in the recognition of a literary character? First of all, the identification and re-identification. There was a famous article by Colin Radford and Michael Weston in the seventies, titled "How can we be moved by the fate of Anna Karenina"?

They insisted on empathy and identification. But identification is nothing without *re*-identification. In order to get a character, we need to recognize that a number of events are one and only being, time after time. Otherwise, every time Anna Karenina would appear, it would be a different Anna Karenina, with a different identity: there would be no possible sum of all occurrences of Anna Karenina, and no character at all.

Any character assumes an invisible identity, removed from sight, unifying various manifestations of a possible person. Playing with that unification is always an option: ALP is not always Anna Livia Plurabelle in *Finnegans Wake*, and gets as many names as occurrences; one can be many, as in Dostoyevsky's *The Double*, or many can be one, as in Virginia Woolf's *Orlando*. At any rate, the character is the manifestation of an invisible oneness.

★

But the character is never the whole identity of the person. Even when trying to complete transcripts of a lifetime, the character remains a selective collection of acts and appearances of the person. When Uwe Johnson wanted to describe in four volumes *A Year in the Life of Gesine Cresspahl* by using heterogeneous materials, newspaper abstracts or poems, he still offered a limited perspective in time and space on what his character was supposed to be in her youth.

A character is a selective oneness of a wholeness. Why? Because it is the core of a person, the invisible oneness of each and every one. It is what, of someone, is to be judged.

★

Any character is the invisible substrate of acts and occurrences of a person, and it is assumed that characters are responsible for their actions: it changes, but it remains the same. It thus embodies the moral unity of a lifetime.

For this reason, everything they did and was selected can be attributed to them. This is very important: characters are always the ground of a possible moral judgment, because they are the subject of a manifold of acts and apparitions.

★

A character is nothing but the invisible essence of a person, bound to keep his or her identity, his or her unit, which extracts and selects most of his life, in order to be read, which means to be understood and maybe judged, by us.

★

What we mean by "character" in a novel, is not very different from what we call, in any kind of religion, a "soul": the very principle of one person, the invisible part which rests in one's life, identity, unity, and may be subject to some judgment.

In order to write a novel, one needs to create characters and, as materialistic as one can be – as I am – one should admit that we are producing a literary *analogon* of what we used to call the "soul".

## Narration and salvation

What are these souls written for?

In "Sinuhe the Egyptian" one of the earliest preserved human stories, the character, who was exiled, is suddenly taken by the fear of dying away from home. He prays for a return to his homeland: "May god pity me (…) my arms are weak… My legs have ceased to follow, and my heart is weary; I am near to dying. May they lead me to the city of Eternity !"[14] He then receives a written invitation from the King to return. The fear not only to die, but to be forgotten, in a foreign land, where there will be no burial, where he won't be remembered and he won't be judged, is likely to be responsible for the narration. Why tell a tale? To be remembered, buried and delivered.

In the "Epic of Gilgamesh", characters do not feel as sure about their destiny and the sense of the whole world as Lukàcs thought. It may already be a novel in Lukácsian terms. Remember Gilgamesh's distress after Enkiddu's death, and his unsuccessful quest for immortality, his failure. Delivering a lamentation for Enkiddu, Gilgamesh recalls all of their adventures, he wants to tell them, and then break down and cry. Looking for Utnapishtim, Gilgamesh obtains what he was seeking, but is betrayed by sleep. He loses immortality, and what he gets is fiction, to become a character.

The first human stories we know about are haunted by the need to bury, to mourn, to remember, to preserve a life from utter destruction; why tell? Because something needs to be saved. What? Images? No: the invisible unity and identity of someone through a lifetime.

★

In return, it seems that, in many religions, the questions of salvation and narration are two halves of the same whole. Anubis is weighing the heart of humans, but his decision depends on his listening to the list of one's sins and good deeds.

Never is a life saved on the basis of an image in human cultures. What is to be judged is a life, in the precise sense of the narration of a life.

It might be that the need to order events of a life in a story is linked to the conception of a final or cyclic trial, and a hope for salvation.

To exercise any judgment, we do need to hear a story. And what we are looking for, as a consequence, in every story, is a possible judgment about lives: whether they were worth it, or not; whether they were successful or failed; what remains, which is lost.

When Kafka writes at the end of *The Trial:*" it was as if the shame would outlive him",[15] he is deliberately using the narration as salvation, and getting nothing but shame as an end result. Something remains, which is neither glory or hope, but shame.

★

Considering the novel as a trial for souls allows us to think a specific interplay between religion and the novel: while religion needs narration to give a content to the soul, to explain what of a soul is to be judged (the narration of its life), the novel needs religion in order to get a final form. What should happen to characters seen as souls? Passing through time, they ask for remembrance, celebration, forgiveness.

When the clock strikes at the end of *The Garden of the Finzi-Continis*, the narrator laughs: "What a great novel!"[16] The novel deals with the passing of time, and the use of memory, but with the weighing of souls as well. It may be the soul of the writer, casting himself as a character, from Augustine and Rousseau to Leiris and Sartre. It may be done as a moral exercise, by the Abbé Prevost, Laclos or Thackeray: "Ah! *Vanitas Vanitatum!* Which of us is happy in this world? Which of us has his desire? Or, having it, is satisfied? Come, children, let us shut up the box and the puppets, for our play is played out."[17] It may be done without any dramatic nor ironic tone, just summing the living and the dead at the end of the novel, as did Solzhenitsyn: "Some people did not survive. He did."[18] It may be apotropaic, saying something while hoping that the opposite will happen: "I'll be forgotten quickly", at the end of one of Houellebecq's novel.[19] The novel ends with a wish to be forgotten, while it is obviously a work made to be remembered.

★

There is no hope for salvation without a narration, there is no narration without salvation. Even if a novel in its content is leaving us with nothing but death, oblivion and Nothing, the novel in its form orders various lives, creating characters, as a support of acts and manifestations, and conducts their trial: anybody, while reading it, can perform as a temporary judge.

Even the more trivial, anecdotal, novel, dealing with frivolous affairs, is a secret question of salvation and deliverance. We peer at the remaining life of dead souls. No matter how materialistic, irreligious, ironic, a novel can be; it always fails to give us nothing but the perspective of the remaining on the ever-changing, ever-dying.

## Nothing but fiction

This is the very meaning of my intuition, when I was reading Lukàcs as a teenager: contrary to what we all may have thought, while studying the modern history of the novel, the novel is not related to secularization. It is a form of narrative, which existed in polytheistic, monotheistic and in secular societies; it is a form related to many categories which are *analogon* of those of religious thought. It signifies that the human mind, while reading a novel, may engage in similar operations to those at work in religious belief – including the identification of souls behind the body, and the quest for a deliverance of these souls.

★

In modern novels, this impulse has often taken the form of a secular search for a memory or of a burial of the dead, as in the work of W.G. Sebald or of Roberto Bolaño. In both cases, it is indeed a non-religious attempt to save something missing, dead and forgotten.

But I think that what we seek in every novel, mystery, science-fiction, fantasy, *autofiction*, is to acknowledge the existence of something permanent in changing bodies, a permanently invisible identity of everyone – each character, even the more trivial, being like a soul. And we want to get a point of view on souls: which is wrong, which is right; which succeeds, which fails in the end. When reading a novel, one is always looking for a concrete point of view on souls.

★

One might think that I argue that the novel is nothing but an artistic illustration of religious impulses of the human mind. But, in my opinion, the novel shows a lack of religion as well. Human beings do not content themselves with religious precepts, but they go beyond precepts by writing and reading stories, which may become novels. I think that novels expose what every precept of every religion always miss, because they are too generic.

In any novel, good or bad, the soul becomes singular and sensitive, since it is a character.

As a price to pay, those singular and sensitive souls, fulfilling some religious needs of the mind, are fictitious. And because of fiction, they are at the same time irreligious.

★

A novel presents the senses with an invisible world that is beyond the image, which passes through the language. It achieves a religious non-sensible world intuition. But a novel also exhibits the world as fictional. The essence of a novel is to present a world where there are actual souls, where lives can actually be preserved and maybe judged, but as a fiction.

In a novel, human mind is contemplating a non-sensitive, invisible world, a religious world, as its own creation – while in a religion, the human mind contemplates this creation and does not identify it as its own.

## The most religious and the most irreligious of all

The novel is both the product of religious categories and an irreligious work.

Being irreligious, the novel shows that, without fiction, there is no soul or salvation. The need to put things into fiction, the need to tell lives and to create characters meets the desire of unveiling the part of fiction in our beliefs. If there were effective souls and possible salvation, then we would not have to invent them. Every novel is showing that we indeed need fiction in order to get some soul and salvation. Every novel emphasizes how much religious categories of thinking rely on *fiction*.

*

Because of the novel's use of fiction, and because it strongly relies on religious categories, a novel always operates a secret identification between religious belief and fiction,
and it is, indeed, irreligious. But a novel is not exhibiting an irreligious world, a secular
utopy; on the contrary, it embodies the religious intuition, in so many human cultures,
of an invisible reality where lives are souls, at last, visible, sensible and judge-able.

*

And this is the condition of a writer.

The only souls that can be saved or redeemed are those that were created, and
they can only be redeemed by who created them; in a novel, nothing is redeemable
but what was created by fiction.

Any novelist is willing to save something of reality – true memories, people,
scenes, sensations or ideas; but, as far as he or she is operating with fiction, the only
thing he or she can save is what *he* or *she* created, not that what once inspired him
or her in reality.

We are writing to save something from this world, but we are condemned to
save nothing but what we invented in another world – of fiction.

This is the very condition of novelists: wishing to save something from their life,
from their world, they get an opportunity to save something by creating it. And in
the end, nothing is saved in the novel but what was created by the novel, although
the novel *has* to express the hope for saving something else than itself.

A god cannot save something he did not create – neither can the novelist.

## As a conclusion

So, what happens to the novel when gods return?

Is there some sort of competition? It would be a mistake to believe, as we did
in secular times, that the novel was secular in itself. It would now be a mistake to
believe that it is absolutely compatible with any religion.

I guess the novel, as a form of fictional narration of lives, is the exact point of
contact – and at the same time the open contradiction – between the unveiling of
a reality that was not created and that has no destination to be and the depiction
of worlds full of invisible souls, made visible to an audience, where everything can
be remembered and judged.

In that sense, every religious belief is a novel that does not recognize itself as a
fiction, exactly as every novel is a religious belief presenting itself as a fiction.

*

In a novel, we all contemplate what a world would be in which our lives might
have meaning, could be judged from the outside, and maybe saved – who knows?

We contemplate what a world would be like where the world could be contemplated by somebody. That is what we call fiction: the *seeing* of a world *made to be seen*.

And we all have to guess that the reason why we need to write or read such worlds of fiction, where the whole world is shown to somebody, to us is because we might think that reality as a whole is without any audience. That is because we are deeply irreligious that we need some fiction.

★

I am not saying that there is no God, no soul, no hope and no salvation. I am simply making the case that anyone who writes or reads a novel must respond to a very irreligious need: the need for the expression of religious categories of thinking as an explicit fiction.

Maybe this could explain why the minds of fanatic believers do not need fiction, since they consider it as an enemy to faith; but this should also explain why absolutely incredulous minds do not hold fiction in high esteem, since they consider it to be a common lie.

And the more religious you become, the less the novel really matters; the more irreligious you become, the less the novel really matters too. When we were children, for example, and being spontaneously religious *and* irreligious, most of us easily cared much for novels.

★

The novel seems to attest at the same time that religion is partly fictitious, and that fiction is partly religious.

Going back to our initial idea, we could now consider the novel not as a product of secularization, of a world abandoned by gods and religions, but as a contradictory product of culture, an *analogon* of a religious world in its content, an *antilogon* of a religious world in its fictitious form. When gods are absent, and when they are present to the human mind, what happens to the novel? The novel stays the same: neither secular nor desecularized, it is a way for us to be highly religious in our irreligion, highly irreligious in our religion, to stay desperately faithful and unfaithful at the same time.

## Notes

1  G. Lukács [1971], p. 88.
2  Ibid., p. 90.
3  G. Kepel [1994], "Around 1975 this whole process went into reverse. A new religious approach took shape, aimed no longer at adapting to secular values but at recovering a sacred foundation for the organisation of society." p. 2.
4  J. C. Monod [2002]. From Hegel to Nietzsche, and then by Löwith, Weber or Blumenberg, Jean-Claude Monod draws an history of secularization in German philosophy as a "mondanization of Christianism" and a will to translate schemes and patterns from theology to politics, and aesthetics.

5  S. Huntington [1996], p. 64.
6  P. Berger [1999], p. 6.
7  Ibid.
8  A. Toscano [2011].
9  J. P. Sartre [1950], translated by Gert Hoffman in *German and European Politics after the Holocaust: Crisis and Creativity*, Rochester, Camden House, p. 288.
10  Ibid.
11  Jean-Paul Sartre to Madeleine Chapsal, 1960, quoted by Paulina Sperkova, "Mauriac et Sartre. La liberté des personnages", sens-public.org, 2008.
12  D. Diderot [1994], p. 154.
13  J. Conrad [1979] is discussed by Ian Watt, "Conrad's preface to *The Nigger of the Narcissus*", NOVEL: A Forum in Fiction, vol. 7, no. 2, 1974, pp. 101–105.
14  R. B. Parkinson [1997], p. 35.
15  F. Kafka [2000], p. 176.
16  G. Bassani [1965], p. 230.
17  W. Thackeray [1998], p. 656.
18  A. Solzhenitsyn [2005].
19  M. Houellebecq [2001], p. 260.

# References

Theodor W. Adorno, *Notes on Literature* (1958), trans. Shierry Nicholson Weber, New York, Columbia University Press, 1991.

St Augustine, *Confessions*, trans. John K. Ryan, New York, Image Books, 1960.

Giorgio Bassani, *The Garden of the Finzi-Continis* (1962), trans. Isabel Quigly, New York, Atheneum, 1965.

Peter Berger (ed.), *The Desecularization of the World: Resurgent Religion and World Politics*, Grand Rapids, MI, Eerdmans, 1999.

Roberto Bolano, *The Savage Detectives* (1998), trans. Natasha Wimmer, New York, Farar, Straus & Giroux, 2007.

Joseph Conrad, Preface to *The Nigger of the Narcissus* (1897), New York, W.W. Norton & Company, 1979.

Denis Diderot, "Paradox of the Actor" (1773–1777), *Selected Writings on Art and Literature*, trans. Geoffrey Bremner, London, Penguin, 1994.

Fyodor Dostoyevsky, *The Double. Two Versions* (1846, 1866), trans. Evelyn J. Harden, Ann Arbor, MI, Ardis, 1985.

Fyodor Dostoyevsky, *Demons* (1872), trans. Robert A. McGuire, London, Penguin, 2008.

Andrew George, *The Epic of Gilgamesh: The Babylonian Epic Poem and other Texts in Akkadian and Sumerian*, London, Penguin, 2003.

Lucien Goldmann, *Towards a Sociology of the Novel* (1964), trans. Alan Sheridan, New York, Tavistock Publications, 1975.

Patricia Highsmith, *The Talented Mr Ripley*, New York, Coward-McCann, 1955.

Michel Houellebecq, *Platform* (2001), trans. Frank Wynn, London, Vintage, 2004.

Samuel Huntington, *The Clash of Civilizations and the Remaking of World Order*, New York, Simon & Schuster, 1996.

Frederic Jameson, *Marxism and Form: Twentieth Century Dialectical Theories of Literature*, Princeton, NJ, Princeton University Press, 1971.

Uwe Johnson, *Anniversaries. From the Life of Gesine Cresspahl* (1970–1983), trans. Leila Vennewitz, New York, Harcourt Brace, 1975 (t. I–II), London, Andre Deutsch Limited, 1988 (t. III–IV).

James Joyce, *Finnegan's Wake*, London, Faber and Faber, 1939.

Franz Kafka, *The Trial* (1925), trans. Idriss Parry, London, Penguin, 2000.

Gilles Kepel, *The Revenge of God: The Resurgence of Islam, Christianity and Judaism in the Modern World*, trans. Alan Braley, Cambridge, Polity, 1994.

Milan Kundera, *The Art of the Novel* (1986), trans. Linda Asher, New York, Harper Perennial, 2003.

Pierre Choderlos de Laclos, *Dangerous Liaisons* (1782), trans. P.W.K. Stone, London: Penguin, 1961.

Mikhail Lermontov, *A Hero of Our Time* (1840), trans. Vladimir and Dmitri Nabokov, New York, Doubleday, 1958.

György Lukács, *The Theory of the Novel* (1920), trans. Anna Bostock, London, Merlin, 1971.

Claude-Edmonde Magny, *L'Âge d'or du roman américain*, Paris, Seuil, 1948.

George R. R. Martin, *A Game of Thrones*, New York, Random House, 1996.

Jean-Claude Monod, *La Querelle de la sécularisation*, Paris, Vrin, 2002.

Orhan Pamuk, *Snow* (2002), trans. Maureen Freely, London, Faber and Faber, 2004.

Richard B. Parkinson, *The Tale of Sinuhe and Other Ancien Egyptian Poems 1940–1640 BC*, Oxford University Press, 1997.

Antoien François Prévost, *Manon Lescaut* (1753), trad. Leonard Tancock, London: Penguin, 1991.

Colin Radford and Michael Weston, "Can we be moved by the fate of Anna Karenina?", *Proceedings of the Aristotelian Society*, Supplementary Volumes, Vol. 49, 1975, pp. 67–93.

Jean-Jacques Rousseau, *Confessions* (1782), trans. W. Conyngham Mallory, London, Tudor, 1936.

Jean-Paul Sartre, "M. François Mauriac et la liberté" (1939), *Situation* I, Paris, Gallimard, pp. 33–52.

Winfried Georg Maximilian Sebald, *The Emigrants* (1992), trans. Michael Hulse, London, Harvill, 1996.

Aleksandr Solzhenitsyn, *Cancer Ward* (1966), trans. Nicholas Bethell, New York, Dial Press, 1968.

William Makepeace Thackeray, *Vanity Fair* (1848), Hertfordshire, UK, Wordsworth Editions, 1998.

Alberto Toscano, "Rethinking Marx and Religion", www.marxau21.fr, 2011.

Virginia Woolf, *Orlando*, London: Hogarth Press, 1928.

# PART III
# Literature and the poetic

# 8
# THE VARIETIES OF LITERARY EXPERIENCE

*Peter Schjeldahl*

Can the thirteen-hundred-word column of topical art writing, in a general-interest magazine, be deemed literature? If so—and of course the idea thrills me—it may be a telling sign of the cultural disarray that this book seeks to address. I take it that a stage has been reached where no one can say with confidence what is or is not a literary form, who is or is not a literary writer, who is entitled to judge, and how, or whether, those sorts of question matter.

They don't matter, I believe, except as distress signals. They aren't real questions, by the test of what difference any plausible answers would make in anybody's life. Being literal-minded—or pragmatist, to dignify myself a little—I will survey the situation, as I perceive it. I'll do so along two tracks: one of hard, though changeable, facts and the other of soft, but stubborn, values. The state of literature presents a set of facts. What anyone—starting here, with you and me—likes about literature constitutes the values that are at stake.

I've titled my essay with a play on *The Varieties of Religious Experience*, William James's 1901 book of investigations in the psychology of belief. James regarded religion as a response, dramatic in individual cases, to the human craving to feel at home in the universe. I will consider literature in terms of a related though less cosmic desire: to feel at one with ourselves in relation to others, including some among the dead.

I will focus on a practical form of that desire: the poetic. I don't mean poetry. I mean any writing that works by calling attention to its expressive means. The poetic in writing is like the painterly in painting, which emphasizes brushwork and color rather than drawing and shading. The poetic favors cadence and metaphor over logic and explication. Both the poetic and the painterly communicate by aesthetic sensation. When successful, they occasion beauty, the merger of pleasure with persuasion, the good with the true. Liking becomes believing.

W.H. Auden called poetry, in words that fit the poetic, "a way of happening." That's good, because showing what it tells. It doesn't do much for rational comprehension. It illuminates without instructing. The poetic is learnable but not teachable. You can't become educated in it, by study, but only sophisticated in it, through experience. It puts you on your own, responsive and responsible in your aloneness. That's what it's for: connecting solitudes.

With the poetic in literal mind, I'll say things about present-day writing and reading, with some references to art and the art world. I will touch on historical developments and social conditions, without much analysis. I aim to behold literature matter-of-factly on the page, or the digital screen, as a medium not of knowledge, but of wisdom. Let words come first and thinking after. Things being as they are, this will lead us to exotic worldly places.

Words that function poetically don't reliably cluster where they once did, in literary forms. They tend to disport in the open air. Serious works in both traditional and experimental modes, while written and published and read as always, have ever less traction in living culture. This has to do with big, irreversible changes in the world. There's no use in lamenting a situation that, while setting limits, contains the seeds for what will be possible in the arts from now on.

What happened?

For convenience, I date one onset of entropy in literature back in time fifty-four years, two months, two days, and seven hours, to the noon hour of July 17, 1959. That was the moment of Frank O'Hara's poem, "The Day Lady Died." I should say that O'Hara was a figure of my hopeless emulation, when I wrote poems, and is still a guiding light for my writing about art. So I have a personal bias. But I think we'll do better in talking about literature with a significant specimen of it in view than we would without. Please listen to this, a peculiar elegy for the singer Billie Holiday, whose nickname was Lady Day:

> The Day Lady Died
> It is 12:20 in New York a Friday
> three days after Bastille day, yes
> it is 1959 and I go get a shoeshine
> because I will get off the 4:19 in Easthampton
> at 7:15 and then go straight to dinner
> and I don't know the people who will feed me
>
> I walk up the muggy street beginning to sun
> and have a hamburger and a malted and buy
> an ugly NEW WORLD WRITING to see what the poets
> in Ghana are doing these days
> I go on to the bank
> and Miss Stillwagon (first name Linda I once heard)
> doesn't even look up my balance for once in her life
> and in the GOLDEN GRIFFIN I get a little Verlaine
> for Patsy with drawings by Bonnard although I do
> think of Hesiod, trans. Richmond Lattimore or

Brendan Behan's new play or *Le Balcon* or *Les Nègres*
of Genet, but I don't, I stick with Verlaine
after practically going to sleep with quandariness

and for Mike I just stroll into the PARK LANE
Liquor Store and ask for a bottle of Strega and
then I go back where I came from to 6th Avenue
and the tobacconist in the Ziegfeld Theatre and
casually ask for a carton of Gauloises and a carton
of Picayunes, and a *NEW YORK POST* with her face on it

and I am sweating a lot by now and thinking of
leaning on the john door in the 5 SPOT
while she whispered a song along the keyboard
to Mal Waldron and everyone and I stopped breathing

I propose that this poem, besides being inventive literature, was a historic crack of doom for literature as a consensually established and defended, exalted pursuit. It so happened that, around that time, O'Hara gave a reading at a theater in the East Village. (There's a pizza parlor there now.) Jack Kerouac, drunk in the audience, heckled, "You're killing American poetry, O'Harry!" O'Hara snapped back, "That's more than you could do."

Those were lively days, and the nights were pretty interesting, too.

"The Day Lady Died" poem stands in literary history somewhat as the contemporaneous works of Jasper Johns and Robert Rauschenberg do in that of visual art. Johns made material facts of immaterial signs, as by equating the American flag with paint on canvas. Rauschenberg created signs out of junk, such as a stuffed goat with a car tire around its middle. In O'Hara's poem, likewise, art is suffused with reality to the tingling verge of being replaced by it. Johns and Rauschenberg influenced the world-changing movements of Pop Art and Minimalism. Nothing so climactic developed in poetry, for reasons I'll get into. O'Hara's originality remains fresh because literary culture has never really assimilated its lessons. I think the poem marks a pivot point in time, from a relatively secure past to a wildly insecure future. It seems worth a close reading.

The technique of O'Hara's prosody sneaks up on you, behind a first impression of being anti-poetic in its flatness and speed, resembling mere chatter. That's an engineered illusion. The poem is plenty formal. Take the almost subliminal rigor of the line "I am sweating a lot by now and thinking of." Twelve syllables with just two stresses, on "sweat" and "think." If you think that's easy to make seem natural, try it. The style embodies the distraction, the fun, and the vulnerability of life lived to the beat of trains schedules and tabloid headlines.

"The Day Lady Died" stages fleeting circumstances and attitudes of a cosmopolitan dandy. The tone keeps shifting: irritable, with "for once in her life;" companionable, naming a shopping angst known to everyone: "quandariness." There's a hint of indigestion in what must be the first ever appearance in poetry of "a hamburger and malted," consumed on the run. The tone turns comic with the word "casually," as the poet congratulates himself on being so cool, buying French cigarettes from the ultra-swanky "tobacconist in the Ziegfield Theatre." But it is dead-level as he cites Verlaine, Hesiod, Behan, Genet, and the poets of Ghana. They are colleagues of his in literature, which he takes seriously. Two significantly jarring notes are the names Patsy and Mike, which can mean nothing to anyone outside his social circle. They mark the private end of a spectrum with, at the public end, *The New York Post*, which was then the most literate and liberal of the city's tabloids. Tacit respect attends the naming of the jazz pianist Mal Waldron—"the *great* Mal Waldron" going without saying. Finally, consider the bank teller who refrains from looking up the poet's balance, which we presume is financially sound though nervously precarious. Her overheard first name makes her symbolic of the myriad individuals, in a city, who are hidden from us behind their functions. Incidentally, I may have found Linda Stillwagon online. A woman of that maiden name and the right age—she was twenty-three in 1959—died in December 2012 in Pennsylvania. A skimpy obituary reports that she was "surrounded by her loving family"—as we can only wish for ourselves, someday. I wonder if she knew that her last name had done literary duty by foreshadowing the end of a revolutionary poem: "*Still*-wagon."

One word needs explaining: "whispered," in "she whispered a song." In her last days, Billie Holiday's voice was broken. Also, she was performing in secret, illegally, having been banned for drug offenses by the New York District Attorney.

What happens when you stop breathing?

You may start again, after the tiny preview of when you won't. "It killed me," we say of a sublime art work or performance. "It knocked me dead."

More to my point, what happens to literature when it is overrun by ambient and personal actualities in a blaze of simultaneous outward awareness and self-consciousness, ending in silence? The literary as a zone of privileged expression is pretty well wrecked, albeit entertainingly. O'Hara absorbs familiar features of narrative and essayistic prose and of lyric verse so thoroughly that they seem no longer quite transmittable, except as lingering charms.

Concerning lyric poetry, compare the line "I am sweating a lot by now and thinking of" to the start of Keats's "Ode to a Nightingale": "My heart aches, and a drowsy numbness pains." The DNA of Romanticism is structurally intact in O'Hara's line, but drained of reproductive spunk. It's as if he let Keats's nightingale out of a gilded cage—freeing it from literature—to hob-nob with the pigeons on Sixth Avenue, whose company it keeps to this day.

From the heat of midtown one July day, how do you climb back to the snow-capped, timeless heights of canonical poetry? You don't, if your common sense endorses Arthur Rimbaud's injunction, "*Il faut etre absolument moderne*." O'Hara plainly pledged allegiance to absolute modernity. I presume that many if not most of us do too, or we wouldn't conceive of literature being in crisis. Fidelity to the present is a kind of all-determining principle that, as O'Hara wrote in another connection, "comes as a kiss and follows as a curse."

In the four years before his accidental death at the age of forty in 1966, O'Hara wrote few poems, searchingly experimental but not very satisfactory. He drank too much, but he always had. I imagine that he had grown unsure of what a righteously up-to-date poem was or could be, any longer. I struggled naïvely in what seems to me, looking back, exactly that fix until I gave up and redirected my energies to the more tractable discipline of columnizing about art, which I had done half-heartedly to that point. The career change shored up my sanity, improved my social life, and, not incidentally, began to pay my bills.

Someone is bound to notice my omission, so far, of O'Hara's friend and the last supreme poet in English, John Ashbery. For me, Ashbery's genius is unaccountable, floating outside, while alongside, the common course of literature. He spews poems. Some are better than others, but all have something like a floor beneath them that is a ceiling for anyone else. He was once asked how he could be so prolific. He said, "Well, it's like television. There's always *something* on." Hearing that, when I was still trying to squeeze poems out of myself, made me sick. I remain in awe. So, yes, I tiptoe past John Ashbery.

Meanwhile, I am aware of the danger of generalizing about contemporary poetry from my personal disappointment. Many poets today, better than I was, carry on the art of the ragged right-hand margin. But I take it as undeniable that poetry has declined as a force in culture and a recognized occupation in society.

It's easy to forget how luxuriantly poetry flourished, for a while, in America a half-century ago, with the Beats, the New York School, the avant-gardism of Charles Olson and his followers, the vogues of the Russians Yevtushenko and Voznesensky, a conservative but still energetic modernism in academe, and assorted populist wags and balladeers. For what ensued, I'll retell an oft-told anecdote.

Sometime in 1961, friends of the late bohemian's bohemian, Taylor Mead, took him to hear an obscure young folk singer at a MacDougal Street coffee house. It was Bob Dylan. At the break, Mead remarked to his companions, "The poets have *had* it." I remember being shocked and indignant, when someone relayed that to me. Later, I was appalled by news reports and photographs of Allen Ginsberg, our bard, sucking up to Dylan like an honorary groupie. Of course I loved Dylan, but he wasn't a *poet*. The truth hurt. Dylan and the waves of singer-songwriters who arrived with and after him abducted, Pied Piper-fashion, the core audience for poetry, of hungry souls in their teens and twenties. The culture ceased to incubate poets. From that day to this, any young person with extraordinary verbal ability is apt to be found dandling a guitar or rapping the night away.

The killing blow was poverty. Logically, visual fine art might have foundered, too, after Andy Warhol. Warhol's dead Marilyn Monroe squared up Frank O'Hara's dead Billie Holiday—as a more negotiable saint of the new cult of tragic fame—and he likewise choked high art, while mastering its means, with imports from the everyday. The critic Arthur Danto keeps insisting that Warhol's silkscreened replicas of Brillo soap-pad boxes finished art off. That fantasy is like Francis Fukuyama's "End of History," which confused history with failed theories about it. And go preach the end of art to the people today who regularly pay tens of millions of dollars for single silkscreens by Warhol, as also for, say, recent squeegeed paintings by Gerhard Richter, whom Warhol decisively influenced. Painting can't decline. Money won't let it.

In the present phase of every art, financial viability is the one and only viability that speaks for itself. Look no farther than that for history.

The shaping of culture by cash isn't new. Careers in the arts typically begin as individual breaks toward freedom and fame and then, if successful, end up where money is. But the patterns and powers of wealth's distribution now have no precedent that I can think of, in terms of scale and impact—steamrolling every sort of criterion of value in art except price. This goes for so-called noncommercial or even anti-commercial work, which siphons from the money reservoir through audience-pandering or do-good institutions. By personal check, museum commission, or foundation grant, a dollar is a dollar.

Of course, visual art is unique among the major arts, economically. Literature, music, and film survive on sales of unlimited copies. Visual art's trade in handmade objects reaps the bonuses of scarcity. Walter Benjamin famously predicted that visual art would falter when mechanical reproductions dispersed the aura of originals. The opposite happened. Like paper currency pegged to gold, reproductions increased the preciousness of the originals. They also made art more popular, which inspired artists with a sense of socially supported mission. But, unlike poets, artists needn't be individually popular to prosper, except with rich elites. The remorseless calculus of publishing consigns poetry to a melancholy niche market, as much as declaring that poems count as pennies in the denominations of cultural, as well as, monetary worth. This crushing insult inevitably warps poets into attitudes of defensiveness or, worse, resignation. Gone is the expansive confidence essential to advancing any art.

I'm not one to disdain the affluence of the art world. Indirectly, by generating public fascination, it affords journalistic criticism a glancing gravitas. The current art game is a theater and an arena of potent symbols, where ineffable and effable values—Eros and Mammon—alternately dance and fight. The challenge for a friend of the ineffable, like me, is to resist cynicism, which would bolster my self-possession but make me a useless observer. I must assume that everyone in the field is doing his or her best, given the opportunities and obstacles of the moment. No one gets up in the morning with the intention of making me feel bad, but whatever they do implicates me. It's about tracking a story while accepting that I'm part of it.

It's an O.K. deal with minor discomforts, such as having to take stands against my temperamental grain. For over two decades I've bumped up against the maddening temerity of Jeff Koons. Picture to yourself one of Koons's huge stainless-steel balloon dogs: an insolent trophy of careless expense and carefree expensiveness, trumpeting the impunity of the monstrously rich. (The pooch is nameless, but it could sensibly be Pluto, from "plutocracy.") Forgive me if you want a dismissal of the work's importance. It is both beautiful and grotesque in ways that, without it, we couldn't accurately imagine, feel, think, and, if so inclined, rethink about the available pleasures and inescapable miseries of our day.

I wish the story of art now were more elevating. But I will settle for winkling out intermittent joys and insights from a decadent regime of Mannerism, which seems to me our blanketing dispensation. On that score, I think that "Neo-Mannerism" would better characterize all levels of cultural production, these days, than any recent post-this or post-post-that banner. Forget Duchamp. Consult Bronzino. Let's widen our historical horizons beyond the last and the next-to-last newness.

Why not look on the bright side of the collapse of theories of history? It licenses knowledge and imagination to roam across time, discovering commonalities any-where. Why not, for example, conceive of "contemporary art" as the class of every art work that physically exists, be it four days or four millennia old? Abstract analy-sis stumbles if deprived of a goal. But when we awaken from dreams of progress, the past blossoms with vicarious novelties; and being alive, moment to moment, becomes the ground zero of all meaning. The rangy immediacy of Frank O'Hara may not be recoverable, but it's a reference in the right direction.

If today's unbounded vistas make us anxious, remember what Kierkegaard called anxiety: "the dizziness of freedom."

Literature shares in the condition that I'm calling Neo-Mannerist, an ecology of miscellaneous species of artifice without a common style but demanding stylistic commitment. Everything is a kind of thing. We read new writing, as we look at new art, with automatic reference to what it typifies. The best of it is the most openly conscious of precedents and affinities.

I sometimes visit art schools and observe students, who are far more sophisti-cated than art students used to be, selecting the kinds of thing that they will make or do, as if from a menu of post-minimalisms and conceptualisms that hasn't fun-damentally altered in thirty years. The kids are like quick, clever squirrels, adroitly spinning the wheels in chosen cages. I don't mean that their work is bad. Most of it is skilled and smart, and some of it is terrific. But nearly all of it falls into generic roles that art plays now in gallery and museum cultures. You mostly can't tell what older artists the students have been looking at, but only what brands.

Artists now, like writers and really all of us, navigate mazes of reflecting surfaces, for excellent reasons. Nothing like a creative philosophy coheres except superfi-cially. Go an inch deep, and chaos roars. You can see this as an effect of globalization: aesthetic languages homogenized into a sort of portable Esperanto, everywhere equally readable, while equally banal. But the whys of the condition are many and moot. How might it deepen?

Lacking sensible ends, art and literature are stuck with means. Therein lies the only way forward that I can imagine. There has been a tentative but intriguing revival of painterly painting lately, characterized by strangely deliberate recklessness. Go and Google Albert Oehlen, Cecily Brown, Dana Schutz, and Josh Smith, to see types of it. The trend isn't terribly satisfying, so far, but it holds promise by forcing dissatisfaction to a head.

Again recalling William James's *The Varieties of Religious Experience*, I think of his accounts of faith kicking in not at the crest of consciousness but at the bottom, with personal survival at stake. Strikingly, the most profound of them center in the sixteenth century, the tumultuous period of the Protestant Reformation and the Catholic Counter-Reformation and, not coincidentally, of Mannerism in the arts. Martin Luther had an ally in Lucas Cranach the Elder and St. Theresa of Avila, a painterly fellow traveler in El Greco.

I propose that today there's a similar tension between restless souls and synthetic styles. Religion is out of the picture, but pressures build that can only, though with exasperating vagueness, be termed spiritual. In literature, the right instrument both to gauge and to exploit those pressures is the poetic.

The poetic works in mysterious ways but is technically practical. It entails alertness to the sounds of words and to how the sounds affect understanding. The use of a word is poetic if it reverberates like a struck bell, with one clear note haloed by semitones. It must convince as exactly the right word for what it denotes, but shaded, and given depth, by the resonance of its connotations.

Recall Keats's phrase "a drowsy numbness pains." Its meter is antique, but, recalling Auden, its "way of happening" is imperishable. Each of the four words, including "a," vibrates with memories of its former uses. The memories don't blend. If the words were people, they'd take no more notice of each other than mutual strangers on a bus. Listen again: "a drowsy numbness pains." What can "numbness" have to do with "pains," or either of with "drowsy?" And what's with "a," implying the existence of other drowsy numbnesses? Despite themselves, by being thrust together, the words trigger the recognition of a state of mind.

The poetic is among the chief pleasures of having a mind that is subject to states. People will seek it, come what may. The poetic abounds even when diffused and adrift, as it is throughout present culture. We get whiffs of it from songs, of course, and also from plays and screenplays and television scripts, and sometimes from journalism—often on sports pages, whose only reason for being is pleasure—and even from advertising, where the ingenuity of the desperation to sell us something lets us savor the play of feelings involved in being sold. The poetic popped up occasionally in a speech by Barack Obama, commanding not only enjoyment but votes. Superior oratory is the poetic, weaponized.

Imagined as an animal, the poetic hunts by instinct, but it doesn't mind subsisting parasitically. It needs only an immediate purpose: something enough worth saying to be said with value added. Displays of verbal facility and wit are characteristic but not sufficient. Some meaningful work must be done. This needn't be important work, but it must make a difference.

Disrespect for the poetic infects society with a degenerative disease of the ear. The malady is epidemic in the effusions of the million-yammering-headed Internet. Everybody writes, and nobody rewrites. (Every good writer knows that writing is only the crude prelude to rewriting.) And much academic writing positively suppresses the poetic by favoring toneless abstraction, wrenching words from their dictionary sense and stripping them of connotations. Tortuous pains are taken to evade any personal responsibility of the writer. Thus we get abstract nouns weirdly personified, robot-like, as when one idea is said to "interrogate" another. (Try to picture that, for a second.) Thus the deadening word "practice" applied to creative adventures, as if we were dentists or accountants in clinics or bureaucracies of the imagination. And thus the grotesquerie of writers diagnosing cultural demoralization in prose that demoralizes.

To be fair, jargon is endemic to specialized fields, from cultural studies to garage mechanics. It's a brutal expedient in the kind of writing that has to be written by people who aren't really writers for people who have to read it, for professional or educational reasons. A poetic style in that line might be like whipped cream on gruel; and the captive reader might think, "Oh, get on with it!" So I'll recuse myself from judging academic prose while taking my stand on writing that we read because we want to, and we want to because we like it. The poetic is my kind of writer's bread and butter, with emphasis on butter. I must routinely please for a living. I'm a culture-section journalist. As such, I try to find appropriate uses for the poetic in journalism, which has troubles of its own these days.

Journalism was once said to be history written by flashes of lightning. The present illumination is more like the flickers of numberless fireflies, a continuous dim glow perhaps revealing that something is there, but only fuzzily what it is. Opinionators riot in the fog. This puts a premium on styles of description. I have in mind the radical sense of a three-word sentence by Gertrude Stein, a talisman for me: "Description is explanation."

Say adequately what something is, and what it means will dawn. The information conveyed may include thoughts and feelings, but tethered to perception. Never plead, or even think, that anything is hard to describe, let alone indescribable. The determination is all. It won't let you be lazy or glib. It will make of your subject a gift to readers, who appreciate having enough cues to think and feel for themselves. Readers are funny that way.

Description, in Stein's sense, concentrates a writer's scattered energies and capacities, as a laser organizes chaotic light. The form that you adopt uses you, rather than you using the form. This is crucial to first-person essays. The essay form—in my case the magazine column, as strict in its way as a sonnet—edits the mess of the writer's personality and character into an efficient persona. Manners, in the sense of etiquette, enter in. As a writer for a respectable magazine, I accept the suppression of aspects of myself that might be shameful or dumb, which my poems used to indulge. But, at whatever level of candor, a rhetorical form is, besides a medium, mediumistic—sort of spooky, when you think about it.

Forms save fuss. The decay of literary conventions handicaps literature. I remember when, as a young poet smitten with Dada and Surrealism, I loathed Robert Frost's wisecrack, "Free verse is like playing tennis with the net down." But he had a point. Free verse was alleged to liberate poetry, as it really did and then, by stages ever more distant from musical speech, overdid. Poets starting from the apparent informality of Frank O'Hara, like painters from the seeming wildness of Jackson Pollock, lacked the formal grounding that makes those liberties sing. The requisite degree of preparation is long gone from schools of literature and art. Today it most strongly informs hybrid mediums, such as the novelistic television series. My nominee for the twenty-first century's best creative work so far is "The Wire." I have my daughter to thank for knowledge of that. She got tired of her mother and me being clueless, and she gave us the boxed set for Christmas.

I'm lucky to work in a line that no one has bothered to liberate. Like any serviceable form, the review column prescribes hard work toward making it seem easy. I'm addicted to it, for reasons that become clear to me when I attempt longer essays and articles. If any of those have succeeded, you can bet it's because my superb editor, Virginia Cannon, held my hand and led me through vales of tears. At any great length, I can't seem to keep a firm enough grip on myself to lose it—to lose myself—as the poetic requires.

I'm reminded of Paul Valéry's wonderful definition of poetry as something written by someone other than the writer to be read by someone other than the reader. And also of another of Rimbaud's visionary declarations, which I Americanize as "I is somebody else." That seems to me common sense for good writing in the first person. I—whoever that is—swears by it.

Not to be lofty, I admit that mine is a humble discipline. Topical art criticism is a second-handed craft, trailing after art—making something out of the something that artists have made out of nothing. Criticism is properly a shabby-genteel suburb of literature's shining city on a hill. I intrude downtown only because we seem agreed that the city is burning.

Regarding somebody-elseness, I defer to writers of fiction, whose stock in trade it is. I'm a dilettantish reader of short stories and novels, knowing what I like but only approximately how and why. It may be that journalism's loyalty to facts paralyses narrative imagination. Perhaps so does an overdeveloped devotion to the poetic. Dave Hickey, the best rhetorician in American art writing, once aspired to fiction, like his childhood friend Larry McMurtry. He told me that McMurtry had said to him, "Dave, you know and I know that you are a better writer than I am. But you will never write a novel, because you can't stand to put in the boring parts."

I am immaculately incapable of fiction, not only averse to the boring parts but no good at making stuff up. Twice, long ago, I attempted detective novels, inspired by the poetic wonderments of Raymond Chandler. After a couple of chapters, in each case, I had a corpse on my hands and not the remotest inkling of who might have murdered it, and why. My hard-boiled heroes looked to me plaintively for their next moves. Sorry, guys.

With that caveat, I remain an evangelist for the poetic, as the optimum performance of any task, in fact or fiction, for which writing is fitted. I would welcome feedback from fiction writers, who now appear only somewhat less beleaguered than poets. I set aside genre authors, who are doing very well. They are definitive Neo-Mannerists, whose books practically write themselves. Serious fiction writers must confront the dominance of genre and of movies and television, in popular storytelling, and with the termite aesthetics of performance arts, in what passes for the avant-garde. It makes sense that some of the most dedicated migrate to coterie tastes and academe. This does not make them snobs and obscurantists. No writer sniffs at achievable glory. You can't play a hand of cards you weren't dealt.

As I approach the end of this essay, I anticipate objections to my aestheticism. I've been skating over ethical and moral, broadly political motives for writing. I do so to lodge a plea for the primitive drive of congenital writers and artists. Respect for that drive is at one with the maximum possible vitality of literature and art, always subject to the kinds of cruel social condition that give rise to political thinking.

An all but universal cruelty of our time, affecting nearly every career in art or literature, is that of people forced into doing what they can get paid to do, in competition with others for the rewards of eminence. This burdens artists who must churn out product for the next art fair, and the next and the next. It afflicts writers whose unavoidable day jobs amount to para-careers, supporting their real work but constituting most of the real work they do. Economic tyranny outrages the idealism of anyone ambitious to make a difference in the arts. It spurs rebelliousness. As a young writer or artist, you want the world to be a certain way. It isn't like that, so you want to change it. You grasp at any hint that a change may be possible, perhaps in a political tendency. But the displacement is at odds with your formative dream of a Great Good Place, of which you are the chief and the ambassador.

Good writers and artists make poor partisans. I think of my hero Oscar Wilde's essay "The Soul of Man under Socialism." He fancied that a revolution would leave him happier in doing as he liked, because less pestered by his social conscience. If you are a political activist and an artist says that you can count on him or her, be kind. Smile and nod. But don't believe it.

There is certainly an ethic proper to art and writing. It's quality—not as an absolute, Lord knows, in a culture that knocks absolutes to pieces and the pieces to powder. I mean a case-by-case measure of the cultivation of *qualities*, in the plural. It's about sharpening shared means for producing fresh perceptions, as needs and appetites for them arise.

The poetic needn't lack for social effects, so long as they aren't predictable. When applied with a will, the poetic is a scalpel. The social body subject to exploratory surgery may be grisly: already dismembered, with zero prospects of recovery. Like anyone, I would love to have inhabited the wedded creative and worldly dynamisms of Periclean Athens, the Renaissance, the Baroque, the flowering of modernity in Paris, and, as I did briefly, during its last phase, New York triumphant in the sixties. Instead there's wall-to-wall Mannerism redux.

I have little scholarly knowledge of historical Mannerism, beyond the common wisdom that artists in mid-sixteenth-century Europe couldn't conceive of what to do beyond gorgeously perverting the legacies of a Michelangelo or a Dürer. I will note only that the Mannerists whom we remember—the likes of Parmigianino, Tintoretto, and Holbein—didn't whimper about their lot. They started where they were and did the best they could. Then along came Caravaggio, and greatness was in play again.

Caravaggios happen, but don't waste your time trying to anticipate them. The future will build on or, more likely, trash our achievements in ways that we can't begin to imagine and, if we live long enough to see them, may very well detest. For now, enough with cutting edges! See what can be done with cutting middles.

I hope I've given a boost to the pragmatic value of poetic license: literature as immunized testimony, be the news welcome or repellent and delivered in whatever mediums and forms come to hand. What is done should only be done well. It must seduce. Good writers are honest sex workers of the spirit. It must teach by example, promulgating the principles that guide it. And it must mind its manners, be they good or bad. Literature is manners on parade.

These are simple-minded ideas, if they are ideas at all. They must operate as common sense does, blinking in the face of every contrary imperative and compunction. They are indefensible except in their access to the well-springs of life, which they channel to enhance or to disrupt, to bless or to curse, the present— outside of which, no one lives and nothing is.

# 9
# INTELLECTION, COGNITION, CONTRADICTION

*Laurent Dubreuil*

We read and write literature to make our lives livable, to think different things, and even differently. This text mainly deals with the latter question and tries to situate the challenge of literary *thinking* (rather than *thought*), in its dual relationship to the event of an oeuvre and to the course of human *noēsis* as "we" can understand it now.

What is happening when I read to you the following lines by Charles Baudelaire: "Je suis la plaie et le couteau! / Je suis le soufflet et la joue! / Je suis les membres et la roue, / Et la victime et le bourreau!"—"I am the wound and the dagger! / I am the blow and the cheek! / I am the members and the wheel, / Both the victim and the executioner!"?[1]

A shared noetic space is opened, and in this space we try to stand and understand what is at stake in the poem. We certainly hear the rhythm, we see forms, feel emotions, process meanings; we remember that all these words have been uttered, and we can attach to them semantic features they do not usually carry. We recall other verses by Baudelaire and others. But we want more, and to grasp what is being said: how could "I" be "the" blow and "the" cheek at the same time? And, by the way, who is this I? Is it ours, or us, or him, or me? Nobody, or everyone? Even besides the particular *adunata* of this stanza, literature seems to be tied to entire sets of impossibilities that are nonetheless made possible "in a sense" by the very fact of writing and reading.

Many different strategies may be used to tentatively solve the puzzle of Baudelaire's text. One can argue that all this is either a plain lie, or a mere play on words; either the dictation of the unconscious that knows no rational bound, or the conflicted expression of sadomasochism; either the invention of a syphilitic brain, or, just "a manner of speaking." All these "solutions" have been in use in literary criticism for a while. The accusation of lie, for instance, is at least as old as the attacks of Xenophanes against Homer and Hesiod; it permeated the (post)Greek culture through Plato's appropriation of the motif; it is still active in a certain conception of fiction as *un mensonge qui dit la vérité*. All these solutions could even be valid, at least up to a certain extent. But they all leave our main problem untouched. Our question was: how are we able to think (and think through) this stanza? And how do we "think literature" each time it leads us to the limits of the unthinkable? (That is, in my view, each time literature thinks.)

At this point, I need to confess that I am not going to offer a full commentary of Baudelaire's poem "L'héautontimoroumenos"—unfortunately, I do not have enough time and space for this. Rather, I am unapologetically using this text as my pretext, and, in closing, as my post-text. I do not even want you to consider that, in my mind, uttering contradictory statements would be the highest achievement of the literary—but this is undoubtedly a symptom of the *clear* opacity that *produces* literature. Literary scholars who would like to avoid such difficulties have in fact very little to do with the shared space of thinking that oeuvres transiently construct.

Our present moment is saturated with "new" approaches to literature that precisely do their best to obliterate the act of thinking *through* texts. This makes this book all the more urgent, and, I believe, decisive. There are more and more promoters of "distant reading," whether they are obsessed with titles of novels or the geographical origin of the authors. Smart and bright critics who speak of books they did not read are also easy to find. In parallel, an ever-growing number of scholars try to turn to cognitive science (neuroscience or evolutionary psychology, in particular) to reinvigorate the study of literature. There is some *logic* to this move, inasmuch as thought exists thanks to cognitive operations (in the brain and in neuronal-like supports). But I think it is an abysmal error to admit in advance that a literary text is a sole matter of cognition (be it embodied, reenacted, or "affected").

What I am about to give now is an outlook on some conditions of possibility and impossibility for the *event* of literary thinking. It is also an oblique response to the current scholarly context I just briefly referred to. It is finally a partial and fragmented description of the path that led me from both the study of thinking in literature and my interest in the extraordinary to the research I undertook a few years ago, about the limits of cognition, in machines, humans or other animals (such as my friends the eloquent bonobos[2]).

Were literary criticism a "science" (and not the opportunistic pseudo-discipline it has to be, as long as it re-asserts the epistemic and noetic transform of literature), were it an actual "*Literaturwissenschaft*" or a "*science des textes*" or even a "*science humaine*," as so many have claimed, then, I could provide you with a summary of some major "discoveries" or "demonstrations" or well-accepted hypotheses.

This is not the case, but let us be counterfactual, and imagine that the developments of literary criticism and theory from the 1940s to the end of the last century were quasi-consistent. In this fictional world, we would find several main points of convergence. Here I just intend to keep and mention two of them, before elaborating some on my own suggestions.

The first convergence lies in the idea that *a literary text is not entirely reducible*: no commentary is complete and "definitive," no translation of a sonnet grasps the entirety of the poetic effect in the original, a tragedy is not abbreviated without *significant* loss or change, a novel is not a sum of information plus some style plus some appropriation of preexisting conventions, mutually incompatible readings are not always the sign of an error (in the book or in the readers' mind), etc. Language is key, and the literary has often been perceived as the only possible discourse beginning where Wittgenstein's *Tractatus logico-philosophicus* ends ("Whereof one cannot speak, thereof one must be silent."). That the "right to opacity" Édouard Glissant famously reclaimed be consubstantial to human verbal language, or thought; or that it would be revealed, mobilized, or forged by literature are very different options. So is the amplitude of the divergence within the convergence, but suffice it to say that, from phenomenology to most authors associated with the so-called French-American "age of theory," that from the Frankfurt School to Jean Bollack's renewed philology or the long aftermath of Russian formalism, literature remains in excess of its content or even its grammatical form (be it syntactic, metric, or conventional). Of course, we are also well aware of the fact that, from semiotics to narratology, many other "critics" exhibited (and still exhibit) a foolish hope in their ability to completely codify and summarize the irreducible. This is foolish, but also quite in line with a long-term practice of criticism, the one that ruled for instance the normative discourse on theater in 17th-century France.

Our second point is this: *writing and/or reading literature is tied to atypical thought.*[3] The most extreme position speaks of trance-like states, according to the ancient theory of inspiration, with Georges Bataille's inner experience serving as a backdrop for literary "strong communication." In my first book, I have shown the role of literary possession in the post-Romantic poetics of reading—and how it has been shunned through the motifs of spectrality.[4] This echoes a long debate, going from Plato's ironical depiction of the poet as someone being "out of his mind" (through *ek-phronesis*) to the insistent exclusion of *Dichten* from the realm of *Denken* in Heidegger, or Gilles Deleuze's stubborn desire to severe the arts from anything like a concept. For many philosophers (often named "Continental philosophers" on this continent), some atypical activity of the mind could be *elicited* by literature, but this has to be more rigorously *expressed* philosophically. I am afraid that Alain Badiou, for instance, and in spite of all his claims, does exactly that: systematically "correcting" and "translating" the lines of the poem into a conceptual index, when, he glosses "the Master" from Mallarmé's "*sonnet en x*" as "the Master of language" in his *Handbook of Inaesthetics*, or when he turns "rien n'aura eu lieu que le lieu" into the philosophical motto "rien n'a eu lieu que le lieu."

Then, in contradistinction with the widespread faith in the "anterior regime" of literature, I posit the literary in a *post hoc* moment, and certainly not at the beginning, the origin, the source, or the *Urgrund* of anything. Literature says what has already been said, but it weaves words and sentences so differently that it *undoes* previous speeches (proverbs, dictums, fragments of conversations, philosophical demonstrations, fictional situations...). In this *response* that creates the unheard does the literary emerge: it emerges as something other (as an exact quote, a paraphrase, an allusion, an echo, an *expolitio*) and as itself. The *non sequitur*, the faulty reasoning (once it has been cut and metamorphosed) perform and exhibit the discontinuities and weaknesses of the previous order (epistemic, social, political...), while being able to *signify*. Literature is both *defective* and *significant*; furthermore, it is created by the failures of so-called ordinary (and ordered) language, it is a strategy to "do something" in spite of the most intense defectiveness; thus it serves as a warrant for signification within verbal language, demonstrating that even the meaningless or the marginal may signify. Signification is not *subjective* (as opposed to *objective*): it is singular, and it arises from a textual object into the fugacious site of the *I*. As a result, the gesture of historicizing literature, for instance, has simply no signification, as long as history is not made "literary" in its own turn, i.e. as long as the defectiveness of the disciplinary standing of history is unable to be converted into some *poiēsis*. This remark applies to all the discursive disciplines or ordered speeches, including, of course, literary criticism and theory.

So, yes, I do think that literature thinks. Literary *thinking* does not coincide with the development of opinions, with a phraseological or dogmatic content: all of these aspects could encompass what would be called "literary thought" if you want. But *thinking* occurs as the text responds to other words and ideas, as it speaks and transforms them. How does one think here? With *notions*—i.e. the fragmentation of untenable concepts the disciplines of knowledge usually try to keep still. With *contradictions*—it all begins with the very reality of fiction, and my willful participation in this; it is constantly reenacted through verbal discrepancy and syntactic disloca- tion, supporting a non-consistent use of informal logic. With *significations*—or the vital outside of fixed senses, rationalistic constraints, and cognitive routines.

Thus qualified, literature is also a name for an experience in/of thinking that is at odds with what we could call "the cognitive program." I use this term anachro- nistically (the same way Horkheimer and Adorno spoke of *Aufklärung* in classical Greece) and I want to refer to a set of epistemic prescriptions. This set is to be found across continents and historical periods, even though its Greek form is still directly, and indirectly, the strongest influence in Academia. At any rate, the cognitive pro- gram under its maximal form requires from its practitioners (1) *an obedience to ordi- nary protocols of consistence* (determining, among other things, non-contradiction and non-entangled truths), (2) *a double ideal of objectivity and reducibility* (this encompasses the search for reproducibility and/or statistical identification), (3) *a conceptual and deictic use of language* (through formalized notation, or not), where most of the gaps and excesses of the so-called natural languages would be practically neutralized or principally overruled. To these features are linked a concern for "the general" or "the universal" (these two words translating the Aristotelian *katholou*) over the *ad hoc* and the indeterminable—and a quest for some methodic compression, or *automaticity*. Both the universal and the automaticity of *laws* (of nature, of history, of human groups, of the unconscious, of the mind, of language, etc.) serve the purpose of objective reducibility, where *noise* is suspended for the sake of the signal (as in information theory). Whereas contemporary researchers from "the sciences" could appear as being much "truer" to the cognitive agenda than most scholars from the humanities, it needs to be said that—despite strong critiques, both internal and external—the dominant and post-global organization of knowledge, in *all* its disciplines, depends on even a partial ratification of the program.

Literary thinking, as we characterized it, is the wild grass that grows in the many cracks of the cognitive edifice.

Now, the mistake would be to approach the literary as something *below* the cognitive threshold or as the counter-image of the program, i.e. as a myth, an outburst of childish imagination, a kind of delirium. What literature has in common with "madness," superstition, or hallucination is its factual rejection of the cognitive as the only (or superior) mode of mental activity. But literary oeuvres, in their undoing of the cognitive, speak to us from beyond the threshold—and invite us to go a few steps further, from the cognitive plane onto the intellective space.

The cognitive, then, is not something made up by contemporary cognitive science. What most researchers coming from functional neurobiology, artificial intelligence, analytic philosophy of mind or experimental psychology are working on is the operative image of the rational, formal and disciplinary enfolding of thought. Here, knowledge and thought are taken as a summation of automatic operations, being a-semantic, transparent, consistent, as well as fundamentally non-defective, repeatable and reducible (even though they are practically defeasible and alterable). Contrary to the old rationalism, the renewed cognitive program tolerates (and sometimes promotes) some (non-Freudian) unconscious; it presents the *res cogitans* as a *res extensa*. After decades of research, we could say that the operations of cognition literally and undoubtedly make us *think*, but that this is not where we stop. There, what I name *intellection* is the *variable* and *processual performance* of *cognition*. The *cognitive* is the retroactive enclosure of what I think on the operation of its cognition; the cognitive program promotes that enclosure as the best or higher tactic. But the *intellective* stems from the extension of extended cognition. Furthermore, *the intellective space* is a putative space where thought and knowledge are performed and shared (as thinking and knowing), and not only computed according to universal laws that would "speak" to us directly, and autonomously.

It will come as no surprise that, in most cases, the current attempts at using the methods (or, more frequently, the findings) of cognitive science for the interpretation of literature are just able to identify very, very generic and low-order devices (that are virtually present everywhere in animal and artificial cognition), and end up with oversimplified theories that do not even look for their experimental or experiential validation. (In a *diacritics* article on "experimental criticism," I have underlined some of the pathetic pitfalls that "Darwinian literary criticism" and other cognate approaches are currently facing, so I will not go back to this critique here.[5]) But the problem has less to do with cognitive science as such than with a misplaced (or underdeveloped) theorization of the literary. If we consider the literary space to be part of the intellective space (and a poem or a play to be one of the shortcuts toward the supplemental noetic manifold), then, by difference, cognitive studies could help us situate *where* and *how* literary thinking separates itself from the cognitive order—and give us some insight on the subsequent consolidation of the intellective into the cognizable. Understanding the *intellective* activity of the literary offers a chance of avoiding being trapped into the repetition of the cognitive program. For the scholars that we are, such a task comes with two associated conditions. On the one hand, as soon as we speak of thought and thinking, we'd better acknowledge the role of cognition (and be able to grasp to "exchange" with practitioners from the sciences of the mind), and all the more so if we are invested in the defects of the cognitive. On the other hand, we must acknowledge for our own modes of exposition and methods the creative role of opacity and of poetic performance—against well-entrenched disciplinary habits.

This is *not* a conclusion. Let us return to Baudelaire's stanza, "Je suis la plaie et le couteau! / Je suis le soufflet et la joue! / Je suis les membres et la roue, / Et la victime et le bourreau!" On a cognitive level, we can do very little with these four lines, or we might show that there is nevertheless a strong recourse to cognitive structures (not limited to syntax, but including the anaphoric "I am"; the scansion granted by exclamation points; the rimes, the meter, the echoing rhythm (for lines 2 and 3), the alliteration of [u] contrasting with the repetition of "and;" as well as the alternating genders for the attributes of what *I* am: dagger, blow, member, and executioner are masculine in French; wound, cheek, wheel, victim are feminine). But this support makes the "cognitive dissonance" (to use a term once coined by the psychologist Leon Festinger) even more palpable. The significance of this dissonance is affirmed at the external gates of a cognitive reading—and I am suddenly this I that is both the victim and the executioner, and… The intellective space where this unacceptable string of words signify is transiently accessed through the performance of cognition, which includes the demise of its very algorithmic progression. In the last few decades, some logicians have developed entire subfields of formalized languages to describe propositions where at least some contradictions and incompatibilities are not lethal (or, more technically, not "explosive" or "trivial"). In my own forthcoming essay on *The Intellective Space*, I have tried to use some of these notations;[6] I will spare you these formulae. The short version is: even when we compute with more than 0s and 1s, even when we accept both *alpha* and *non-alpha*, i.e. even when we do not forbid nor categorically rule out the possibility for thinking to pass by and to bypass the cognitive, we also normalize the intellective through its formalization or theorization. Perhaps is it impossible to keep some sense of discipline, without finally attempting to reduce the irreducible. Perhaps is it necessary to both show the heuristic gain of simplification as well as its costs.

Well, once you have the cognitive schema of literary thinking, everything *else* is yet to be expressed and created, each time anew: so is its signification. To put it differently, *the algorithmic sustains the poetic, but it does* not *equal it*. What I just wrote is still a cognitive rendition of some cognitive inability.[7] In more intellective terms, this non-equation (that is still an equation) leads to a stronger proposition, this one: *the poetic is incommensurable to the algorithmic that nonetheless allows it*.[8]

Literary thinking, as enacted through the production of an oeuvre, invites us to consider that our mental life is not only ruled by the possibility of mechanical failure (when "this is not true," "this can't be," or "this makes no sense" lead to an error message or to "abandon")—not only governed by processes of trials and errors (with the brain working as a Turing machine, or in the praise of cybernetic and epistemic *bricolage*)—and not only a matter of neuronal plasticity (coupled with a desire to turn the organ of the brain into a semi-metaphysical *organon*). Literature reminds to our minds that thinking sometimes occurs from the precipice, where no bridge could be found. It is on the intellective space that we have a chance to do more than failing, operating, or inventing—a chance to *create* with and through the incommensurable of *noēsis*. Could it be that the task of literature, in addition to providing ideas, emotions, and recollections, is also to teach us how to think beyond human cognition, or to think beyond ourselves?

## Notes

1 Charles Baudelaire, *Les fleurs du mal* (1861), LXXXIII. English version from *The Flowers of Evil* (Fresno, CA: Academy Library Guild, 1954) trans. by Aggeler, 265 (with my corrections for the last line).
2 The Wamba family documented in various books, articles and documentary movies including: Sue Savage-Rumbaugh, Stuart Shanker and Talbot Taylor, *Apes, Language, and the Human Mind* (New York: Oxford University Press, 1998), or Pär Segerdahl, William Fields and Sue Savage-Rumbaugh, *Kanzi's Primal Language* (New York: Palgrave Macmillan, 2005).
3 Or "alien thought," as Stathis Gourghouris calls it in this collection.
4 Laurent Dubreuil, *De l'attrait à la possession: Maupassant, Artaud, Blanchot* (Paris: Hermann, 2003).
5 Laurent Dubreuil, "On Experimental Criticism," *diacritics* 39–1 (2009).
6 Laurent Dubreuil, *The Intellective Space: Thinking Beyond Cognition* (Minneapolis, MN: University of Minnesota Press, forthcoming), §§ 52–53).
7 By the way, this is my non-cognitive take on the still unsolved "P vs. NP problem" in computer science.
8 In this, I may be close to Gilles Châtelet; see *L'enchantement virtuel* (Paris: Rue d'Ulm, 2010), 245–252, in particular, for his reading of Roger Penrose's *Shadows of the Mind* (New York: Oxford University Press, 1994).

# 10

# HEINER MÜLLER'S LYRIC LONELINESS AND THE MYTHICAL BODY

*Stathis Gourgouris*

The impetus in my book *Does Literature Think?* (2003) was to restage the ancient quarrel between poetry and philosophy by exploring the terms of what might be called poetic (or *poietic*) cognition. While at the time the inquiry was conducted with the philosophical text as the primary object, as a sort of target, in recent years I have been trying to reconfigure the argument by turning to poetic text itself. My interest in poetry is, of course, deeply personal and more ingrained and long-lasting than any of my other passions (including philosophy), except perhaps for music. Speaking as a poet, I would argue that poetry has always been directly implicated in the problem of thought, which is a philosophical problem (and political, no doubt, although I won't discuss this now), and not merely from the standpoint of analysis or criticism. Poetry itself is a specific mode of thought, as experimental and factual as scientific thought and as speculative and analytical as philosophical thought, even if it does not follow their rules of verification and classification.

Accounting for poetry as a mode of thought is surely not reducible simply to a matter of poetics, to examining poetry as a literary genre, but a matter of *poiesis* in the broadest sense: engaging with the process by which specific social and historical imaginaries (or mentalities) encounter and often alter their world in unprecedented creative/destructive ways, with poetic language in this process being a particular, and one might even say peculiar, modality. The peculiarity has to do with poetry's tense relation to writing, which is arguably as archaic as any problem in literature. As an oral/musical form allows itself to submit to the regime of notation, however we determine this to be, it calls forth an essential performativity that retains itself by pushing up against (and sometimes exceeding) the permutations of written form. This is an off-hand way of stating what is both obvious and yet inordinately open to question, which I take nonetheless as a simple presupposition.

This matter of excess is all the more relevant in my choice of Heiner Müller as a terrain for discussing poetry, given the prevalent tendency to doubt whether Müller can even be considered, strictly speaking, a poet at all. Even more, choosing to speak of Müller as a *lyric poet*, or if you will, to speak of him in the idiom of the lyric, knowing full well how this idiom itself is but an excessive category whose contours and trajectories are open to contention, makes this decision even more disputable.[1] Recognizing that, by phrasing matters this way, I have dredged up, yet again, the chimeric phantom of genre, I will nonetheless insist on approaching this question as particular and esoteric to Müller's work, even though obviously it pertains to a broader range of problems. In this respect, I will not theorize the question of the lyric, but approach the matter by foregrounding a set of parameters and configurations whose language is internal to the admittedly problematic history of a specific poetic practice. My insistence on a metaphorics of internality will resonate, as we will see shortly, with a particular poetic gesture that is unabashedly esoteric.

My interest in Heiner Müller has been a long one, at least since seeing the performance of his play *Cement* at Berkeley in 1979, directed by Sue Ellen Case, which was the first professional performance of Müller's work in America – the initial one being a student performance of *Mauser* at the University of Texas, Austin, in 1975, during Müller's first of many visits to the US. This interest was widely exercised over the years by an always anxious urgency not to miss a performance of Müller's work in the vicinity of my existence – and I've been fortunate to witness some truly great ones. But after Müller's death in 1995 – and especially as the collected *Gedichte* was published in Germany – I shifted attention from theatrical performance to the poetic text, discovering, much to my astonishment (and this is an embarrassing admission), a truly inspiring poetics that brought into a new horizon the core relation between the poetic and the political, which has been for years a consistent field of research for me in all kinds of ways. This discovery led initially to my translation of nineteen of Müller's poems into Greek in May 2000, but the underlying theoretical problem never got a chance to be addressed otherwise until this occasion.

There is a conventional argument that wants Müller to have begun as poet and ended as a poet, having distinguished himself in between as a dramatist. There is an equally conventional line that considers Müller's poetry to have been always a kind of rehearsal space for his dramatic texts – the idea being that his poems are fragments of various theatrical work-in-progress phases, but do not stand as works in-themselves and are to be valued only in conjunction with their various reincarnations in the body of specific dramatic works. The third conventional line of argument – that Müller is the only valiant heir to Brecht in German theater, which cannot, however, ignore Müller's famous statement: "to use Brecht without criticizing him is treason" – draws its energy from the examination of Müller as a dramatist, not a poet: a position that, if nothing else, also disregards Brecht as a poet.

Against these, I would put forth an equally conventional – one might argue – response which takes for granted that dramatic texts are poetic texts, with the proviso that this is decided by virtue of their performativity and not by whether they belong to the formal language of verse. I understand and accept that there may be some argument against this proviso, but the tradition of the theater across the centuries weighs heavily on linking poetic thinking to performativity as much as to a specific style of verse-making. In any case, the point is not to settle this issue (a non-issue, really), but to combat the perception of Müller as an occasional poet, or an idiosyncratic poet with a minor poetic oeuvre that must always pale before his gigantic status as one of the greatest dramatists of post-Beckettian theater.

My own elementary sense of this case is that the categories "dramatist" and "poet" are consubstantial. Müller's greatness as a dramatist is predicated on the fact that he is first and foremost a performer of words, a performer *with* words, lending his texts an internal performativity which precedes their theatrical realization. This is the primary level at which we must encounter him as a poet: "I have real difficulty writing prose. I don't believe in literature as a work of art to be read. I don't believe in reading."[2] Of course, we might say that this formulation disregards the performative element of reading, but here Müller's target is the conventional understanding of literature as a singular and private encounter with the text signified entirely by the act of silent reading. Moreover, this provocative thought process is also reiterated conversely when the target is the conventional notion of theater. There, "literature has the task of offering resistance to the theater." But what sort of literature? "Only when a text cannot be done the way that theater is conditioned to do it, is the text productive for the theater."[3] Taken together, the two formulations are meant to resist, indeed subvert, the way that both categories "literature" and "theater" expect to exercise command over the poetic act.

In any case, this is why Müller's deconstructive-Brechtian trajectory (which would be erroneously considered post-Brechtian) is characterized specifically by a kind of dramaturgy that keeps the text open (often with minimal or no stage directions), a kind of dramaturgy that resists the transformation of dramatic material to drama (*Hamletmachine* and *Medeamaterial* being the most famous examples). This dialectical trajectory might be considered to follow a twofold path. First, from a formalist aspect, Müller's deconstruction of dramatic language entails the most rigorous or most extreme application of the Brechtian *Verfremdungseffekt* on language itself – or more accurately, on dramatic verse itself. In this respect, those of his poetic texts that are nominally recognized as theatrical texts dismantle any traditional anchoring on the dramatic monologue as a poetic form. Second, from a historical-philosophical aspect, language for Müller is primarily mythical, that is to say, phantasmatic, indeterminately linked to history, irreducible to analytic determinations, and most of all, feasible only in a performative framework.

Müller had a very clear sense, not only of himself as a poet, but what it means to be a poet theoretically and what sort of openings the poetic text provided to his authorial practice, generally speaking. Although I still consider that we best encounter an author's self-description with suspicion, nonetheless, we cannot ignore Müller's frequent remarks that one can be more innovative in poetry than in drama.[4] Nor can we ignore his consistent reminders that the theater is nothing other than the space where the impossible is sought after in an orchestrated universe of performative gestures, in which he includes language itself: "Without [a] step into absolute darkness, the absolutely unfamiliar, the theater cannot continue… Theater won't be interesting at all unless you do what you cannot do."[5] Seeking the impossible is one of the most succinct ways to designate the poetic, the realm of *poiein*, which, regardless of what might be the mode of articulation (poetry or philosophy, agit-prop pamphlet or dream text), pertains to humanity's capacity to imagine and create things heretofore unknown, unthought, nonexistent – in a word, alien to our cognitive parameters.

From this standpoint, it's difficult to account for Müller's theatrical production using the traditional terms of dramatic textuality, including what is understood as dramatic poetry in the conventional sense. Most of his dramatic work is composed of hyperextended poems (if I may put it this way), or just suspended poems, without beginning or end, oftentimes nebulous as to the poetic persona that authorizes them textually or, in plain English, *speaks them*. Other times, poems are literally suspended in *medias res* of other texts, by which I mean, spatially situated in a more or less recognizable dramatic text but entirely decontextualized in relation to the terms of this text. Although such poems – which by the way are oftentimes explicitly mythological – are called interludes, one is baffled by them if one seeks to approach them that way. They have no recognizable metaphorical, or even allegorical, connection to the dramatic action in which they allegedly intervene. They are not interludes; they are just plain interruptions. To put it simply, Müller's dramatic language becomes dramatic solely in the instance of performance. There's nothing generically (meaning, inherent to genre) dramatic about it.

After the publication of the collected poems, a first classificatory glance on the oeuvre could consider Müller's poetry to bear three tendencies: the mythological, the political, and the lyrical. Even though, ultimately, I would dispute this mode of classification let us go ahead with it in order to see how it breaks down – indeed, that it breaks down esoterically. This classification would mean to identify three strains correspondingly: 1) the thematic or imagistic configurations of Greek myth (where names, stories, or events from Greek tragedy are restaged in a contemporary setting); 2) the historical myths of Germany and Marxism (whose entwinement Müller conducts inimitably and against the grain of the great tradition in German letters that might inform it); 3) the mythographic rendering of the authorial "I" which is repeatedly orchestrated by an extreme, sometimes even brutal, mapping of the body. Notice that the notion of myth pertains to all three categories, which is one way of me saying that the categories are already compromised as modes of distinction (even if one can certainly corroborate them by Müller's poetic patterns), but is also meant to isolate the element that reminds us of the performative horizon of these poetic texts – indeed, all poetic texts.

Before I elaborate on the notion of myth, permit me a quick digression. A number of years ago I published an essay titled "Communism and Poetry," which was written as a draft for an exploratory project that aimed to examine the curious phenomenon of certain highly experimental poets, belonging roughly to the modernist tradition and very accomplished as far as the canon goes, who were avowed communists, although somewhat maverick in their relation to party politics.[6] My interest was to meditate expressly on this, by all accounts, incompatible pair – incompatible because, conventionally speaking in both cases, "communism" suggests a signifying framework of praxis by a collective subject that ultimately bears the forces of history (often teleologically, that is, by means of a perfectly defined logic), while conversely, "poetry" suggests a signifying framework where an individual subject pursues a visionary praxis that, in the last instance, aims beyond history (or claims to aim beyond history) in the sense that it engages with an imperfectly defined un-logic that invokes, as Adorno would have it, a transhistorical mode of understanding via the intransigence of subjectivity.[7] My argument was that these poets confounded both these categories by dialectically undoing the expectations of each: on the one hand, their poetic intransigence raised an obstacle against the disciplinary boundaries of a politics that never dared think beyond history; and on the other hand, their political commitment raised an obstacle against the disciplinary boundaries of a poetics whose presumption of transcending history granted artistic experimentalism a kind of autoscopic, self-consuming, identity.

Heiner Müller may be said to be one of the last such poets, since this pair of categories lost its historical reality in his lifetime. But I invoke it here specifically as a way to recast my title pair "lyric loneliness and the mythical body" in light of "communism and poetry" in a way that will hopefully illuminate my choice of terms. It's doubtful that we can forge a direct correspondence between these two couples. An easy gesture would arguably be to associate poetry with loneliness and communism with myth. However, even if we keep this configuration, I would rather that we place it in a chiastic relation, where it becomes, if nothing else, more provocative, so that poetry can correspond to the mythical body and communism to lyric loneliness. Whatever the case, the chiasmus is only interesting if the signifying vectors of correspondence are continuously shifting, forming a kind of mobile double helix configuration.

The most fluid, perhaps we might say promiscuous, term in this framework is myth. It's easy to say that in large part Müller's texts are notoriously mythological. But all his texts are mythical; his thought is mythical. As I elaborated in *Does Literature Think?*, "mythological" refers to texts that enact/restage various myths, as opposed to "mythical" which pertains more to a certain mode of performance and surely does not depend on specific mythological content. By which I mean that Müller is an expressly mythical poet, who also explicitly favors mythological content but not always – and this "not always" is what interests us here. In this respect, as a point of departure, a reading of the "mythical body" as a motif easily involves the most comfortable mode in Müller's writing, wherein, literally, the mythological body is called upon to do poetry's work.

A classic example of this would be the case in *Hamletmachine* (1977) where the existential dilemma of the hero is resolved by a transgendering desire: To be or not to be is not really a question because Hamlet wants to be a woman – the utterance is all too succinct: "I want to be a woman." Indeed, to be more precise, Hamlet wants to be Ophelia, because he desires to change proper names as much as proper sex, the two being equally anchored in the predicament of identity. When, later in the play, Hamlet closes his long monologue of theatrically (poetically) configuring this irreparably ambiguous self with the echoing declaration "I want to be a machine," he underlines the dead-end logic of identity, not only sexual and personal (gender and name), but 'human' identity altogether: the body itself, in its outmaneuverable degeneration, marks the insufferable limit where one's history – one's place in history – is splayed open (*Hamletmachine*, 55–57).

Another such example could the case in "The Liberation of Prometheus" (Die Befreiung des Prometheus) – one of the interlude texts in *Cement* (1972) – where Hercules, in his effort to scale the mountain in order to release Prometheus from the rock, encounters an enormous obstacle.[8] As the text says in so many blatant words, the thousands and thousands of years of combined fecal matter from the shackled prisoner and his torturer creature, which have been encrusted on the rock as layers and layers of sedimented experience, an experience of struggle, of being eaten again and again, of decay and regeneration – a corporeal experience now utterly petrified but nonetheless still organic because the putrid stench that it emits assaults the visitor from thousands and thousands of miles away (might this, too, be another obstacle produced by divine envy against the prisoner in order to avert his emancipation?) – all these, then, thousands and thousands of encrusted temporalities – for time, entwined with the stench of waste and decaying flesh, has become an element that belongs entirely to the realm of the senses – produce an equally mythical (in terms of scale) spatial detour, divergence, digression, as Hercules tries to figure out a different way to approach the mountain, encircling it and encircling it for thousands and thousands of more years, in a condition signified only grammatologically at the level of the sentence, a sentence that itself seems to last a thousand years and cover a thousand miles.

To illustrate the point, I quote the full text in its breathless splendor:

Prometheus, who brought lightning to the humans but did not teach them how to use it against the gods, perhaps because he took his meals at the table of the gods, which would have been less sumptuous if shared with the humans, was commanded by the gods – either on account of this deed or conversely his omission – to be chained by Hephaestus the blacksmith to the Caucasus, where a dog-headed eagle devoured daily his perpetually regenerating liver. The eagle, who considered him to be a partially edible rock formation capable of small movements and, especially while being eaten, of discordant song, also took to emptying his bowels all over him. This excrement became his nourishment. Transforming it into his own excrement in turn, he passed it along further to the hard rock below, so that when Hercules, his liberator, climbed the desolate mountain after three thousand years, he could already discern the fettered prisoner from a great distance, sparkling white from bird shit. Yet, repulsed again and again by the wall of stench, the liberator had to circle around the massif for another three thousand years, while the dog-headed one continued to eat the liver of the chained one, while nourishing him with its excrement, so that the stench increased at the same rate as the circling until the liberator became accustomed. At last, helped by a rain that lasted five hundred years, Hercules was able to draw within shooting range. There he held his nose with one hand. Three times he missed the eagle, because he had involuntarily closed his eyes, dazed by the waves of stench which struck him when he took the hand from his nose to draw the bow. The third arrow slightly wounded the prisoner on his left foot, the fourth killed the eagle. It is said that Prometheus wept not for his wound but for the eagle, his only companion for three thousand years and provider for three thousand years twice over. "Am I supposed to eat your arrows?" he screamed, forgetting that he had ever known other nourishment. "You peasant, can you fly with this feet of shit?" And with this, he vomited from the smell which Hercules carried around ever since he had cleaned the Augean Stables, because the horse shit stank to high heaven. "Eat the eagle", said Hercules. But Prometheus could not grasp the meaning of his words. Very likely, he also knew that the eagle had been his last connection with the gods, the daily pecking his only memory of them. Never more restless in his chains he cursed his liberator as a murderer and tried to spit in his face. Meanwhile, Hercules, doubled over with disgust, tried to find the fetters which bound the enraged one to his prison. Time, weather and shit had made flesh indistinguishable from metal and both indistinguishable from stone. But now, loosened by the violent rage of the prisoner they did become discernible. It turned out that no chains existed, already eaten by rust. Only at the point of his cock were the fetters intertwined with the flesh, because Prometheus, at least during his first two thousand years on the rock, occasionally masturbated. Later he must have forgotten even his cock. The liberation left a scar behind. Prometheus could have easily freed himself, disarmed and exhausted from the millennia though he was, had he not feared the eagle. His behavior during the liberation showed that he feared freedom more than the bird. Roaring and foaming at the mouth, with teeth and claw he defended his fetters against the liberator's grip. Once freed, on his hands and knees he howled from the misery of trying to crawl with his numb limbs, and he cried out longing for his peaceful place on the rock under the wings of the eagle, where nothing ever changed or moved other than the occasional earthquake decreed by the gods. Even after he could finally walk upright, he struggled against the descent like an actor who does not want to leave the stage. Hercules had to haul him off on his shoulders. The descent to human-ity lasted another three thousand years. While the gods tore the mountains to bits, so that the descent through the frenzy of broken stone was more like a fall, Hercules bore his precious burden so that it did not come to harm, like a child clinging to the breast. Clasped to the liberator's neck, Prometheus indicated in a soft voice the direction of the projectiles, so they could avoid most of them. Meanwhile, screaming aloud to the heavens, which had dark-ened by the whirling rocks, he declared his innocence in the liberation. There followed the suicide of the gods. One after the other, they hurled themselves down from the heavens onto Hercules's back and disintegrated into rubble.

Prometheus worked his way back onto the shoulders of the liberator and struck the pose of the victor, who rides on a sweating horse to meet the cheers of the people.[9]

The vociferous drama ingrained in this text came to the forefront for me when I saw it performed, not as an interlude in *Cement*, but disengaged and staged in its own right as a music-drama by Heiner Goebbels on a moonless summer night at the ancient Delphi stadium (June 23, 1995). Staged for one actor (the great Ernst Stötzner), unmasked and uncostumed, and two musicians – Heiner Goebbels on keyboards and samples and David Moss on drums and vocalizations – against the archaic darkness of the Delphi landscape and escorted by the random sounds of goat bells in the surrounding hills, the experience came the closest to what I can imagine to have been the Aeschylean theater. What to this day remains engraved on my memory cells down to the bone is especially the ingenious gesture in Goebbels's score to register the unsettling power of the voice of pain through Moss's remarkable vocalizations. For it rendered brilliantly the subversive gesture of Müller's text to equate, without explicitly saying so, Prometheus's cries of pain caused by his eternal torture with his cries of rage (and pain) against the event of his liberation. The voice that expresses the pain of torture is the same voice that resists liberation, a desperate voice in both cases: pain as habitus and as source of expression, which in Goebbels's hands becomes a musical language inasmuch as it is already a poetic language. I cannot imagine a more concrete manifestation of how Adorno eventually responded to his own widely misunderstood statement that "to write poetry after Auschwitz is barbarism" by inserting the exception of the tortured man's right to scream: "Perennial suffering has as much right to expression as the tortured man has a right to scream; hence it may have been wrong to say that after Auschwitz you could no longer write poems."[10] In what sense this scream is poetic – in what sense the very thing that is inarticulate, a mere scream, is in fact a poem, or the image of poetry as such – is the inordinately difficult question opened up by that the historical exigency of Auschwitz.

If read against the grain as an autonomous lyric instance – given that otherwise, as a mythological text in the midst of a play, it marks a readable norm in the framework of Heiner Müller's writing – this piece complicates the reading of the poems that follow. Like P.B. Shelley's own famous play, Müller's interlude is a modern sequel of the Aeschylean instance (which is lost in its ancient manifestation, except for some interpolated fragments): Prometheus unbound. And if Aeschylus' staging of the myth of Prometheus is not only an exposition of a certain anthropogony (of how humans come to be – that is, *be humanized*) and, at the same time, an exposition of the human predicament in relation to the law (obedience, defiance, etc., which is part of the predicament of humanization as well), it is also – though rarely considered so – a staging of the gift of *poiesis*, indeed of poetry itself as an incendiary, illuminating, profane, and anarchic act that marks the terrifying capacity of the human.

From this latter standpoint, the presumed distance between the mythical and the lyrical is alleviated, even within the text itself, as Prometheus's resistance to being liberated, his literal attachment to the rock and to his petrification (*putrification* might be the perfectly resonant neologism here), thus making of the rock mass an animate entity, is drawn in direct conflict with the animal-like persistence of the liberator Hercules, who becomes the next bearer of the gift, the humanizing gift not of fire this time but of transgressing the law. From Aeschylus – who, as a Pythagorean, had a precisely Hippocratic notion of the ailing body – down to Müller's remarkably graphic sensitivity to disease, decay, and degeneration extends an uncanny line, beyond the obvious theatrical proclivities. Bracketing the explicit political dimensions of the piece – an elaboration of which would take us far afield – the poetic excess of both the characters and the text, of both imprisonment and liberation as torture, of both animate and inanimate matter (history and nature, life and death, body and chains, body and ideas – of transgression, punition, and liberation), all embroiled and entwined, captures concretely the entwinement of the lyrical with the mythical.

So with this in mind, I turn my focus to an odd type of poem, mostly produced after Müller's knowledge of his cancer and up until the point of his encounter with death. These poems are odd because they defy the categorization of Müller's poetics; they are profoundly and unabashedly personal. It is also curious that these poems are dated, as if the historical reality of their temporal dimension cannot be outmaneuvered even within a mythical performative mode.[11] The poem "ICH KAUE DIE KRANKENKOST DER TOD" is dated just 18 days before Müller's death, while "Zahnfäule in Paris" is even odder, because it precedes the disease – or the knowledge of the disease – by more than a decade but it is also dated, equally personalized, entirely unlike the rest of the work at the time, and in this sense propelled into the order of the later poems of progress toward death.[12]

I confess that every attempt I have made to construct a general hermeneutic of these poems has produced in me a sense of triviality. I say this without the least intention to idealize the position of the allegedly untouchable text or the position of the untouched critic, untouched by the poem's invitation to play the game of interpretation, a guessing game, if there ever was one, although most of the time conducted in the midst of – or indeed, generating – a whole variety of theories. It is common and important to speak of the unspeakability of the lyric, even while attempting to determine the speakers that it mobilizes. There is indeed a kind of "poetics of constraint" here, even in an unusual grammatological instance. For Müller specifically, this becomes dramatic in that the radical personalization of his poetic space-time is engaged in such unconcealed fashion that it almost makes room for the confessional. Or so it would seem at first sight, if it weren't for the fact that nothing in Müller's work could ever stand on mere subjective reality. While life itself in a radical sense is poetic material (even with biographical corroboration – whatever that means), *poiesis* is always inevitably mythical, and one remarkable aspect about Heiner Müller is how alert he remains, even under the most confounding situations (personal and historical), to the *co-incidence* of the existential-historical with the mythical.

In this light, I am drawn by these poems of the cancerous body – which I dare call lyric poems – because of their intransigent internality which, I argue, signifies an entirely different meaning of the mythical body, different from what we tend to think according the standard categorizations of Müller's poetics. The body in these poems performs its own mythical idiom of crossing the path of history, which is present here in dramatic – yet not dramatized – fashion and entirely focused on the body as the singular event of this drama. This idiom is unburdened by the mythological weight of the examples I mentioned earlier (Hamlet/Ophelia, Prometheus/Hercules), but it is mythical nonetheless because, while being enunciated by an "I," the body ultimately takes over the subject position. I would not quite say that it embodies the "I." Nor would I say that, in taking over the subject position, the body produces a disembodied "I." Generally, I think that discourses of embodiment need to be deployed with alertness as to their politics. Certainly, I would be the first to sign on to a sentient dimension of knowledge or of making sense of things – *making* sense, here, taking on the meaning of *poiesis* par excellence.

In any case, let us remember, that there is nothing about the body that is pure. Its domain is marked precisely by continuous mutability; the very conditions of organic matter require a continuous passing, the constant demise of cellular structures, giving way to alteration – some might say regeneration, but if that's the case, it is always partial; regeneration is never fully possible. The body predictably and remarkably decays; cellular structures are sooner or later driven to the plenitude of death. Plenitude might be apt as a way to refer to what is most of the time signified as nothingness because only at the point of death might we say that the significational framework of the body is complete. We might speak of "form embodying consciousness" – as one often hears in discussions about the lyric – but we must account for the fact that forms, insofar as they embody anything, become at once, at that moment, impure, mutable, elements of alteration and decay.

If there is a motif I would accentuate in these poems it is ingestion. But this is ingestion of matter without any notable digestion, which seriously subverts any metaphors of the organic body. The body here is entirely at the mercy of either history (external forces of authority – science and technology, medical experts, etc.) or at the mercy of itself. We could say that it might also be at the mercy of the "I" but this "I" is written as external to the body, not as a lyric "I" that authorizes itself and the poem.

| Zahnfäule in Paris | Tooth Decay in Paris |
| --- | --- |
| Etwas frisst an mir | Something is eating me up |
| Ich rauche zu viel | I smoke too much |
| Ich trinke zu viel | I drink too much |
| Ich sterbe zu langsam | I'm dying too slowly |
| (1981) | |

Notice the significant difference between *Ich* and *mir* in "Zahnfäule in Paris" ("Tooth Decay in Paris"). One might say the speaker might be eating himself up, but this would already be an external reading. If he is in fact eating himself up, by virtue of the rules of the esoteric performance of the text, this is unsignifiable. The only thing we see is that "something" is eating him – this something could be him, but not necessarily. To be playful, this "I" could be what's eating him, but that becomes possible only because this "I" is elsewhere, acting on something else – it is the "I" that smokes (too much), that drinks (too much). Moreover, the verb used here (*fressen*) means "to eat" specifically in reference to an animal – the verb referencing the eating of a human-animal is *essen* – and, perhaps for that reason, it also means to eat voraciously, insatiably. This image of binge-eating forms an interesting liaison with "*zu viel*" – the excess of "*Ich*" – but contrasts with the slowness ("*zu langsam*") of the self-precipitated death. It too serves to dislocate the "self" from the "something"; continuing along these lines of play, we can say that it *animalizes* the "self". Whatever is eating me up, this "something," is directly linked to whatever drives me to smoke and drink myself to death, to slow death. One cannot avoid noting the irony here, for the poetic persona speaks of slow death, while everything we know of the poet's life was the extraordinary speed and scale with which he rode his health to its demise.

| *ICH KAUE DIE KRANKENKOST DER TOD* | *I CHEW THE HOSPITAL'S DEATH-FOOD* |
|---|---|
| Schmeckt durch | Through the taste |
| Nach der letzten | After the last |
| Endoskopie in der Augen der Ärzte | Endoscopy in the doctor's eyes |
| War mein Grab offen Beinahe rührte mich | My grave was open I was almost moved |
| Die Trauer der Experten und beinahe | By the mourning of experts and almost |
| War ich stolz auf meinem unbesiegten | Proud of my unvanquished |
| Tumor | Tumor |
| Einem Augenblick lang Fleisch | In a flash flesh |
| Von meinem Fleisch | Of my flesh |
| 12.12.95 | December 12, 1995 |

In addition to the externality of self, the reiteration in "ICH KAUE DIE KRANKENKOST DER TOD" ("I EAT THE HOSPITAL'S DEATH-FOOD") is to suggest the externality of death. Here, death becomes the site of hospitality and subsistence, and already determined as ground (grave) by those agents of hospitality and subsistence. This is to be contrasted with the inveterate internality of the body's own growth ("my unvanquished tumor"), which only the institutional order of the hospital sees as a site of otherness. In this situation, the body is proud of itself in perhaps the only instance of denoting itself as the site of subjectivity: i.e., an instance – a flash in the blink of an eye (*Augenblick*) – of self-possession, even if in a Biblical idiom (*Fleisch von meinem Fleisch*), as well as, in an entirely perverse way (typical of Müller), the prolonged site of auto-generation, *autogéstion* we would say in French, which means self-determination: a kind of autonomy that, as I have argued, is always linked to a poetics of self-alteration.[13] The utterly personalized idiom of disease as self-determination is but an extension of Müller's consistent stance, much in the same way that the lyrical body is one more instance – perhaps the last instance? – of the mythical. That art (*poiesis*) is life is hardly metaphorical. It is the very site of generation and degeneration, of irrecoverable growth and decay:

Art can after all be a disease. It's possible that's the disease we live with. In our lifetime we don't run the risk of recovering our health. We have to live with this disease and with the paradox that we are parasites because we exploit this world.[14]

One of Müller's best known late poems, "Herzkranzgefäss" ("Coronary Vessels"), is perhaps the most alienating in the terms we are speaking, and the only one – barring the previous Biblical reference – that allows a mythical name to enter it (the Sphinx). *Ich* is entirely absent here. It may be presumed as addressee, but what is really addressed and mapped from the very first verse is the body itself. Its spatial coordinates are marked clearly, transparently one might say, but also its temporal coordinates are produced as a consequence. *Frist* is a peculiar word that means essentially a limit point of time, but in addition to the obvious "deadline" (which suggests time ending: death) it also means "lease" and "prolongation" – a new lease on time: a time after the disease, a time of cancerous living, which the author (to leave the poem for a second) relished in a perverse way, propelling out of himself enormous creative energies.

---

### Herzkranzgefäss

Der Arzt zeigt mir den Film DAS IST DIE STELLE
SIE SEHEN SELBST jetzt weisst du wo Gott wohnt
Asche der Traum von sieben Meisterwerken
Drei Treppen und die Sphinx zeigt ihre Kralle
Sei froh wenn der Infarkt dich kalt erwischt
Statt dass ein Krüppel mehr die Landschaft quert
Gewitter im Gehirn Blei in den Andern
Was du nicht wissen wolltest ZEIT IST FRIST
Die Bäume auf der Heimfahrt schamlos grün
21.8.92

### Coronary Vessels

The doctor shows me the x-ray THIS IS THE SPOT
YOU SEE IT YOURSELF now you know where God lives
In ashes the dream of seven masterpieces
Three flights of stairs and the Sphinx shows her claws
Be glad if the attack stops you cold
One less cripple cruising the landscape
Thunderstorm in the brain Lead in the veins
What you wanted not to know TIME IS THE DEADLINE
The trees on the way home: shamelessly green.
August 21, 1992

---

*Frist* may also mean "respite" or "reprieve" – once again, suggesting, that finality is part of the trajectory, a resting point. "Time is up" could be an interesting rendering in English of *Zeit ist Frist*, in the echo of *"etwas frisst an mir"* – "something is eating me up" in the poem "Tooth Decay in Paris" – the long process of which has brought the time of decay to a final standstill. I also imagine that this phrase echoes the common usage of *Zeit ist Geld* – "Time is money." The sarcasm in the resonance is inescapable. Especially, as it provokes us yet again to consider the issue of speed versus slowness, as we saw it in the mythical scale of the liberation of Prometheus.

I have foregone the choice to translate it simply TIME IS THE LIMIT, even if this would work, because the English expression has lost the ambiguity inherent in limit. Müller relishes the perverse instance of affirming what is inevitably destructive. In the interstices of this contradiction resides the *poietic*.

In the end, if we assume that these are lyric poems and if the poet Heiner Müller opts, against the grain of most of his writing, to stage himself as the mythical body – the last mythical body of his textual oeuvre – then we can say that Müller's lyric prevents a discourse of redemption. The body is the deadline. It is itself, much as it eats itself. It does not embody form, nor does it pretend to help forge a transcending form. What it does is the work of trans-formation, a work always marked by the finitude of mortality, which in the realm of the living is the work of internally conducted othering, the work of self-alteration.

## Notes

1 A crucial reference here is the work of Virginia Jackson and Yopie Prins, which culminates in their anthological intervention *The Lyric Theory Reader* (Baltimore, MD: Johns Hopkins University Press, 2014).

2 "Answers by Heiner Müller: I am Neither a Dope- Nor a Hope-Dealer" in Heiner Müller, *Hamletmachine and Other Texts for the Stage*, Carl Weber ed. and trans. (New York: PAJ Publications, 1984), 138.

3 Heiner Müller, "Literature Must Offer Resistance to the Theater" in *The Battle*, Carl Weber ed. and trans. (New York: PAJ Publications, 1989), 160.

4 See Heiner Müller, *Contexts and History: A Collection of Essays from the Sydney German Studies Symposium 1994*, Gerhard Fischer ed. (Tübingen: Stauffenburg Verlag, 1995), 269.

5 Heiner Müller, "Conversation in Brecht's Tower" in *The Heiner Müller Reader*, Carl Weber ed. and trans. (Baltimore, MD: Johns Hopkins University Press, 2001), 229.

6 Stathis Gourgouris, "Communism and Poetry" *Gramma* 8 (2000), 43–54.

7 Theodor Adorno, "Lyric Poetry and Society" in *Notes on Literature Vol. I* (New York: Columbia University Press, 1990), 37–54.

8 The notion of obstacle, the inveterate rock itself, extends metaphorically to the entire venture. To quote Heiner Goebbels, who creates a music drama out of this interlude as a free-standing poetic text: "*The Liberation of Prometheus* is a prose text which Heiner Müller has dropped into his play *Cement* like an erratic block – a real stumbling block for the theater which cannot be done justice with ordinary theatrical methods." From the insert in Heiner Goebbels, *Hörstücke* (ECM Records, 1994); also found in: www.heinergoebbels.com/en/archive/texts/material/read/516

9 This is my translation. I have borrowed extensively from Marc Silberman's pioneering translation of *Cement* (*New German Critique* 16, Winter 1979, Supplement), as well as Alan Miles' s version used by Goebbels for his music drama: www.heinergoebbels.com/en/archive/texts/material/read/516

10 Theodor W. Adorno, *Negative Dialectics* (New York: Seabury, 1979), 362. This little phrase has been entirely forgotten in the wake of the other thoughtlessly reiterated (and in fact misquoted) phrase – "there is no poetry after Auschwitz" – that has become a sort of meaningless motto. Certainly, Müller's entire work can be considered as the distilled elaboration of Adorno's 'self-criticism' as to what poetry after Auschwitz might signify. His most succinct account of how Auschwitz is not an exception but part of history and in this sense perfect material for the theater can be found in the interview: "Auschwitz ad infinitum" which appeared originally in *Drucksache* 16 (1995), the program brochure for the Berliner Ensemble's 1995 production of Bertolt Brecht's *The Resistible Rise of*

*Arturo Ui*, directed by Heiner Müller, and is posted here: http://greatwritersfranzkafka2.
blogspot.com/2012/04/auschwitz-ad-infinitum-discussion-with.html

11  The three poems discussed here in my translation can be found in Heiner Müller, *Die Gedichte* (Frankfurt am Main: Suhrkamp Verlag, 1998).

12  I have learned a great deal from Alexis Radisoglou's insightful discussion of Müller's late poetry in his *Keeping Time in Place: Modernism, Political Aesthetics, and the Transformation of Chronotopes in Late Modernity* (PhD Dissertation, Columbia University, 2015). Crucial is his argument that Müller embraces the inevitable prospect of time ending as a project, as a poetic work open to the future. This endows finitude (the space of life ending) with yet another order of time, indeed a space of time (*Zeitraum*), which works as a kind of creative/destructive interruption – in my terms, as the opening of *poiesis* itself.

13  I must confess, by way of an anecdote, that I did not perceive the Biblical echo here until I translated this poem into Greek, because Biblical language is known to me in Greek (including the translated Old Testament Hebrew) and essentially unrecognizable in either English or Martin Luther's German.

14  Heiner Müller, "Writing Out of the Enjoyment of Catastrophe: An Interview with Horst Laube" in *Germania* (New York: Semiotexte, 1990), 193.

# 11

# THE ROUTE OF THE IMPOSSIBLE

## Aesth/ethics of Paul Celan's *The Meridian*

*Paul Audi*

If by "thinking" we mean unfolding and articulating a meaning, firmly attached to constantly renewed questioning, we should say that the question of thinking or re-thinking literature only finds its own meaning and scope on condition that we take the full measure of a crucial fact: that it is first of all, and above all, literature itself which thinks – or better: which thinks *us*. Not in the sense that literature is the reflection of our being-in-the-world, but in the sense that our being-in-the-world already conforms to what literature thinks of it. Is it for this reason that, as Pierre Macherey expressed it, "what an epoch thinks about itself is up to literature to say"[1]?

In submitting to the exercise of "re-thinking literature" it would seem that we are still pursuing a *critical* design. But there are no ways of attempting to "re-think literature" without drawing near to Thebes, with its hundred gates… And there is no doubt we shall ever be able to open only a few of those entrances. Here, my approach will be of an aesth/ethical order as I call it. In other words, I will try to stand at the crossroads of ethics and aesthetics. And for reasons which will soon become obvious, my guide in this approach will be the poet Paul Celan.

*

*The Meridian*[2] is probably Paul Celan's best-known text. There are many who consider it to contain not only the quintessence of his poetics, but also the essence of his idea of poetry. The text is nonetheless an occasional work: a publicly held "speech", in which the author strives to wind up all the springs of his eloquence; in particular he gives multiple signs of skill and dexterity towards the audience who came to attend the award of the Georg Büchner Prize in Darmstadt on 22 October 1960.[3]

It is true that the poet is never alone, unlike his work — which, if we are to believe Celan, is condemned to suffer a constitutive, intrinsic solitude; for that is the poem he never communicates (in the truest sense of that verb), whatever he says, for in truth there is never a *common* poetic idiom. If Paul Celan's experience reached a conclusion, it is really the necessity to raise poetic language in general, and the language of the poem in particular, to the level of the highest common factor. Anyone who claims the opposite, praising the civilising, soothing, conciliatory mission of poets, would immediately be unable to grasp the absolute singularity of Celan's *poetic adventure*. Whilst politics aims for the common language it needs if it is to be united, or more commonly "to make connections", poetics is quite a different matter. In this concert of voices which call on the One, a concert which always ends in dissonance, not to say vociferation, screaming, bellowing and invective, the poetical has the honour of playing the role of the inestimable joker. Indeed, we have known this since Plato: poetry attempts the impossible — as if to make us unlearn the herd's way of speaking. So, if the poem never communicates itself to anyone and remains, in a certain way, for itself, *nobody's rose*, the poet on the other hand, in these honorific circumstances just as much as any other life situation (including those shadowed by misfortune and suffocated by lack of air) is never "lonely" (34a): he writes in and for the world; he writes so as to render to every being, every other, what is "the most essential aspect of the other [...]: its time" (36b). For the world's time challenges every individual's time, inasmuch as it makes appear, or allows within its span, that which it dooms to disappear from its very inception. Under the yoke of this senseless "law of succession", as Hölderlin called the world's time, nothing lasts, nothing persists, not even the day in which each thing comes for a time to take its place and testify to the existence of a certain "reality". This time, which depends on no one but on which everyone (and everything) depends, is such that Fate rules as master — and, concomitantly, is "full of mortality and to no purpose" (44). Yet this "pointless" does not spare the work of the poet which, whatever one says, will always be as tenuous as the breath which brought it into being.

And yet: the poem preserves an unarguable singularity which gives it its entire dignity and distinguishes it from all other forms of linguistic expression: by its *very date* it raises a question (one that could well be seen as one of protocol if it were to take on a reflexive status, which it never does) — it raises the question *from what point of the real, what sort of impossible, what type of encounter, what factor of contingency — in short, from what chance or miracle can the poem gain access to itself?*

Alone in being alone, such is the poem. Its aloneness comes from the fact that it is always *one* and always also *unique* in its kind, as indeed is every entity answering to the name — and upholding its status — of "creature" (cf. 31e). Being created, the poem is so much so that it is precisely as a creature that it makes use of speech. "But the poem does speak!" (31a), cries Celan at the heart of his speech. However, to say that the poem speaks is to say that it does so in the first person; that the poem, and not only the poet, is able to say "I". And it says "I" — it speaks *itself* — to the extent that it is endowed with a singular essence, a selfhood — or, as Celan prefers to say, a personality. If the poem is a creature, it appears in fact as the fruit of a personification. That is why it is natural to conclude that when the poem speaks, it speaks "always only on its own, its very own behalf" (31a).

But then, what is *the truest* name of the poem? Is it Poetry? Or Art? If we agree that it is the poem's prerogative to *name* all things with its words, how can *it* be named? How can it name *itself*? Would it choose the family name of Art? Or wouldn't it rather take the name of poetry, so as to avoid asking something *broader* or more *recent* than itself to provide it with a name? But in that case, what status can still be given to the distinction between Art and Poetry – that distinction which shines at its brightest *in* the poem, *from* the poem and with a *view* to the poem?

Things become yet more complicated. For in speaking in its own true name, not only does the poem also speak in the name of that Other which ceaselessly expects it to grant it its name (if naming is indeed the poem's prerogative), it also unrolls a skein of images and sounds. It pulls this thread horizontally, as it were, from trope to trope, like the line called a tropic on a Mappa Mundi; and although it speaks in this way, following the line of figurative meaning, it never communicates anything of what it *perceives*. None of what it hints at which "is perceived and is to be perceived" (39b) can be shared. For any meaning attached to its necessarily singular idiom to be communicated, i.e. shared, would suppose at least that the language the poem's speech is based on would be common, and consequently embody a certain community. Is that the case? If it were the case, there would be no reason for the poem to exist.

But to understand why this is so we still need to attempt an answer to this question: what is the proper place of the poem, the place which belongs to it even though it is where the poem is the most "strong in itself", it becomes, is, and remains truly *itself* [4]? This is the fundamental question Celan poses in *The Meridian*.

★

*The Meridian* gives us an example of prose which has been thought about in every detail (every word, every punctuation mark) and which, in the very unfolding of its phraseology with its measured rhythmic, gives considerable scope to the meaning it seeks to deploy through the accord it seals with everything which, from the very first word he writes, Celan chooses to draw out, hold and reflect from the works of Büchner. It is doubtless traditional for a prize-winner to pay homage to the writer whose name the prize bears. But on this occasion chance seems to have played a positive role, since this prize ceremony gives Celan the opportunity to return to the poetological foundations of his art, which he had already (but too elliptically) questioned in his short speech in Bremen, given a little over a year earlier. His reflection this time leads him to go back to the ultimate meaning of poetry's attachment to art, an attachment which justifies the quite modern transformation of the poet into an "artist". Is this absorption of poetry into art as evident as it is said to be? Do art and poetry share the same flesh, the same bones? Should we not think, on the contrary, that they are the subject of a dispute? More than that, if ever the difference between them does exist, does it not rather take on the aspect of a disagreement? For that is what this or that extract from Büchner's work seem to suggest, provided we pay them very close attention. Except that these passages do not testify that Büchner was sensitive to the possible existence of a disagreement between art and poetry, but on the contrary that he was not sensitive to it at all – and with reason: the disagreement only begins to appear when poetry, which no one can doubt is an art form, notes the fact that it is no longer possible to "enlarge art", in the words of L.-S. Mercier (in his *Traité du theatre*, 1773) which Celan quotes twice, when enlarging art – however desirable it may be from the point of view of art itself – turns out to have become quite impossible, or at least when it reaches its limit in the very nature of facts or events chosen for representation, i.e. in the refusal certain facts or events impose concerning their possible presentation, representation or figuration. And in fact, if there is a fact or event whose truly awful reality will remain forever absolutely impossible to represent, it is the Holocaust. How could this fail to have consequences on the poet's reflection? In those times of extreme distress, shouldn't that distress extend to embrace the essence of the *poetic*, provided it is still possible or now impossible – but that, precisely, is the whole question – to *detach itself* from all attachment to art, supposing we understand the word in the classical sense Büchner claims here and there in his work?

Celan was already firmly convinced in 1959 (ten years later he expressed it aphoristically) that even if nowadays poetry "is no longer an obligation" for anyone, it should still be able to go on "showing itself"[5]; that it even has *the duty* not only to take the initiative, but also to go "outside" (31f),[6] under the strong impulsion of writing whose poetical essence is now to be "*en route*" (34a) – when it is not (and this would be more just) the way itself, in that the way is there to lead man to grasp the meaning of the human adventure, this *historical* adventure which will end with the meaning of all real otherness being completely undone in the Nazi gas chambers. Armed with this awareness of this duty *of* the poem, the poet then resolves to affirm something like "I, the poem, I speak" – not in the least ignoring that everything the poem has to say "today" must be said "always only on its own, its very own behalf" (31a) and must also – now that the worst has happened and left everyone, in the strongest sense of the word, *speechless* – "at the edge of itself" (32b), i.e. according to that "strong tendency to fall silent" (32a) which the distress of the moment cannot fail to inspire, maybe even command, in him. For just as there is no longer any poem worthy of the name which does not keep "its own '20th of January' inscribed in it" (30a), in that it only consents to break silence in memory of the most deafening silence ever known and in testimony to the most "frightful" of all possible "mutings"[7], likewise it is no longer acceptable for the language of the German poet Celan to continue giving itself to be shared without first being the object of a remarkable *crossing* – a passing-through about which Celan spelt out that it had to "pass through the thousand darknesses of deathbringing speech".[8] Of all forms of expression, poetry is indeed the only one known to man which has the possibility of turning language back on itself and above all *against* itself, so that the breath of utterance is directed from the only side where, through that breath itself, something quite other than the echo of the murderers' crimes can come to resound.

This is the perspective in which Celan evokes nearly all the works of the exiled poet who died at 23 – *Danton's Death*, *Woyzeck*, *Lenz* and *Leonce et Lena*. He does so each time under the auspices of one single question: what appearance does "art" (the first word of Celan's speech) – art as a notion, an idea or a simple word, but (as we shall also see) as the personification that notion supposes, perhaps even involves, because of the status acquired by art in the West and *not understood* until Celan – what appearance does "art" carry in Büchner's writings? Celan insists that it means reconsidering Büchner's conception of art in general and literature in particular, not only because literature appears paradigmatic, but also because it is from literature, i.e. making one's way among the quoted references, that one can glimpse, as if by contrast with what the said references immediately require us to think, what is the ultimate state of the "poem today" (19 and 32a). In other words, it means once more grasping Hölderlin's old question: *Wozu Dichter?* but this time displacing, even changing some of its terms. For the question *today* can no longer possibly concern the *why* nor *the poets*, but rather the *how* and *the poem*. And we can already understand the reasons for this substitution: because the answer to the question of *why* cannot depend on anything other than the status and function of art, which poetry knows it belongs to *de facto*. The question is not that of art, but of poetry; and if poetry requires us to put the question of *how*, it is not in the sense of art either (i.e. the *manner*), but only in the sense which emerges from the fundamental question Celan ends up putting at the conclusion of his speech: *how, that is by what means and under what conditions, is a poem "itself"?* Which is to say that the *how*, although it does not refer to art nor to poets, bears on the grasp of its selfhood (its being itself) by this creature which is much stranger and more singular than poets, by this creature which is incomparable, even in terms of the extensive relations of language, the poem: supposing of course that there is such a thing as "*the* poem"? But then who is to say that the poem, like the poet and every other creature, is a *living* being? It is said by the whole of Western aesthetics, one of whose most eminent representatives in modern times could well be Büchner, to whom Celan was asked to pay homage at the moment when signal homage was being paid to him, Celan. Indeed, this is the passage Celan quotes from *Lenz* to indicate his own starting-point: "The feeling that what has been created has life [...] is the sole criterion in matters of art" (12b). In matters of art, surely; but is it the sole criterion in matters of poetry?

"Ladies and gentlemen, please, take note [here Celan quotes Büchner]: 'One wishes one were a Medusa's head' [and Celan completes the quotation like this]: in order to ... grasp the natural as the natural with the help of art!" And immediately Celan adds: "*One* wishes to does not of course mean here *I* wish to" (16b). What justifies this precision about the text of *Lenz*? By making *critical* use of that quotation, Celan is pursuing two ends. First he wishes to distinguish art's way of achieving its "grasp": a way which is always anonymous in itself, and according to which the grasp never bears witness to *the person* who grasps, but only the object grasped, that is – always – "the natural", that natural (in other words: life) which moreover sees itself in and through its arti-factual, artificial grasp, identified as itself, petrified in its essence which nonetheless has nothing fixed about it. Secondly he wishes to differentiate the way of doing things which is proper to poetics from that of poetry, which consists in *piercing* the magic circle of art (drilling through the curtain wall, undermining self-sufficiency and undoing the artwork's self-referentiality) to reach, beyond that limit, what is now no longer *foreign*, i.e. life in the immediacy of one's experiencing-oneself. This is the critical basis on which Celan develops his poetology.

★

Two theses are formed through *The Meridian*; gradually taking shape with the addition of small touches; little by little they also come into competition. However, neither of these two theses is summarised in the form of a pronouncement: it is only the reader's or listener's understanding which would lead them to see them that way. More than that, the whole speech encourages us to juxtapose them, to place them side by side, given the remarkable fact that they even have truth value. But as they occupy the same rank whilst also saying the opposite of each other, the disagreement arises as soon as we aim to hold them together and at the same time. "Today" indeed it has become impossible not to accord them the same rights. Such is the condition of existence of the *poem today* – a phrase, I repeat, which occurs twice in the speech, and which Celan deliberately isolates the second time between two dashes, as if to deprive the adverb of its entire *historical* weight – yes, such is the poem's *current* historical condition that the two theses aimed at it, and which are directly opposed to each other, really need to learn to *coexist*. A non-pacific coexistence, true, given that it is a *disagreement* for which there is nothing that would make a solution possible. And it would be no use appealing to the judgement of history, now that history occupies the outposts of a "truly radical calling-into-question of art" (19) which some have given the name of *modernity*.

That said, let us formulate the two theses.

The first maintains that "poetry is art". This pronouncement does not merely mean that poetry is an artistic form; it also means that poetry *stricto sensu* is of the order of *poetics*, the word extending to the meaning of Greek *poiesis* which, according to the objects and contexts, refers to producing, creating, making, constructing, composing, doing. To say that poetry is a matter of art therefore supposes that the poem is an "artefact", i.e. the result of a non-natural process – a process of production, composition, creation – and that this result is in addition to what already exists (what is part of the "natural", including the "second nature" which is custom). Even if this point of view first of all characterises everything which, in Enlightenment Europe, would end up being classified under the name of "aesthetics", one could say that this consideration of the nature of art (art as *poiesis*) is where the Ancients and the Moderns, so rarely in tune with one another, are in harmony. Celan alludes to this, particularly when he says that it is fatal for the poet to "start" from art "as something given and absolutely unconditional". (19) In other words, the poet himself has to ratify the equation poetry = art, an equation whose validity has been founded in reason for millennia. But if the poet has to start from there, must the poet also arrive or return there? This is where a second thesis arises, attempting to answer just that question.

This second thesis stipulates that "the poem is only fully itself on condition that it escapes, at least in part, from the conditions by which a work of art is achieved". Poetry is *not-all poiesis* (to pick up a famous phrase of Lacan's): something in it evades the artistic. Or, another formulation of the same thing, the poetical is something which *poiesis* can neither explain nor completely absorb. Which is as much as to say that the "place of poetry" (23) *is not solely limited* to the space occupied by "images and tropes" (37b), by "tropes and metaphors" (39b), to which the perspective given and sustained by "art" has reduced it ever since poems have existed. The proper place of poetry or the poem is firmly located elsewhere. But where? What is that virgin country for all art which would properly locate it? This question haunts our most recent modernity. We are its contemporaries. And yet, all we are able to conclude, as a prelude to an attentive hearing of *The Meridian*, is that the second thesis is not so much a matter of aesthetics (indeed from the point of view of aesthetics it seems nothing less than absurd) as of ethics. But here again, what ethics are we talking about? The ethics of the poet? Should it concern this man's values, or his beneficent behaviour in life? Never. For what we are talking about here – singularly, and let us also say exclusively – is the ethics of *the poem*, i.e. that unconditional demand by virtue of which a poetic text – like a person wanting, if not to be master of his destiny, at least to be able to answer for his acts – takes up the cause of its own freedom, deciding to free itself – to "extricate itself" (*Freistezen* is a verb which occurs in various forms no less than six times in the text) – from all that logically precedes it and which would tend to determine it because of that precedence, i.e. all that has always had to be "presupposed" as a foundation for the poem's authority, starting with its identification with art (*poiesis*). This ethic underlying the poem, this demand for self-liberation is the condition for the poetical to reach its essence, for the poem in the end to be itself, to be *truly and freely* returned to itself.

But how can something which partakes of art be liberated from art? How can one escape oneself ... in order to be oneself? How is the poetical to be restored to art, if indeed the role of that art, with its practical codification and theoretical criteriology, is to suffocate it or even devitalise it? Clearly that is the question running through the second thesis put forward in the speech. As for the desired liberation, as for that extrication or indeed that "step" (23) whose mere advance makes Celan's oeuvre something *absolutely modern*: a poetry which refrains from holding poetry to the *poiesis* which give it its being, the better to attach it to everything which, come what may, seeks to break the thread of that old equation, i.e. to resist the distancing art always imposes in the name of its work, Celan has no illusion that it opens an "impossible way". For the poet, he says, it is even "the route of the impossible" (50a) – and for today's poet, the only possible way. At once necessary and impossible – is that not what marks the essence of the tragic? No doubt Celan's aesth/ ethics emerges from a tragic backdrop, since the starting principle is the need to play one's poetic hand well in the game of *poièsis*. But the way it is achieved has nothing tragic about it. *It is even, essentially, an act of rejoicing: for it means turning toward phenomena, questioning and addressing these* (36a)*, it means accomplishing an intimate disposition to welcome, as if by "need"* (35a) *that event which is the Other.* Celan's text names this free disposition, this vigilant openness, several times, and differently each time (each of the names for this disposition connecting the poem's ethic to an infinite perspective)[9]: "the testing and the thought" (*das Verhoffen und der Gedanke*, 31f); "perceiving" (*Wahrnehmenden*, 36a); "attention" (*Aufmerksamkeit*, 35c); and finally, "concentration" (*Konzentration*, 35c). And indeed, no poem could lay claim to it without itself (i.e. in its writing) resolving to go "in search of oneself" (46), of its own proper place. In fact, this demands of the poem that it *forces* both the syntax and the semantics of a language whose possibilities are already more or less exhausted.

If Celan sees no other choice but to qualify the way of the poem as impossible, it is because following such a way supposes that the poet begins by suffering a logical-aesthetic contradiction which is only resolved by an existential miracle, when not so much the poet but his work – the poem, that is – happens to *meet itself*.

That is why it is incumbent on the poem to explain itself to itself. But what is the act of self-explanation, if not that which above all gives ethics its content? And yet – this is the whole meaning of *The Meridian* – in the particular case of a poem in search of its *selfhood*, the task means self-explanation to that *other (or that true/ false) "oneself"* which everyone has known and recognised since time immemorial under the name of "art".

There is no doubt that by "showing itself" poetic speech becomes "voice" (46), but that is exactly how the poem becomes a "work of art". In our Western climes, poetry has always been received as a work of art, in the sense Büchner used to understand it with all its array of criteria – art being, perhaps (keep that "perhaps" in mind from now on) that which from its origins has aimed at bringing about the end of poetry … Indeed, if we are to believe Celan, there is an end to poetry, not an end to art as Hegel thought. An end inflicted on poetry by art itself … What a curious paradox! What a strange existential status clings to the poem! Although it makes its way between an "already-no-longer" (when it is received under the auspices of art) and an "always-still" (since it does not want to give itself up) (32b), does not the poem have to hold itself (hold itself back) every time on the crest of a present (*Gegenwart*) of pure presence? The "unique, momentary" (36b) present of the poem anyway means that in all circumstances it remains an *orphan*, i.e. without any specific ancestry; that also means that there is nothing "ecstatic" (in the Heideggerian sense of the term)[10] about its temporality – that is, it has no temporal anchor other than that which is reduced to its own absolute detachment, that *step*, that *position of liberty* which Celan indicates by speaking very simply (although he has Mallarmé in his sights) of its *actualisation*.[11] An actualisation which, it will be understood, above all depends on the poem accomplishing an act – *being* an "act of freedom" (7b) if its role is indeed – such is the secret of its poetic character – to depart from the overdetermination of the Other which an already-formed language can impose, in order to build its own idiom, its own most proper language, which can only appear in the light of the inherited language's meanings and syntactical articulations as a "counterword" (*ein Gegenwort*, 7b).

That this "speech" of the poem bent on *countering* language, reducing it to silence, if not to block it in a way, that this speech should itself be the fruit of an act, or an acting-out, where the true destiny of liberty is played out, this is indisputably what makes the poem's essence resemble a movement. A responsible movement, as it is at the opposite extreme of any sort of fixation (of meaning) or of stopping (on an image), and thus as far as possible from any effect of *petrification*, contrary to the fate art ineluctably assigns its object if we are to believe Büchner who (as the worthy inheritor of a multi-millennial tradition) would have had no hesitation assimilating the powers of art to those of a Gorgon or a "Medusa's head" (66), capable of turning to stone whatever meets its eye, whatever its gaze "represents" to it. Celan says that "whoever has art in view and in their head" is in no less than a state of "self-forgetting" (20b), inasmuch as they limit the powers of art to those of representation – which, to say the least, omit that which represents to the benefit of that which is represented. This is why it is never art – whose function consists by definition in *imitating*, in being thoroughly *mimetic*: either in a "naturalist" sense (recalling *Lenz*, Celan rightly reminds us that art is defined as "to grasp the natural *as natural*" (16a, my italics) – or in an "artificial" sense – recalling *Léonce et Léna*, he evokes art in terms of the fabrication of automata by means of "cardboard and watch springs" (3a) – but much more poetry which deserves to be assimilated to becoming-shape,[12] the equivalent of personification, giving a personal face and voice.[13] Indeed for Celan the figure of the poem (the poem as a figure or person) is such that it is expressly placed "under the sign of a radical individuation" (33b). For its part, art remains on the contrary irremediably deprived of any face, unremittingly anonymous, inexorably *inhuman*, since by privileging what is represented to the detriment of what represents, its work always "creates I-distance" (20d). In addition, it is none other than this position of externality, which is always a matter of an unspoken "stepping beyond what is human" (17a) – it is this position which if need be ensures its success. It is only on the basis of this achieved, conquered, openly declared externality that the work of art – defined as a glimpse or a taking-in by the gaze – can grasp its object. But each time a shadow takes the place of its prey. This however is not reserved to poetics: in that it never puts its object at a distance, in fact it is not strictly speaking concerned with any object. Hence it knows neither prey nor shadow. Pure subjectivity in action, liberty liberating itself, liberating its liberty, it is an I which – since it speaks – possesses the power to say I. And that is not without obligations, in more than one respect. It has to answer for itself, for its presence – or, better, its presentness – but must also have it in its power, as is actually incumbent on each of us, to call upon its Other as a Thou. Why? We can start by asking about the Other of the poem. For the poem, what is other than itself would logically mean non-poetical use of language. On this point, *The Meridian* essentially distinguishes itself from all earlier poetical treatises; among the innumerable non-poetical uses of language we should include its *artistic* use, which supposes that the speaker occupies an external position and takes on an anonymous status. Detaching from *this* Other, the poem takes on the figure of a way (*Weg*): a way which leads it to "show itself" between the two way-markers of *already-no-longer* and *always-still*. These two way-markers play the role of *poles*. At the summit is the pole of *becoming-art*, that becoming which is always already accomplished, which means that what it contains of power, like its power itself, is where it always comes from; in other words, its becoming (potential) is its past, since it would appear fatal to the poem to be received as a work of art. And there is the pole of *being-poetry*, that being which it always has *to be*, in the manner of what a "blueprint for being" (46) generally prescribes. This is to say that it should be possible to distinguish the poem's future from its becoming, i.e. the liberty of its actuality from the fatality of its potentiality. But if the poem's essential presentness is well and truly founded on a becoming which is declined in the past tense ("already-no-longer") and a being declined in the future tense ("always-still"), it is because it never stops going from self to self, to go beyond its *place* (the "place of poetry" [23]), starting from what is *not* its place but nonetheless claims to be; art, considered the site of poetry.

★

No doubt the fact that the poem's being does not entirely consist in respecting the rules of art demands to be proved. Yet we have made a start on providing a proof if we glimpse that poetry "today", unlike art which has always sought to be timeless, has to affirm its *actuality*. For in the end, everyone can see that it can no longer play at being anhistorical. With Nazism, surely recent history has *interrupted* – I am deliberately using Celan's word – and interrupted with the most strident conflict, the most atrocious screams, the dream of eternity in which art had been wasting away, far removed from all reality, since the dawn of time? What we also have to realise is that the poetical, by its very actuality, means to express itself in the name of *another self* – let us call it the "human" (17a) as Celan does – whereas art, from its essential inactuality, has only ever expressed itself in the name of *another who is "totally other"* (31b) – that is, of the artefact (in antiquity) or the artifice (modernity) it produces. From a particular point of departure ("poetry = art") there opens up a chiasmus so perfect that it seems truly staggering: while the poetical speaks of itself in the name of the Other, art speaks of the other in the name of itself. One is based on the otherness of the Other, the other on the strangeness of the Stranger.

In fact, the aim of the poetical is that whatever is destined to takes its place as signified as well as referent with regard to the elements of language it uses, that these intentional correlates of "speech" gain access through poetics – that is, in writing – to their essential *otherness*. On the other hand, it is thanks to the artifices the poem articulates that its meaning is able to demonstrate its real *strangeness*, whenever it exists. With regard to the question raised, that of the poem's selfhood, Celan has no difficulty believing, at least at first, that ultimately there are "two strangenesses" and that they are "close together" (28). They are in such close proximity to one another and have such a strong resemblance that they keep being mistaken for each other. One is continually enveloped in the other, to such an extent that the history of Western thought has found this to be one of its most insistent motifs … On one side, there is indeed the Other of the poem, the Other which makes its mark on the poem's selfhood, although the poem only achieves its self-being by *bespeaking* itself to the Other,[14] i.e. by committing to that Other; and on the other side is the Other the work of art *is*, where the "natural" (that for which art is a stranger to that which is strange to it) achieves its proper identity (its being *as* natural) by *compromising* with it.

What does this mean? That because of, or despite a certain terminological vagueness surrounding the notion of *Unheimliche* (42b, 42g), "uncanny" (17a), we need to distinguish, in any poem worthy of the name, what is the familiar strangeness of the artistic (often this is its rhetorical, theatrical aspect [cf. 6a–7a] – more cerebral than cordial, in any case) from the strange familiarity of poetics. And what exactly are we to say about that? If the Other with regard to art is the "uncanny" (42g), if every work of art is by essence, and thus by definition, uncanny, what are we to call the Other with regard to the poem? This Other seems so difficult in itself to identify that one could be tempted to think – and Celan does not escape the temptation[15] – that there was never any other *nameable, hence identifiable* Stranger than the one in whose name art came from time immemorial and as if from outside to make contact with humanity and "idealise" it. How indeed are we to think of, and name, the "other" Stranger – the Stranger who is not "uncanny", the ("familiar"?) Stranger who is One with the body of the poem? How are we to think of, and name, this inherent *gap* in the unity and uniqueness of the poem, if indeed they do exist? In other words, what would be the physiognomy of this way within the self, this "detour" (46) which goes from self to oneself, which the poem always has to follow to measure its idiomatic place?

But wait – admitting the evidence, affirming the proximity of poetry and art, for example by defending the idea that the first is only ever a species, a modality, a particularisation of the second, itself conceived as a genus, is that not denying their possible differentiation its true status of *disagreement*? That disagreement well and truly exists – and Celan is its courageous explorer in this speech which has no equal. So much so, that what he means to make us understand is that there is no *circular* reply to this last question. True, the poetical always goes via art and is sanctioned by art, but if it makes this detour it is only so as to return to itself. Misfortune befalls any poem which stops partway; it will never be totally itself. To be totally itself, a poem can do no other than *return* to poetics. The poetical is only reached on the way back; it is "a kind of homecoming" (*ein Art Heimkehr*, 46). Which means that one never "leaves" poetics, one only "returns" to it.

Celan expresses this by noting in one paragraph that the poem's movement (since the poem is an action, or better: it accomplishes an act – that is, it forms an event which has the virtue of redistributing meaning from the moment of its emergence and as a function of that emergence, and thus of sharing meaning according to a new organisation) – the poem's movement does not go from one point to another, but it is "a circle" (42f). This topography then leads him to explain that the poem, because of its always already-accomplished assimilation to a work of art, has a duty to carry out (such is its destiny) a detour between two figurations of itself, between two figures of the self which are positions of otherness one for the other. An otherness of alienation in one case, an otherness of strangeness in the other. An Other as self on one side, and a self as Other on the other side. A first pole marked by the snare and danger of losing oneself, and a second where the self finally *meets itself*. The place of the "poem today" is located between these two othernesses of the self, of which one is the fruit of becoming, the other the fruit of the future. Between these two arises its destiny (*Schicksal*, 5b) which consists in going from self to self, from an other self to another self, i.e. from art to the poetry which the poem also is. It thus exchanges the fatality of its becoming for the liberty of its being. Its whole selfhood is there – in the fact of being destined for itself by going from self to self, explaining itself to itself.

Ethics finds its clearest definition in this task, this call, this necessity to explain oneself to oneself. In *The Meridian*, Celan summarises the matter of, not the poet's, but the poem's ethics by evoking a movement: the "a sending oneself ahead towards oneself, in search of oneself" (*ein Sichvorausschicken zu siche selbst, auf der Suche nach sich selbst*, 46). In these terms, *The Meridian* ensures the conjunction of ethics and aesthetics, of poetics and the artistic, but not without crystallising it first in this aesth/ethical injunction, also addressed not to the poet but to the poem, i.e. to poetry as it has to be written today: "To the contrary: go with art into your inner-most narrows. And set yourself free" (42e). Here the circle engenders its tangent.

But what, then, is the "direction" (*Richtung*, 5b) or the "making toward some-thing"[16] of this tangent? If the poem is on its way and the poetical is a way, it is because both of them, one like the other, one with the other or one for the other, are directed/oriented toward the "heartland" (*Herzland*).[17] This word, used in Bremen, this "land of the heart" or "cordial space" designates the soul's country where "perhaps" – since we must at least suppose this if we are to cast out nihilism – there is "an addressable reality".[18] The Heartland, then, is an uncommon place, foreign to all commonplaces, a properly "u-topian" (40b) place where every exist-ing being would not only speak to the heart but would also reveal itself capable of being the object of an interpellation, a nomination, *in the second person*. In other words, the Heartland is defined like this: a place with no spatial coordinates where it becomes possible – possible because impossible – where it is even required to say Thou to all things. But to find the place without place where the poem comes from, there is a condition: in its poetic version which is connected to "breath" (23, 29a), language has to agree to suffer the trial of breathlessness, of exhaustion, in the same way as man, in the figure of the Jew, was forced to suffer the trial of martyr-dom and extermination. Indeed: if it has to make its way through this trial – that is, if it has to attempt to make the two vectors of its communication, syntax as much as semantics, overcome the barrier of the possible – the very barrier which its "speech" (*sprechen*) reinstates every time – then in this case, and only this case, the poem has a chance of reaching its most proper place. This is what Celan underlines when he writes that the poem only comes to occupy this place on condition that its speech remains, at every stage of the crossing which leads it to emerge from the field of communication, "mindful of the borders language draws and of the pos-sibilities language opens up for it" (33b).

★

In the various works of Büchner, Celan points out what he considers a "radical calling-into-question of art" (19). This questioning is itself questioned by Celan by the simple fact that, although he prefers Lenz, he gives the tragic character Lucile from *Dantons Tod* a superior value: Lucile, "blind to art" (6c) as she is, embodies the being of poetry. "I believe that I met poetry with Lucile and Lucile perceives language as shape and direction and breath" (23). We owe it to Lucile to have *interrupted*, by actualising her untimely words, the "artful words" (6b) of those who, through the potency of their *technè*, think they are on first-name terms with the heights of History. She gives a human figure to speech, direction to meaning (which, although always already significant, becomes fully meaningful) and breath to that which only comes to life through her breath. However, this questioning does not so much constitute the primary task for Celan as the task which has to be accomplished by *poetry today*. No longer can anything lead poetry nowadays to pretend to do without, to claim it has anything else to do, than to have it out with what, in the eyes of history, gives it its very power: art. This poetry can no longer avoid what the times expect of it: to interrupt the eternal monologue of art, this buzzing which is going nowhere, in order to replace it with its opposite — a "conversation", even a "desperate" (36a) one, whose springs it is the self-appointed mission of *The Meridian* to reveal. Yes, a new sort of dialogue, confronting the third person of art and the I of poetry, such a dialogue needs to happen — it needs to commit poetry to disengaging from the death-dealing, petrifying game of art which defines it in principle and which, in a certain way, has always given it its direction. Why is art the destiny of poetry — its fate, if you like? If it is fatal to a poem to be received as a work of art, doesn't that reception strengthen its scope? Or is it not the contrary? What about the art-becoming of the poem? Is that its only destination? But here a question suddenly tears into Celan's critical homage to Büchner. It is not aimed at questioning Lucile's counter-word, "Long live the King!", although it does go against the strides of history, and evades the proprieties of what is *understood*. No, the question is different; and one could say of it that the whole of Celan's reflection in *The Meridian* is anchored to the hook of its inverted question mark. It is expressed in this form: "may we [...] should we before all [...] think — let's say — Mallarmé through to the end?" (19) Nothing more is said: in the next line we are back to Büchner. The name of Mallarmé shines as long as a shooting star; as for the supposed final consequences, we know no more of them after than before this very fleeting mention.

Admittedly the entire context pleads in favour of what, in the field of structuralism extended to post-structuralism, would soon be called "the death of the author". There is no exaggeration in thinking that this is the theme with which the whole of *The Meridian* (not to mention the perspective in which Celan envisaged the act of writing — in a word, his refusal, his rejection, one could even say his horror of all anonymity as well as all decontextualisation of poetic speech) claims, loud and clear, the right if not the duty to disagree. The speech's editors, Bernhard Böschenstein and Heino Schull, nonetheless explain in a footnote that with the clear invocation of Mallarmé and the evocation, sometimes elliptical, of the final consequences which could rightly be drawn from his point of view on poetry, he returns to a text by Valéry in which the author of the *Coup de dés* is quoted as saying to Degas that "it's not with ideas that you make verse, it's with words".[19] Why not? Although it would be just as appropriate, if not more so, to refer to one of his most memorable aphorisms, "The work implies the elocutory disappearance of the poet, who cedes the initiative to words, set in motion by the clash of their inequality." But that is not really the most important thing: in the background of all these conjectures there is a hypothesis which alone would fully justify Celan, at the very moment when he was concerned with thinking about his forthcoming speech in which, the fact is, his job was really to draw final conclusions from *Büchner's* conception of art, in insisting on speaking the name of Mallarmé, particularly in the perspective of *his* "final consequences". This hypothesis – which as far as I know no commentator has yet considered – is that the author of *The Meridian*, when he was writing his speech, had a certain book by Maurice Blanchot at hand (Celan had long been familiar with Blanchot's work): *The Book to Come (Le Livre à venir)* which had just been published a few weeks earlier, and whose principal concern consists in giving pride of place to Mallarmé's phrase celebrating the elocutory disappearance of the poet, consequent on the initiative the poem yields to the words. It should be maintained that with regard to *The Meridian,* Blanchot's *The Book to Come* plays the role of a true but very "obscure" *hypotext*; more precisely, that Celan's entire thinking developed in *The Meridian* – even where he is deliberately and explicitly talking about Büchner – seems to me to be *a reply,* a way of responding point by point to one of the chapters of Blanchot's book: the last, which is also the most important as it bears the name which Blanchot also gave to the whole.[20]

*The Meridian*, then, contains an *Auseinandersetzung* – an "argument" – which eats into the domain of contemporary criticism, because its object is not so much Blanchot himself as the author, himself a poet, in whose wake Blanchot, in his 1959 book as in previous writings, thought he could, and even must, answer the very question Celan was asking himself at the moment he was working on his poetical declaration of faith, the question "Where is literature going?" The author in question, it will be clear, is Mallarmé.[21] So this hypothesis about the context in which Celan wrote his speech suggests that we think he was unable to resist the desire to take a position in relation to a speech which, although it hails firstly the elocutory disappearance of the poet and secondly the non-existence of any poematic actuality or actualisation, would ultimately lead to the overthrow of poetics *and* its investiture by art. As for the way he takes his position, the hypothesis I am supporting also calls on us to think that Celan strove to reply, retort and almost systematically contradict the Mallarmé quoted by Blanchot, or the Blanchot who draws his inspiration from Mallarmé. In short what has to be properly understood is that far from seeing Mallarmé's poetology as the spearhead of a poetical thinking "to come", Celan sees it much more as a past, even outdated discourse, one which belongs to the past even though it emerges from the most stable, recognisable axis of Western aesthetics; he sees in it what his speech quite idiomatically calls "art", not what *he* names (just as idiomatically) poetry – poetry which only achieves its full consistency in a strictly aesth/ethical context where the poem, going against any initiative yielded to the words, finally finds a way of being *itself* – that is, to affirm its time which is the *present* of its actualisation (as preserved by the memory of its dating) at the same time as the poet, in the poem, affirms his elocutory *presence*.

A table will serve better than a long speech to lay out the hypothesis of my reading:

| The Book to Come (quotations from Blanchot and Mallarmé) | The Meridian (replies of Celan) |
| --- | --- |
| – The book without chance *(hasard)* is a book without author: impersonal. (226) | – […] language is something person-like … (6c) |
| – […] the book must remain anonymous: the author will restrict himself to not signing it ("allow the volume to bear no signature"). There are no direct relationships, and even less ownership, between the poem and the poet. The poet cannot attribute what he writes to himself. And what he writes, even if it is under his name, remains essentially nameless. (227) | – "One wishes one were a Medusa's head" in order to … grasp the natural as the natural with the help of art! — *One* wishes to does of course not mean here: *I* wish to. (16a–b) |
| – Nature is transposed by language into the rhythmic movement that makes it disappear, endlessly and indefinitely; and the poet, by the fact that he speaks poetically, disappears into this language and becomes the very disappearance that is accomplished in language, the only initiator and principle: the source. (229) | – But the poem does speak! […] For sure, it speaks always only on its own, its very own behalf. (31a) |
| – The "omission of self" […] makes poetry into an actual sacrifice … (229) | – But language actualized, set free under the sign of a radical individuation that at the same time, however, remains mindful of the borders language draws and of the possibilities language opens up for it. (33b) |
| – […] the essential demand of the work. Its solitude, its accomplishment starting from itself as if from a place, the double assertion juxtaposed in it, separated by a logical and temporal hiatus, of what *makes* it and of the *being* in which it belongs, indifferent to "making" … (229) | – Then the poem is – even more clearly than previously—one person's language-become-shape, and, according to its essence, presentness and presence. (33d) |
| | – He who has art before his eyes and on his mind […] forgets himself. (20d) |
| | – Art creates I-distance. Art here demands in a certain direction a certain distance, a certain route. (20d) |
| | – Can we now perhaps locate the place where the strangeness was, the place where the person was able to set himself free as an – estranged – I? Can we find such a place, such a step? (25a) |
| – We also know that Mallarmé denies all reality to the present. "There is no present, no – a present does not exist." "Badly informed is the one who proclaims himself his own contemporary" (230) | – But the addressed which through naming has, as it were, become a you, brings its otherness into this present. Even in this here and now of the poem – for the poem itself, we know, has always only this one, unique, momentary present – even in this immediacy and nearness it lets the most essential aspect of the other speak: its time. (36b) |
| – "Here anticipating, there recollecting, in the future, in the past, under *a false appearance of the present*." – Beneath these two forms, time expressed by the work, contained by it, within it, is a time without present. (230) | |

| | |
|---|---|
| – The work must then be the consciousness of the conflict between "the moment" *("l'heure")* and the game of literary time, and this discord is part of the game, is the game itself. (231) | – Perhaps one can say that each poem has its own "20th of January" inscribed in it? Perhaps what's new in the poem written today is exactly this: theirs is the clearest attempt to remain mindful of such dates? (30a) |

Finally, a last clue in favour of my hypothesis, the most surprising thing about *The Meridian*: this rain of *veilleicht*, this shower of "perhaps" (I have counted seventeen, fourteen of them in the space of three pages). This is the word Celan requires to mark the rhythm of the meaning he intends to give his declaration of faith. What is this incredible repetition, this mad insistence due to? Or at least, to what or to whom are they secretly trying to signal? The answer is: the one he has decided to detach himself from, the pure representative of that poetic art which obliges the poem to say *We*, to say *They*, to say *He*, and absolutely refuses to say *I*: Mallarmé. Once again, Mallarmé as Blanchot deliberately highlights him right at the end of *The Book to Come*. For it is with a quotation from *Un coup de dés...* that the book literally closes – the line is this: "EXCEPT *on high* PERHAPS..." (EXCEPTÉ *à l'altitude* PEUT-ÊTRE ...), precisely like that, in small capitals.

★

I shall conclude with two short remarks.

1.  The poetical of which the "poem today" partakes denies *a priori* the autonomy which modernity attributes to the existence of a work of art, an autonomy (or self-sufficiency) whose primary manifestation remains the attachment to that *beauty* which even Sade wanted "impervious to outrage", starting with the outrages of time ... More generally, the poetical ensures the intrusion of heteronomy (i.e. an other making the laws) into the artistic context where the rule of the beautiful is applied with all the greater ease in that it seems more or less sufficient unto itself. This is to say that the poetical no more finds its law in the rule of the beautiful than in any other non-temporal "criterion in matters of art" (12b); its law, if indeed it needs one, is summarised exclusively as not leaving the sphere of the human (67). The circle of art, the sphere of the human: this is the only topography recognised by the poem, or rather the much-sought *place* of poetry – that place which, as Celan keeps saying, is only opened to the poet's understanding thanks to a certain extrication, a veritable *Freistezung*. There is indeed no phrase which better explains the content of this liberating openness than this: what dictates its law to the poem, to which art is deaf, writes Celan, is that "something not completely fearless, that listens beyond itself [i.e. above *poiesis*, which the poem always, but only in part, already derives from], and the words [hence beyond images and other tropes engendered by the use and articulation of words]" (48c). This phrase is of capital importance in every way, even though it indicates that what legislates

for poetics, beyond the artistic, is a certain disposition or availability, listening to what comes, openness of the work towards the unpredictable, unsuspected, absolutely contingent arrival of the Event. To put it even more exactly, the only *obedience* the poem can or should subscribe to is *self-disposal to the encounter with what comes*. In this way the much-sought place of poetry is revealed at the same time as one acknowledges the fact that the poem stands "in the encounter – *in the mystery of the encounter*" (34b).

2.   Celan's entire "poetics" unfolds in an aesth/ethical context. For – this is its core – while it would always be *impossible* for him to deny that poetry is an art – who would reject the idea that poetry is an art of language? It is no less *impossible* for him to affirm that it is the poem's duty, supposing that it goes in search of itself (an encounter which is only possible because poetry *exceeds* the limits of art, i.e. is *truly* part of art whilst not being *completely* part of it), to submit to conditions of representation and thus of externality and putting at a distance, which are the conditions of art. We cannot repeat often enough that it is contradictory and therefore absolutely impossible to hold together, and at the same time, the two propositions – the first which is both ancient and modern (aesthetic), the second which is, let us say for want of anything better, contemporary (aesth/ethical). But it is just as impossible *today* not to hold them together and at the same time. Without wanting to be too schematic, that is the *crux poeticum* which Paul Celan had to bear, and it is what he decided, given the occasion, to examine in *The Meridian*.

So what does *The Meridian* say, beyond noting this twofold impossibility? That the poem is so sublime that it erects this cross in a subliminal way. In other words: every poem gives form to a "crossing" (50c) by drawing the line which goes between metaphors and other tropes – this is the *aesthetic* vector of the poem's achievement – and by adding this horizontal line so that it crosses a vertical line. What vertical line? If we identify the horizontal line as that of the *tropic*, the vertical line will take on the appearance of a "meridian". Here the meridian represents the *ethical* vector of the poem's achievement. There is nothing but running between two poles: the pole of the artistic (arrangement, form, the beautiful, everything which relates more or less closely to aesthetics), where the poem is *no longer* or *not yet* itself (i.e. poetic) and the pole of the poetic itself, where it arrives at its destination – that is, it happens that the poem, not having given up on (being) itself, gives the slip to its own becoming, and if only out of respect for what is to come (hence in the name of be-coming), fortunately, encounters itself.

## Notes

1  P. Macherey, *À quoi pense la littérature?*, Paris: PUF, 1990, p. 199.
2  Paul Celan, *The Meridian: Final Version – Drafts – Materials*, translated by Pierre Joris, eds. Bernhard Böschenstein and Heino Schull, Stanford, CA: Stanford University Press, 2011. References to this edition are indicated by paragraph numbers. I will also refer to the bilingual (German/French) edition of the text in Paul Celan, *Le Méridien & autres proses*, translated by Jean Launay, Paris: Seuil, coll. "La librairie du XXIe siècle", 2002.

3  Philippe Lacoue-Labarthe's commentary has notable qualities but suffers from a constant desire to draw Celan over to the side of Heidegger, as if this heuristically rich supposed connection between them was obvious. No doubt he was right to point out, and regret, that André du Bouchet's translation in French (Fata Morgana, reprinted in 2014) omits the *thirteen* "Meine Damen und Herren!" which structure and scan his oratory (cf. *Poetry as Experience,* translated by Andrea Tarnowski, Stanford, CA: Stanford University Press, 1999, p. 105). Even if suppressing this *leitmotiv* removes nothing from the innovative beauty of this version, one cannot help deploring the incomprehension such an act demonstrates. Incomprehension, because the very essence of *thanks* indicates that it always calls, more or less explicitly, on the Other, even the Wholly Other, even if it has to suspend the gratitude it is seeking to express to another with a view to transcendence, and even if the object of thankfulness (in this case the jury members) cannot be confused with that Other or Wholly Other *before whom* in such a case one is responsible for one's own gratitude, if it is true that what expressing any kind of thanks is about is exercising a *responsibility.* As to the fiction which would have us believe that Celan's thought is only comprehensible in the light of Heidegger alone, I should like to take this opportunity to pay homage to Jean Bollack, to whom we are indebted for doing justice to this entirely *catastrophic* association (see his important study "Le Mont de la mort: le sens d'une rencontre entre Celan et Heidegger", reprinted in *La Grèce de personne,* Paris: Seuil, coll. "L'ordre philosophique", 1997, pp. 349–376, or, in a more diffuse but equally convincing manner, *L'Écrit. Une poétique de l'œuvre de Celan,* Paris: PUF, coll. "Perspectives germaniques", 2003).

4  It is important to pay attention to this sort of formulation, characteristic of *The Meridian*: "Perhaps the poem is itself because of this…" (29c); "It stands fast […], the poem stands fast at the edge of itself" (32b).

5  "La poésie ne s'impose plus, elle s'expose (26.3.69)", cf. P. Celan, *Le Méridien & autres proses,* p. 51. This aphorism, written in French, was first published posthumously in the review *L'Éphémère,* Summer 1970, p. 184.

6  The expression is Büchner's, and taken up by Celan.

7  "Speech on the Occasion of Receiving the Literature Prize of the Free Hanseatic City of Bremen" (1958), *Selected Poems and Prose of Paul Celan,* translated by John Flestiner, New York, W.W. Norton, 2001, p. 395.

8  Ibid.

9  I shall soon return, in a non-Celanian context, to this quintuple appellation for the disposition which liberates the poetical in art.

10  It can never be said enough how far those who seek to interpret *The Meridian* on the basis of the temporality of the *Dasein* described by Heidegger in *Sein und Zeit* are from the thinking Celan expresses.

11  The poem: "language actualised, set free …" (M1, 33b).

12  The poem: "one person's language-become-shape" (M1, 33d).

13  Celan notes that Lucile, in *Danton's Death* by Büchner, is the character who, although "blind to art", nonetheless considers that "language is something person-like and tangible" (T1, 6c), as indeed is the case for every poet.

14  "The poem wants to head toward some other, it needs this other, it needs an opposite. It seeks it out, it bespeaks itself to it." (35a)

15  After suggesting that "perhaps there are two strangenesses *(es gibt vielleicht zweierlei Fremde)"* (28), Celan surprises himself by acknowledging a little later that "Art […] in the final analysis is perhaps only *one* strangeness" (42g). Evidently here everything depends on the repeated use of *vielleicht* …

16  P. Celan, "Speech on the Occasion of Receiving the Literature Prize of the Free Hanseatic City of Bremen" (1958), p. 396.

17  Ibid.

18  Ibid.

19  Paul Celan, *The Meridian: Final Version – Drafts – Materials,* p. 229 (Appendix; note #17).

20  Maurice Blanchot, *The Book to Come,* translated by Charlotte Mandell, Stanford, CA: Stanford University Press, 2003.

21  It is no surprise that in the drafts of *The Meridian* published as part of the "Tübinger Celan-Ausgabe", the name of Blanchot only appears once – and, what is more, in a note alluding to Hölderlin, not Mallarmé (cf. *The Meridian: Final Version – Drafts – Materials*, p. 198). For it is not Blanchot Celan is arguing with here, it is Mallarmé. My hypothesis consists only in claiming that 1) the expression "through to the end" is an allusion to the consequences Blanchot drew from Mallarmé, or rather his slanted reading of Mallarmé, in *The Book to Come*; 2) the link between *The Book to Come* and *The Meridian* is thus only a link of concomitance, as the first book from the first line to the last is an answer to the question to the problem haunting Celan at the time of the Büchner Prize, i.e. "where is literature going ?" – implying *today*, so that he had to have it out with the destiny, presented and clarified by Blanchot, which in the previous century Mallarmé had assigned to the poetry *"to come"*, i.e. that which it had now become (the difference being that the Holocaust had happened in between, and that Blanchot did not then integrate this fracture in history in his overview of the "The book to come"); 3) the expressions Mallarmé's name is supposed to relate to when he is mentioned in *The Meridian* – those with which Celan believes he has to disagree, are the very ones Blanchot chose, almost at the same time although a little earlier, to take into account and quote in the last chapter of *The Book to Come*. Perhaps it will be objected that in the index of names that of Mallarmé also appears only once in the drafts. My reply is that unlike the name of Blanchot, that of Mallarmé appears in the final text of the speech, and the question where he is cited involves its central thematic. That being said, I find it difficult to believe that Celan had not received or bought Blanchot's book at the moment of its publication, a moment which perfectly coincides with that of the gestation of his speech. It is only a short step from there to imagine that it is the reading of Mallarmé which Blanchot unfolds in his book which inspired the theme Celan chose in order to write his speech and render homage to Büchner. I confess I should have been highly tempted to take that step, if my lack of taste for speculation had not held me back.

# PART IV
# A new subjectivity

# 12
# RE-THINKING, RE-FEELING LITERATURE

*Camille Laurens*

I have been much concerned lately with the need to re-think literature and have devoted an entire book to that little prefix "re", with which we redo the world, re-speak our convictions, re-begin to write, and are reborn every day, even though others before us, a long time before us, have already done that.

What does re-thinking literature mean to me? Does it mean to return to a reflection which might have been interrupted some time ago? That would imply, as some people fear, that literature is in free-fall, that it is no longer of any interest, no longer driven by intelligence, and that we, in this book, have the noble task to resuscitate it, or at least to re-validate it by distinguishing it clearly from everything which takes itself for it in cyberspace or in communication space, and by rescuing it also from the all-inclusive power of the image? Or is it, more modestly, a matter of rethinking it, of thinking it differently, as one starts a letter again differently, not to redo it in the identical manner, but to dream it more original, more efficient, more important in our lives?

In both cases, rethinking seems to imply the idea of progress: rethinking in order to improve, as one rethinks a machine, a timetable, or the arrangement of a room. But we all know, as Roger Caillois has pointed out, that "there is no progress in the arts", that Claude Simon is not superior to Flaubert, Flaubert not more talented than Madame de La Fayette, nor that Baudelaire is better than a troubadour. No contemporary writer, no matter how much of a genius, can claim to have "rethought" literature in this way, even if one would not have to look too far to find some who boast of it.

To be sure, in literary history one can consider, for instance, that Nathalie Sarraute rethought literature when she wrote *Tropisms*, as she did in a more theoretical manner in her articles and her lectures, by analyzing the "age of suspicion", by engaging in an interrogation on the notion of the character, or by introducing "sub/conversations" in the novel, just as Virginia Woolf was able to theorize her desire for renewal against the old guard of the Edwardian novel and minutia realism. Or again, one can claim that free verse renewed the idea of poetry at the end of the 19th century.

Do we, then, in this early 21st century, need to make an inventory of outdated, outmoded, agonizing forms, to revisit literature in order to liberate it from what is not able to regenerate it, to declare that certain types of prose or of poetry no longer touch us, no longer have anything to say, either about ourselves or our time, do not speak to us while others transport us by means of their newness, their originality, their power of subversion? Some of you may well be eager to sort out this classification which remains of subjectivity, and which always unleashes passions – a reassuring proof if one were needed that literature is still competent. It is in this sense that the novelist and essayist Philippe Forest raised eyebrows when he declared that as far as he were concerned, "the novel-novel", the traditional novel was now "in a terminal coma". He added:

> Today the most interesting novels show a similar suspicion with regard to the old formulas in which, in the guise of imagination, the author passed off to the reader, in a very unimaginative manner, the same stereotyped plots, with cardboard characters, in trompe l'oeil settings. We have had enough of all of that, and we want something truthful.

I'm not going to go over the subject of autofiction, but I do want to go back on the last word, which, applied to literature, remains a source of interrogations, of questions, "we want something truthful".

What is truth in literature? Is the word as pertinent and does it have the same value as when we speak about scientific truth? These last few years, such basic literary questions have come back, front and center, in philosophy and in human sciences, for example in the work of Jacques Bouveresse. Speaking more generally, does literature yield knowledge on which we can count, a wisdom, which, if applied to our own existence, might have some concrete efficacy, a truth that we could verify in life, which would help us live better in the world, better understand others and ourselves? Moreover, is the goal of literature to give meaning and to produce truths?

Proust, for one, thinks so, he whose entire work is based on the truth. According to him, the artist enables us to see real life, which normally we do not see. For the author of *A la reecherche,* literature is the means of going against the stream of supposed ordinary knowledge which our habits and our passions give us and which is more like a *doxa* than knowledge. The artist, Proust says, undoes that type of knowledge, substituting it for, "the most real thing", found in the depths of being, which he renders visible, thus proposing, he writes "the most austere school for life" (Proust, *Time Regained*).

I really like the word "school" as Proust uses it. It applies to the writer who works nonstop and it applies to the reader. Both are in the school of life through their experience with literature. And yet this word is quite mysterious: what is this school? What do you do there? And especially: what do you learn there?

I will quickly skip past the type of didactic knowledge that one can find in novels: of course, novels can make us discover the life of the Incas, the twists and turns of contemporary financial machinations, or the daily life of a supermarket cashier. Of course, all of this is fascinating, and literature has an essential role to play in the fields of politics, sociology and so on; it enables us, as do philosophy and human sciences in general, to concern ourselves with the problems of the world, to become the sort of "pensive reader" that Victor Hugo sought so earnestly. But it is not this cognitive function of literature which holds my attention today. I am talking about another form of knowledge, less exterior, less quantifiable. What interests me today seems more underground, more enigmatic, indeed more elusive: what does literature do for us? What difference could it make for us? What knowledge, what classics, what humanity does literature bring to us?

I will begin with my own experience. The anecdote I will tell you is personal, but I will tell it to you because it deals with the riddle. In 1994, I lost my first child, Philippe. In the months following his death, despite the advice of my doctors, I took no medication, not the least antidepressant. During my painful anguish, only two things enabled me to get through the day: reading and writing. I managed to hold on almost exclusively thanks to these two activities. Mixed of course with tears and lengthy collapses, but the fact is that I immersed myself in literature, that I read and re-read the same works, went over the same lines of poetry, the same maxims *ad libitum*, and the bottom line is clear: literature acted on me, literature did its work. It eased the pain in me, at least as well as anti-anxiety pills. It nourished me with a new knowledge, with a vital strength.

I wonder why, I wonder how; it's mysterious.

First of all, this bandage or this energizing treatment could not have been brought to me by just any literary text, even a sublime one. I know that reading *Madame Bovary*, a novel which I rank very high, would have had no power over me. The texts which I was reading and which helped me, which really *brought me something* were of two sorts. Either they were texts of mourning, read at length – Mallarmé, Hugo, Jaccottet, Roubaud, Forest, Cixous… or fragments, bits and pieces like the debris of literature which acted in the way a charm acts, or rather a magic formula: it sufficed for me to recite to myself this line of Racine's *Bérénice* "J'aimais, Seigneur, j'aimais, je voulais être aimée" ("I loved, my Lord, I loved, and wished to be loved"), or a couple of lines of La Fontaine, to feel, temporarily to be sure, but deeply nevertheless, not consoled, but fulfilled: the verse, its music, its repetitions, filled in the holes left by the Real: I do not dare say "la béance", the gap because Camille de Toledo quite appropriately stresses how much this term has been overused.

In the first case we see clearly what is at work, that Proust analyzes so well: the reader of a love story, or a story of mourning (the two essential elements of literature), this reader appropriates the author's experience to apply it to his own existence, diverting in support of another person, through the effect of what Proust called "a posthumous infidelity", the feelings that the author had expressed with regard to a different one. Literature, then, is like a driving belt of human knowledge, one might almost say pedagogical knowledge: literature teaches us to love, to suffer, to forgive, to resist and even to die. It does not only inform us, it literally forms us. This is not theoretical knowledge, but practical knowledge, a very practical handbook, at least for me. Benjamin Constant's *Adolphe*, for example, enabled me to understand a man I loved, and to draw very concrete lessons, though from darkness – and not only an idea of love or a philosophical point of view about the difficulty of loving. Between the novel at the very beginning of the 19th century, and my own novel, *Ni toi ni moi*, (*Not You, Not Me*), which came out in 2006, between Benjamin Constant and me, there is established a chain of human knowledge which has us following each other, him and me, in a "school of life", which is much less a theoretical link than an apprenticeship that is very close to reality.

In his book, *La Connaissance de l'écrivain* (*The Knowledge of the Writer*), Jacques Bouveresse develops this humanistic conception. He refers to the work of Martha Nussbaum according to whom literature is capable of bringing an essential contribution to moral reflection without condemning moral philosophy to uselessness. That means that she is not content to provide extremely rich and diversified materials for the reflection at hand, she also takes a direct part in it, in her own way, especially by means of her contribution to the moral imagination and the aptitude for practical reasoning.

Nevertheless, in the second case that I was referring to a moment ago, it is not a moral wisdom that was proposed to me, since a single verse without any specific relationship to the circumstances was able to calm me. At that point, it was poetry which carried the day. It is the return of the word, of sonorities, of meter which acted on me, reading, often aloud, and rereading. In *Encore et Jamais* (*Again and Never*), my essay devoted to repetition, I analyze the mysterious effect of calming and jubilation, which, beyond any textual significance, a poem exercises on me.

"The little German boy who", Freud tells us, "delights each time by starting up the spool loud, da, far, there when his mother is away, symbolizing, thanks to this game, her disappearance and her reappearance; thus he calms his anguish of being abandoned, the back and forth movement of the spool, gives promise of the maternal return". In the poem, the sound is like the mama, one is happy that it comes back; the ear and the heart also wait for it in alliterations or assonances, in rhythm. The line of poetry comes back to its beginning and the mother comes back to the house. Whoever loves me comes back, isn't that the secret message of every poem? (*Encore et Jamais*)

Senghor similarly heard the beating of the maternal heart in the tom toms of African poetry. In that sense the poetic text is directly in contact with physical memory, with sensuality, with the most carnal sensibility.

But of course, things are not as simple as all that; we do not have, on the one hand, meaning, with a subject, a theme which concerns us (desire, love, passion, honor, death…) and about which we think that the author must have an innate or acquired knowledge; and on the other hand, melody, rhythm, sonorities, which, beyond all meaning, like music, are going to calm us. Because the two are inseparable. Art, according to Hegel, is situated between thought and sensibility.

Jacques Bouveresse sums up this impossibility of separating content and form by posing the following rhetorical question:

> If some literary truth or other can be paraphrased in a non-literary form, are we still dealing with a literary truth in the sense that it is a truth that only literature is supposed to enable us to both discover and to formulate adequately?

The answer is obviously no. Thus, if after my son's death, someone had said to me "You'll see, with time, you will suffer less", it would have had no effect on me (except to irritate me); whereas repeating to myself this line of La Fontaine "Sur les ailes du temps la tristesse s'envole" ("Her sorrow, on the Wings of Time soon flies") brought me real relief, which stemmed both from a close knowledge of the truth that was being formulated and the musical gentleness of the formulation.

I seem to be stating the obvious because all of us here are convinced that meaning and form are intricately related. But I would like to continue with my tale. There was a text that I read and reread, particularly in the first weeks of my mourning. I read it and reread it many times and Philippe's father read it to me aloud, performing it, and we laughed so hard that it brought tears to our eyes and then we cried all the more. It is a passage you certainly know, from *Voyage au bout de la nuit* (*Journey to the End of the Night*) by L.F. Céline. Right after the death of Bébert, a young patient whom he did not succeed in curing, the narrator buys a copy of Montaigne at a bookstall along the Seine:

> I just chanced to open it at a letter Montaigne once wrote to his wife after a son of theirs had died. That passage caught my interest at once, probably because it made me think of Bébert. Roughly, this is what Montaigne says to his wife:"Ah, my dear wife, don't eat your heart out! Cheer up! ...Everything will turn out all right! .... It always does ... And by the way, rummaging through some old papers belonging to a friend of mine, I've just found a letter that Plutarch wrote to his wife under circumstances very similar to ours ... That letter, dear wife, struck me as so apt, so much to the point, that I'm sending it on to you! ... A splendid letter! Well, I won't keep you waiting any longer, just let me know if it doesn't do a good job of healing your sorrow! [Here I skipped several lines. This is how Céline continues in his ironical-burlesque mode and concludes on the tone of a *moraliste* or a philosopher]: Maybe we go wrong when we try to judge other people's hearts. Maybe they felt real grief. Period grief?" Period grief; grief of the period; sorrow of the period.

Thus the reader sees, as in an off-handed perspective, Plutarch, an ancient, Montaigne – a man of the Renaissance – and Céline, who writes after World War I, in 1932. The first two have an indestructible confidence when it comes to the text, to the power of beautiful language, the prestige of literature. The latter, thanks to the character of Bardamu, develops a radical pessimism, which covers the war, colonialism, and... literature. And yet it is this text of Céline's which restored in me, despite my mourning, a vital force, where, neither Plutarch nor Montaigne could have done it. Probably it is because there was something in his orality, in his irony, in the cruelty of his view of the relationship between words and death, and finally, in the intelligence of his self-appraisal, something that was closer to me, to my "historical" experience of the world, if I may say that. Literature is both timeless and ultra-contemporary: that is why we have to be able to hear in the literature written today its share of today. So much so, that the Céline question does in fact pose itself for me: even if great literary texts have a timeless beauty and an undeniable human actuality, isn't it the vocation of literature to invent and to reinvent a form to express the constant violence of the world, its doubts, its absurdities, its aporias, its gaps? Does it not need to embody, to allow us to hear through its novelistic constructs or their collapse, in language itself, in its clashes, its silences – need it not let us hear "the anguish of being in the world" (to refer to Camille de Toledo's beautiful title), which is peculiar to its contemporaries, does it not need to make us think, to be sure, but especially to feel, to feel physically the *sorrow of our period*? Sorrow is a part of all periods, literatures too. But the novel, the poem takes hold of the pulse of language, the pulsation, the beat which enables us to understand and to feel not only sorrow but also the sorrow our time.

Rethinking literature today is channeled, then, through the acknowledgment that "anxiety has slipped into the body of things" (Camille de Toledo) and that literature is the means for getting us to know and to feel it. (And I remind you that anxiety in French is *inquiétude*, a word whose etymology suggests not immobility but rather constant movement). This "austere school of life" about which Proust speaks is therefore above all a school of doubt, a "school of dizziness" where everything is in movement, in metamorphosis. Nevertheless, and however paradoxical this statement may seem to be, it is not a school of grief, since it proves to the reader that it, and it alone, can revivify him. The most despairing texts can move misfortune away: what counts beyond what the meaning they transmit initially, is their body, their flesh, their voice. To listen to grief struggling in language might be a joy. Literature certainly testifies to the grief of its time, but most of all it testifies to the fact that it enables us to overcome it.

Of course, the knowledge that literature brings to me has a moral, philosophical, sociological, political dimension; its truths allow me to understand the world better. Insofar as I am a writer, I imagine my text to come, I draw both on my experience and on my knowledge: for each of my novels, and especially for my most recent essay, I read and reread texts of psychoanalysis, of philosophy beforehand – Freud, Bourdieu, Kierkegaard helped me to think just as do Beckett, Proust, Michaud, Woolf. One can rethink literature of our time, against or with those who preceded us, but never without them. On the other hand, whether one is a reader or an author, there comes a moment when one is confronted – but that is not the right word – when one is connected, joined up with the body of the text, linked directly to it. Where it is no longer, for instance, a matter of thinking about the phenomenon of repetition or its intellectual or social implications, but to make it ring, resonate, to touch it, to take one's pleasure from it. Then, the text, novel, or poem, engenders desire and satisfies it at the same time.

During his seminar at the Collège de France on *The Preparation of the Novel*, Roland Barthes spoke about books as "sensual objects". Using Chateaubriand as an example, he spoke of reading him as akin to being "swept away by pleasure" and he even added, speaking of the literary text: "it caresses me". One can certainly not deny that Roland Barthes has contributed to thinking literature, and yet his most powerful thought is undoubtedly the following: by refusing to separate knowledge and the theoretical intelligence of the carnal body of the reader, he celebrates literature as that which enables us to feel "the happiness of being alive", what sets us in motion, body and soul. I know that this word soul has become obsolete and has been ridiculed but if one remembers its etymology, it is above all what animates us. To rethink literature, not so much as a source of knowledge than as a source of life, a vital element here and now, that is my proposition today. It is not new but it is good from time to time to repeat things, to say them again.

I would like to dedicate my conclusion to Hélène Cixous, whose language has the unique gift of being open to what is going to happen. By giving its chance to every sentence, she also gives it to the reader; by playing with the signifier while liberating meaning, she also liberates the reader. This aspect of being not thought out ahead of time, not premeditated, is what caresses me in Hélène Cixous' texts. That is why I address to her with gratitude the sentence that an admirer of Michelet said to him in 1851 when he found out that his nomination to the Collège de France had been canceled:

> We learned nothing from you. But our soul, which had been away, came back home to us.

# 13

# HOARDING AS *ÉCRITURE*

## Dodie Bellamy

> [O]ne does fill some with all one takes in, and I've taken in, I dare say, more
> than I've natural room for.
>
> —*Henry James, The Ambassadors*

The linkage of hoarding to writing came to me from the outside. It first arrived
in 2014, when Matias Viegener interviewed me for the *Los Angeles Review of Books*.
His final question, which seemed to come from out of the blue, was, "Dodie, are
you a hoarder?" In my breezy response, I touched upon the associative gathering
of information I find myself and other writers performing in our digital age, the
frequency with which seemingly random data disrupts the logical flow of information. I didn't discuss this so much as enact it. Then, a year later, Suzanne Stein
asked me to write a piece for a series that *Open Space*, the blog/online journal of
the San Francisco Museum of Art, was publishing around issues of "ownership."
Suzanne wrote:

> Someone suggested that I commission a column on hoarding, and I imme-
> diately thought of you, remembering the interview you did with Matias last
> year about Cunt Norton; the subject comes up in a passage about excess,
> overwhelm, and you talk about it as a response to loss, emptiness, lack.

Interestingly, while Suzanne's summary of my interview response is not at all accurate to what I said in the interview, it totally captures all the feelings that came up
when Matias asked me if I was a hoarder—feelings that I was attempting to hide,
not wanting to seem to lose my cool. In this current attempt to unpack my relationship to both hoarding and writing, I've tried to throw open the shutters, so to
speak, to bring my vulnerabilities and conflicts into the discussion. The method I
work in today is one of accrual rather than rational linear progression, and hoarding

is such a brilliant metaphor for that process I can't believe I didn't think of it myself. My title is a nod to Eve Sedgwick's coinage "fisting-as-écriture," which she uses in her discussion of literary superhoarder Henry James.

In August 2015, Kevin Killian and I turned over fifty-five file boxes of ephemera to the Beinecke Rare Book & Manuscript Library at Yale. Negotiations for the transfer, like those in a hostage situation, were long and drawn out, and we didn't know until a month before it happened if the deal was going to go through. So for two years Kevin and I had this big secret we dared only to whisper to a couple of our closest friends—and we still have a big secret because telling anybody how much money we received is considered beyond vulgar. This is painful for both of us. Though we spent thirty years of our literary life hoarding its dejecta, our writing has been committed to spewing all sorts of shit few would dare reveal. Hoarders of information we have never been.

Kevin and I don't have a lot of space. We live in a one bedroom apartment, with a small back porch we use for an office. We used to keep dozens of boxes of whatever in the basement, but one day our landlord made everybody clean out all their stuff, and it sort of ruined our lives. Even with a storage unit three blocks away, boxes are stacked everywhere. The storage unit was so full that in order to organize our archives, we rented a second unit for a year. The artist Kota Ezawa also lent us his studio when he was on an extended out-of-town gig. I feel abject and scattered when I take in the disorganized chaos that surrounds me. Books have overflown their shelves and are stacked in irregular, toppling piles on every available surface. We're getting rid of half these books, we declare. The last time we did a book sweep we made $500, but the will to do another sweep never seems to arise. It's both more and less than laziness; it's the sheer intensity of decision-making that stops us. That book on Surrealism I've had since high school—to remove it would be like tossing away a part of my DNA. Same with my two copies of Julia Kristeva's *Powers of Horror*—even though the parts that matter most to me have long been scanned and stored in the PDF folder on my hard drive, which is backed up both locally and online. As long as there's an internet and I have money to pay for it, *Powers of Horror* will never leave me. But when I touch the books, I'm flooded with memories of discovering the lack around which all my writing would henceforth revolve, my brain sparking, my hand scribbling in the margins, purple, red, black. If I got rid of my two copies of *Powers of Horrors*—even though I know I'll never read either again—it would be as if I were rejecting my younger self, saying to my younger self *I never really valued you.*

Way back in the 1970s my younger self read an interview with the novelist Jayne Anne Phillips—this was before Phillips started publishing with mainstream presses—and I remember her talking about the junk piled around the houses of poor people in the South, how by surrounding themselves with all this broken-down stuff, people who had nothing could feel the comfort of surplus. She somehow connected the lushness of Southern writing to those junkyard houses. I think of the stylistic opulence of my first novel, *The Letters of Mina Harker*, all the sex, cultural references, quotes, puns, poetry, parody I crammed on top of one another—each convoluted sentence screams THESE WORDS MATTER DODIE MATTERS. If only I'd kept my copy of Jayne Anne Phillips' first chapbook of stories, *Sweethearts,* printed in 1976 in an edition of 400. I bet it would be worth something now. That's the problem with choosing—it cannot be trusted. Invariably, non-hoarding lets you down.

Archivists wine and dine and flatter you until they break through your defenses. It's like the archivists are Mommy and you're sitting on the toilet taking your first poo. They say, "Good Dodie!" and you give them whatever they want, even tender bits you know are better kept hidden. What archivists want are singular unique objects, the irreplaceable. All these letters, photos, contracts, yellowed newspaper clippings, flyers, manuscripts—moving my hands across their object auras, the sadness of materiality strikes me, the inevitability of loss. I think of old people getting ready to die and giving away their stuff. I think of schizophrenics who get rid of everything they own, all their money, and set off. I unearth the first two pages of a letter so intense it verges on love letter, but the final page is missing and I can't figure out who it possibly could have been from. Dismay hits me, this sense of a vast past that has vaporized—all that love and anger and realization. My past. The more the papers are organized, I start to think of them as an exoskeleton protecting me from annihilation. The sense of exposure is unbearable. I feel like I'm attending my own wake; I feel like I'm being embalmed. But I bear it because I want the money, want to be remembered—even though the future the archives promise feels impossible. Impossible in that I won't be here any longer, impossible in that anybody would be interested in my life/stuff. And then there's my apocalyptic pessimism—it's hard to believe that human life won't soon be extinct. Posterity, despite the Beinecke's climate-controlled storage facilities, may end up being puny. I gave the archivists everything. Everything except my journals and wedding photos and anything to do with my deceased parents. I kept these tokens out of love and a conviction that I'm not finished yet.

Sometimes I run into someone I know I don't get along with, but I can't remember why. An impression too vague to base behavior or attitude on, yet there it is between us, foggy as scratched Plexiglas. A woman I haven't seen for a decade sticks her face in mine and gives a fulsome apology for some previous bad behavior, and in a fit of claustrophobic panic I find myself saying *don't worry about it, everything's fine, it was a long time ago, I'm as much to blame as you*—even though I have no idea what she's talking about. Friends who teach complain that these *young people* have no sense of history, but I worry that no one can escape our ahistorical zeitgeist, that all of us are tunneling towards a totalizing NOW. I imagine existence as a boundless expanse of dirt and I'm a worm burrowing through it, gorging on it on one end, shitting it out on the other. I read online that the donut shape is the basic organizing structure of multicelled creatures, that the human body is an elongated donut, our digestive tube from mouth to anus, the donut's hole. Our deepest interiority is a slick pink hole. Whatever I haven't written down slips away. My journals prove that I have existed, that I'm a continuation of *something.* Dozens of volumes of fleeting thoughts and emotions—much of it embarrassing and not nearly enough description—waiting for a crack of light, waiting to be shaped, loved.

I worry about my mother's photos—hundreds of them that after eight years are still too poignant for me to sort through—maybe I should have given them to the archive. What if my cultural capital plummets and nobody wants a second batch of my residue. I imagine myself dying alone in a hovel, undetected until neighbors complain about the smell and my starving cats have eaten away my face. My disgruntled landlord, to whom I owe back rent, tosses my belongings into a dumpster, and my mother's snapshots grow soggy—all her smiling relatives and friends—even I don't know who many of them are—their meaning, their index disintegrating. In the archive they'd rest in boxes of acid-free files, waiting for a curious grad student to unearth them, to plunge their obscurities. Writing students have told me that in other classes they've been admonished not to describe photographs because that's boring—but I never tire of writing about them, of staring and staring until I feel like I'm passing through the emulsion and holding a beating heart. Kevin gave all his prints—thirty-years-worth of portraits of literary types—to the Beinecke. Beforehand he scanned them, so he figured he wasn't really losing anything. But I mourn the loss of analogue photo processes. In order to peer *into* digital images, I envision them pixelated behind a shadow emulsion. This imagined emulsion links the iPhone-clicking Dodie to the darkroom-in-her-closet Dodie of my twenties, to the work-study job I had at Indiana University's photo lab, hand-printing group photos from events held on campus. In a darkened room, white paper is inseminated with light then sloshed in a bath of toxic chemicals, its image slowly materializing. Since an image appeared so long after its capture, it always surprised. The film *Blow-Up* is a tribute to the mystery of the image, its power to hold secrets. Only through hyperfocused surrender can one unveil its prize.

In college, I was taught that emulsion was comprised of silver halide crystals dispersed in gelatin rendered from cows fed mustard, which resonated with the Knox gelatin that ladies of my childhood dissolved in hot water and chugged to make their nails grow strong. It was Rose Knox who marketed gelatin to women. After her husband died in 1908, friends urged her to sell the business, but Mrs. Knox cared too deeply about women and gelatin and her workers to do that. When she took over as CEO, she instituted a five-day work week, two weeks of paid vacation, and paid sick days. A sign in the company lobby read "Happiness Headquarters." So. Much. Information. When does one expand? Cut back? Stop researching? When is enough enough? Like Colette's aging courtesan Lea in the *Chéri* books, I straddle two centuries that are drifting further and further apart. Will I, like Lea, quit scrambling for relevancy and simply give up? Or will I like Henry James, who straddled Victorianism and modernity, gain power from contradiction, from *too much*? All those commas and dashes; all those conditionals and misdirections; all those circumlocutions, erratic switches from intimacy to distance, heaps of ambiguous "it"s—in his late fiction, James' sentences simultaneously accrue and self-destruct as if composed with magic ink. There's too much punctuation, too much grammar—but just when we feel we cannot bear another twisted clause, the seduction of plot compels us onward. James' curvy syntax creates a centrifugal momentum that flings away dullness, spinning us into vortices of discovery and erasure, desire and loss. In *Dainty Desserts for Dainty*

*People* (1915), Mrs. Knox, who was as far into her new century as I am into mine, wrote, "The pies and hot puddings of our grandmother's days have waned in popularity, and in their places are to be found cold and frozen desserts." By embracing gelatin's mutability, she forged a new era of sweets. "[Gelatin] may be used in an almost endless variety of ways. It makes possible numberless dishes, not less delightful to the eye than pleasing to the palate, and opens the door to constantly new achievements in culinary inventions." Like Henry James and Mrs. Knox, am I advancing new paradigms? Or am I, as MFA fiction students often treat me, just weird?

When writing happens, my world shifts and like on *Marvel's Agents of SHIELD* a portal opens. Things tumble into it—events memories books movies the endless online garbage I read my body. The longer the portal is open, the more tumbles in. Patterns form, but on some level everything feels—everything *is*—connected so I keep pushing more and more stuff in. For each piece, I gather at least twice as much material as I need—and I buy talismans and souvenirs—snowflake obsidian pyramid, tiny bronze Steampunk rocket ship on a ball chain. Sorting through my notes is exhilarating and arduous. Sometimes I do multiple, progressively longer versions, piling paragraph upon paragraph, hoping that under all that weight startling connections will sprout. When do you close the portal? I don't know. While I'm in the thick of writing this essay, in fact, a male critic complains my pieces go on and on and on, and my confidence stumbles. I download Judy Grahn's 1974 lesbian-feminist anthem *A Woman Is Talking to Death* and reread it. Regretting all the women she didn't love enough, didn't try to save, Grahn writes,

> These are indecent acts, lacking courage, lacking a certain fire behind the eyes, which is the symbol, the raised fist, the sharing of resources, the resistance that tells death he will starve for lack of the fat of us, our extra.

Defending our "fat," our "extra," we starve death. Grahn reminds me that for a woman, too much is always a form of resistance, and I regain momentum.

Collecting is about display. The curio cabinet my mother had for her blown glass clowns, the shelves a friend installed on his dining room wall to showcase his bounty of vintage vases. The vases are turquoise and sinuous, and even though I'm ignorant of their provenance I can tell from their presentation I should be impressed. Hoarding—even if others happen to see it—is never about display. My father's over-loaded workroom in the basement, rows and rows of baby food jars filled with nuts and bolts and tiny nails—which begs the question—where did those jars come from? Was he amassing this stuff since I was an infant? Hoarding is a private act. You feel embarrassment and guilt over your manic accrual. The best writing embarrasses the author—at least a teeny bit—emerging from a compulsion to flaunt what any sane person would camouflage. The reader turns the page and witnesses the uncontainable—*panties around ankles*—and the energy that flares up astonishes. Work where the writer—or the workshop committee—is totally in control fails because its libidinal pressure has been critiqued away. The resultant piece is so polished, so correct, so flat you could bounce a dime off of it.

When my mother died, I started wearing one of her rings, a gaudy band encrusted with crushed diamonds. The week after her funeral, back in San Francisco I went for a Chi Nei Tsang treatment, a form of Taoist internal organ massage. My practitioner, Eréne, was a young woman who stood very erect. Her deep voice and her sternness combined with her excellent posture gave her the air of a cyborg. She occasionally worked with the dying, as a sort of doula, helping them cross over to the other side. So, I was lying on my back on the massage table, and as soon as Eréne stepped up to me, she said, "Is that your mother's ring?" There was a shudder in her voice, as if she could feel death emanating from my finger. "You need to soak that in salt water to get rid of negative energy," she continued, "to allow only the good energy to remain." I didn't want to soak away anything, I wanted to cling to my mother's every last microbe. When Eréne would poke around my belly, I'd go into a trance and have visions. Eventually I'd come to with a huge gasp, just like in the movies. Even before she died, my visions were usually about my mother, as if I had these ancient memories stored in my colon, all the love and pain she and I shared for the 50 years that I knew her.

Nine out of every 10 cells in my body is a colonizing microorganism. These communities of symbiotic bacteria and viruses and fungi that live on and inside my body are known as my microbiome, though I'm not sure "my" is appropriate here. As host, I contribute around 23,000 human genes, while microorganisms contribute over 9,000,000, which is a ratio of 390:1 human to microorganismal. Microorgasmic would be a livelier adjective, all these ecstatic mini-me's popping in and out of my anatomy. I've always suspected I wasn't an autonomous entity, but now there's scientific proof that this person known as Dodie is, in fact, a bio-molecular network. I cannot be separated from my environment; I collect bits and pieces wherever I go. They adhere to me and change me. My physical being is a hoard. After my mother died, her empty house wasn't frightening, like I feared. I felt embraced as I walked from room to room, touching her things, absorbing her. I imagine those mother particles are still tumbling through me. Touching myself, I touch her.

I experience my psyche as similarly spongelike. Each gesture I make leaves a trail, happening within a vortex of communal gesture. Each step I take, my community steps with me. All the shit in my sociobiome, all its wonder, I can never shake off. No matter how othered I feel, I can never be other, not really. It is impossible to write about myself without writing my culture as well, for that culture infuses my personhood, even those aspects I despise. I consider America to be a shameful place—maybe it always has been—but right now much about this country is appalling. Fill in your own examples. If I pretend my writing can stand outside the shame that is America, that my ego-id-superego isn't driven by it, I'm not just lying to the reader, I'm lying to myself. On a recent trip to Los Angeles my plan was to drive directly from LAX to a gallery. I pulled into a mini-mall near the airport, starving and running late, and the only place to eat was HomeTown Buffet. Like how bad could it be? Atrocious, that's how bad. I choked down black-eyed peas with white rice, a few bites of ham, chicken, and salad. One cube of red Jell-O.

Even the iced tea was inedible. Back in Indiana I used to go to a similar place with my mom for lunch—Old Country Buffet—when I was still a vegetarian—and I'd get a big salad and macaroni and cheese or some potato thing. And pudding and ice cream. So, of course, I felt pangs of her absence as I sat there among the overweight families, the old couples, single men. I was the only single woman in the place. I sat there alone—kids squealing with excitement over the desserts—picking at this toxic food. Station upon station of toxic food, and I could take as much as I wanted to—which makes this one of the most American places in the universe—and I thought of my chemo-riddled mother, her great pleasure at feeling well enough to leave the house and do something—anything—to please me—and I felt a loneliness so dense, it was as if the whole place was folding in on me, compacting. I felt sad and bland and utterly unspecial—and bummed that I hadn't eaten anywhere near $15-worth of food. It's a contest between you and the buffet, and in order to win you have to pile your plates high, like toppling high. *You say I can eat all I want—well, let me show you how much ALL can mean. I am the fucking champion of ALL.* Remembrance itself is a type of hoarding, a clutching at love or trauma—those "others" that make us fully human—and all of us are these futile Humpty Dumpties trying to put our shards back together again.

As I write this, my cat Quincey starts dying—more quickly—she's been terminally ill for years. She was my mother's cat, and she and I grieved Mom together. In the eight years I've had her, I've done everything to keep Quincey alive. A $4,000 hospitalization, $200 acupuncture treatments. Life is precious. It is natural to try to keep it around as long as possible. The vet and I discuss her options, when to euthanize. What if she dies at home, I ask. He says I should wrap her body in a plastic bag and put it in the freezer—to keep it from oozing. Having a pet wrapped in plastic in the freezer—that's exactly the type of thing the worst hoarders do, the kind where cops/psychiatrists/distressed relatives cringe while crews wearing surgical masks or hazmat suits haul out their crap. In Los Angeles, Dennis Cooper lived next door to a code-red hoarder—Claire, an ancient white-haired woman. When Kevin and I slept on Dennis' sofa bed, Claire would peer in at us through the long strips of glass on either side of the front door. We happened to visit the weekend they cleared out her place. In my memory, the event is totally silent. Workers carry out stuff, lumbering beneath their burdens like a line of ants hauling bread crumbs as Claire floats down the sidewalk, back and forth, totally untethered. There's not a sound in the air, not even the rustle of palm trees.

I read that I can alter my microbiome, make it more diverse, by spending time outdoors in dirt, by drinking kefir. I purchase kefir grains online and start fermenting. Kefir grains are thousands of years old. No one knows where they came from, and scientists have failed to synthesize them. The grains are said to be a gift from Allah. Some say they are bits of the original manna. Mine arrive dried, and I feed them organic raw milk. Slowly they reanimate, little mummies sucking up protein. As the grains awaken they look like small curds of cauliflower, like scrambled brains. I bought a white cotton cap for their mason jar, a circle of fabric edged with crocheted linen lace. Fastened to the jar with a red silicone band, the cap reminds me of Granny's bonnet the wolf put on in "Little Red Riding Hood." The kefir in its white bonnet is ravenous, requiring more milk each day. Its colonies of bacteria and yeast swell as it readies to enter, to better me. When I lift off the cap to shake the lumpy white liquid, I can feel its ancient presence and my body engorges. Soon I will meld with a time when God just reached down and handed us gifts.

I dream of Quincey. She's on the street staggering around, lost. I'm so glad to find her, as she's been missing for a long time. She's stumbling, one of her front legs injured, so I take her to the vet. The vet is very suspicious. I realize he's called Animal Control and he's taking Quincey away from me. I seize her and try to flee. I end up struggling with the vet. He's on top of me, choking me, and I'm struggling to breathe when I wake up. I wonder if the dream is about my guilt for having put her to sleep, for not defending the last dregs of her life—my fear that she's stumbling around in limbo. A gaunt ball of rumbling love—that was she. This daily energetic transaction. And then poof. No more energy. Like an appliance that's been unplugged. I write the dream in my journal with the awareness that I'd planned on working Quincey into the present essay, and the dream might fit in nicely. Quincey, my mother's cat, was an extension of my mother, the last living beat of her. My loss is infantile, a child on a rug shitting her pants and wailing maaaaaaaaaaaaaahhhhhhhhhhhhh. Yet here I am, caching it away for future use.

On Amazon, I purchase a set of Gigogne tumblers by Duralex—the six-ounce size. At a party I was served wine in one, and a few days later, at a cafe, tea. I fell in love with them, their roundness. For the same reason—this roundness—I replaced my tube-shaped mugs with oversized teacups, breakfast cups—I lick their orbed contours and think of mother's milk. The Gigogne glasses, being heat resistant, are the most popular glasses in the Middle East for drinking tea. I read that there is a photo of Osama Bin Laden holding one—but no matter how much I google Osama Bin Laden + Duralex, Osama Bin Laden drinking tea—I cannot find this image, which I have a passion to see. If I found it, I'm sure I'd save it to my hard drive like a treasured family snapshot. It's humiliating the way I hoard images information kitchenware food. What else—jewelry and clothes. I don't just buy a tin of a favorite tea, I order a whole pound. What else—pens and journals. I first heard of Duralex while translating a poem by Sabine Macher called "sur mon bureau." Even after five years of French in high school and college, my command of the language was so atrocious that my initial read of the title was "on my dresser." Rather than desk. The poem turned out to be a nightmare to translate—a list of objects with few subjects or verbs to contextualize them. Objects out of context, out of use value, become remarkably mysterious, wrapping their meaning tightly around themselves. Some Francophile explained to me what a Duralex "verre" was, and I put the full force of my obsessiveness behind coming up with an American equivalent. Nothing fit. We have Pyrex, but no brand of ubiquitous cheap glassware. So, I left in Duralex as a spot of untranslatability—a site where language and culture stretch and waver—a wooziness that I reclaim in my curvaceous breast glasses. I lift one to my mouth and suck. Glass as tit. Dare/can I get that reductive here? I guess I am/can. In poetry workshops I was taught that separation from my mother—that painful wrenching apart—allowed my entry into the symbolic order—and thus language is about attempting to bridge this irrevocable gap—so that whenever I speak or write it is within a narrative of unbearable loss. I can only say "glass" if the glass and I are tragically separated. I can never fuse with the glass so I'm left with these stacks and stacks of words through which I try to pull the world towards me.

# 14

# CORPSE POSE

*Wayne Koestenbaum*

I have corpse envy. At the end of yoga class we do corpse pose, savasana: dress rehearsal for the morgue. I'd planned to write an essay about how literature should start enjoying its own corpse mode, its oft-foretold senescence; I'd planned to become an expert on corpse pose, to analyze what I feel lying on a blue yoga mat, waiting for the bell to ring, savoring my slack-jawed simulation of interment. I'd planned to divagate on corpse pose's relevance to contemporary literary practice, but then, yesterday at noon, my stepfather died. What if the rigmarole surrounding my stepfather's corpse—figuring out funeral arrangements or letting my older brother handle them while I stand idle—ruins the essay I've promised to deliver? I've sworn to write a piece entitled "Corpse pose," but now I must fly to California to deal with a real corpse.

*

I could write "Corpse pose" on the airplane, en route to California for the funeral. But maybe I'll be too discombobulated. On a plane, I can't spread out my notes. While I paint, in my studio, I jot down notes on lined yellow five-by-seven inch pads. My painting notes aren't literature, though I save them in a manilla folder, as if they were valued drafts. I could transcribe them and reincarnate them as a poem or an essay, but I dread that process. Transforming the notes into literature will involve making sisyphean prosodic decisions. Should I mutate the fragments and phrase clusters into sentences? Should I stack up the sentences paratactically, or integrate them into coherent paragraphs? I might decide that the notes are actually a poem; lyric identity helps me avoid syntactic maturity.

*

Here are five of my painting notes. If you want to help me sculpt them into literature, be my guest.

1.   Add white to black edges to cover up the blue.
2.   Change color of lozenge behind butt.
3.   Lavender heavens deepen Joan's body.
4.   Cover the ultramarine area with Twombly-esque graphisms, using small brush.
5.   Use palette knife. No outlines until I see forms in the smudge.

These notes won't be literature until I shape, frame, or contextualize their stammering.

★

Contextualize: that was what I learned in grad school, a Ph.D. program, not theory-heavy. Contextualize. That meant history. Find the historical context for my close reading of butt-fucking imagery in H. Rider Haggard's novel *She*. The context that interested me wasn't history. The context was my desire to find butt-fucking imagery in H. Rider Haggard's *She,* and to stimulate my class of fellow grad students by audaciously leading them through my sodomitic interpretation.

★

In my stepfather's presence I never referred to him as "stepfather." Perhaps this omission distressed him. One year, for Xmas, I gave him a copy of *The Arcades Project*, an assemblage of notes, a book difficult to read but easy to idealize. I had fallen in love with Walter Benjamin's numinous incompleteness, and wanted to present this ruin to every man or woman I knew who needed fixing, who needed to be made more monumental. My real father (my mother's *first* husband) was born in Berlin, 1928; *father* and *Germanic* are twinned concepts. I thought I could firm up my non-Germanic stepfather by giving him *The Arcades Project*. Or maybe I wanted to make him a bit more ruined.

★

My stepfather, a historian, knew how to find contexts for random information; his specialty was the second world war, and so he could divine a context for *The Arcades Project*. Amelioration, idealization, repair, and obfuscation are the indirect aims of most of the gift-giving I've done in my not particularly generous life. I've given my real father Lichtenberg's *The Waste Books,* Benjamin's *Reflections* (containing "A Berlin Chronicle"), and a CD of Schumann's *Der Rose Pilgerfahrt* (*The Pilgrimmage of the Rose*). Here are prerequisites for a gift to a father. (1) It must be German. (2) It must be fragmented. (3) It must be lionized only posthumously. (4) It must represent ruin. (5) It must do a good job of transfiguring ruin.

★

To the first session of a semester-long seminar I taught on *The Arcades Project*, I brought two personal relics of dubitable relevance: a 1968 Kodak Super 8mm movie camera, and a photo of my great-uncle Walter, a chemist, who died in Caracas in 1956. Born in Berlin, he looked uncannily like Walter Benjamin; judging by my great-uncle's face in the photograph, I could imagine that he'd died of overthinking. The photo, though it served no legitimate pedagogic function, encapsulated my infatuation with *The Arcades Project,* whose incompleteness held my lacunae in a loving, unparaphrasable grip. Because I, like my Uncle Walter, resembled someone liable to die from overthinking, then perhaps I could be trusted as a living representative of Benjamin's auratic incompletion.

★

But why the movie camera? I brought to that first *Arcades Project* class my Super 8mm movie camera to embody the aura of outmoded technologies. This scuffed object—a pathetic, nonmonumental bit of American midcentury flotsam—hurtled me back to photoreproductive crossroads, the fork in the road separating Swann's way from the Guermantes way. I now display this talismanic camera in my apartment's hallway; next to the camera, on its diminutive shelf, are ten back issues of *BUTT* magazine, a Ballantine 1961 paperback screenplay of Fellini's *La Dolce Vita,* and a stack of yellowed books I bought in Berlin, including Benjamin's *Berliner Kindheit um Neuzenhundert (Berlin Childhood around 1900),* and a 1914 edition of Richard Dehmel's *Hundert Ausgewälte Gedichte (100 Selected Poems).* Dehmel wrote the text that inspired Schoenberg's *Verklärte Nacht. Transfigured Night,* like my 1968 Kodak Instamatic, was a bygone innovation I still hadn't adequately studied, an outmoded iconoclasm still waiting, over a century later, to wake me up.

★

Also on this shelf, beside the Super 8mm camera, sits a five-inch-tall porcelain replica of a toilet, my household's half-assed homage to Duchamp's *Fountain,* another outmoded yet still detonating innovation. Inside the tiny toilet's bowl, a transparent glass marble dumbly rests (an instrument of divination, like the fortune-tellers Benjamin finds in the arcades); and in the toilet's chassis, where its plumbing should be, resides a bundle of two by three and a half inch cards—a handmade, nondenominational tarot deck, a gift from Eve Kosofsky Sedgwick, who decorated them with rubber-stamped images of Proust, various bodhisattvas, a Virgin Mary, and other divinities.

★

One night, my mother spilled sugar on the kitchen floor and told my stepfather to sweep it up. She called out for him: "Sugar Boss!" (Henceforth, in my private lexicon, "Sugar Boss" became his nickname.) Already stooped from Parkinson's, he stooped even more to clean up the sugar, whether with a whisk broom or a wet paper towel. He could be boss of sugar, but he could not be boss of her life, her body, or even of his own body, over whose movements he had less and less control. Sugar Boss was sweet, passive, easily trampled, easily ignored, almost speechless. Sugar Boss, now a corpse, posed for me, during the last decade of his life, a nosological dilemma: was Parkinson's the sole cause of his shocked, masochistic inanition, or did Parkinson's continue a process already in motion?

★

My aim, originally, in this essay, before Sugar Boss became a corpse, was to write about a kind of literature that follows in the wake of Beckett, Thomas Bernhard, Joe Brainard, and more recent models—a literature that makes no bones about its corpse-like exhaustion, and that recycles its depletion (its stance of no longer caring about literature) into a new, faux vitality, a vitalism composed of ellipses, blunt honesties, paratactical leaps, silent sulking fits, and a staged love affair with its own posthumousness. If literature's foundation—what I've recently called "the jejune sequentiality" of onward-proceeding speech—has decayed, and we are now writing with invisible ink, could we learn to savor invisibility, and turn this deficit into a new source of energy? (Recurrent bad dream: in a taxi, I'm writing a poem or essay, but the ink turns out to be invisible.) Before Sugar Boss became a corpse, I'd hoped to issue a hortatory call for texts that might take blissful advantage of literature's posthumousness and enjoy their deadness (à la Zizek's *Enjoy Your Symptom!*). I wanted to wake up my own language (or put it to sleep?) with a call perhaps anachronistically and credulously avant-garde; to start writing with more parsimony and less passion; to exhort myself to be cold, meager, scant, illegible, inaudible, and to find in that bleak zone a new repose, the repose of corpse pose; to play dead, in prose, before my time, thereby magically evading actual termination, like Sheherazade with her stories.

★

My new idée fixe is asemic writing—writing that doesn't use words or signs. (Classic examples are the drawings of Henri Michaux, author of *Miserable Miracle*, a mescaline journal in the spirit of Benjamin's hashish investigations.) I'd love to pontificate on behalf of asemic writing—to give you asemic assignments—but I'm distracted by a graveyard in California, Home of Peace Cemetery, where, tomorrow, or soon thereafter, with or without my presence, my stepfather's corpse will be interred in a small plot of expensive land. Another family member is also buried there—my mother's and father's first child, a stillborn boy, nameless, delivered on February 17, 1955. This stillborn baby—who remains a focus of my mother's ruminations—demotes me from my perch as second son. In fact, I am the third son, if we count the first child, who had no out-of-womb existence except as corpse.

★

My mother, who suffered a severe stroke a few years ago, can speak cogently, but she has difficulty reading and writing; she sometimes write words, or groups of letters recognizable as words, though she is mostly unable to decipher them. Now she regards literature as a region from which she has been unfairly barred; and in this twilight world, largely without literature, except for the occasional audio book, except for *Moby Dick* and poems of Emily Dickinson and a few other CDs she plays without apparent pleasure, she engages in eddying rumination. My older brother, who is a cellist but in another life, might have chosen to be an airplane pilot or a psychoanalyst, calls it "perseveration." One subject on which she perseverates, as if making a poem out of thought itself, is the stillborn first child. (Earlier this year, with a rabbi, my mother planned a magical scheme. For a fee of $500, the rabbi offered to perform a ceremony to reclaim the stillborn child's soul.) The great romances of my mother's life have been with the disappeared, the out-of-reach, the forfeited; the stillborn child possesses an irrevocable reality and potential that we four surviving children lack. But now I'm stuck in the cul-de-sac of autobiographical recitation; I need a good dose of asemic writing to wake me up.

*

I'd promised myself to end this essay with a guidebook on how to "go asemic"—how to deterritorialize literature, how to enfranchise the hand, or mouth, or mind—but the only suggestion I can think of is to urge you to find an old bathrobe, shirt, skirt, or towel, to lay it on the floor, and to write on it, perhaps with oil sticks, pastel crayons, markers, charcoal, graphite, or pen and ink; then, if you like, you could affix this item of former usefulness—now serving as papyrus—to a wall, with ordinary push-pins, and enjoy the spectacle.

*

The stillborn child my mother delivered on February 17, 1955 is only theoretically my sibling. The stillborn child is my mother's preoccupation, her pet corpse, her philosopher's stone, her pact with the unfinished and the unfinishable; he is her grudge, and she is (as am I) a tapestry of grudges, intricate as a codex Bible. (According to my older brother, who dutifully keeps apace with my mother's perseverations, she recently contemplated belated legal action against the hospital or doctor connected to that 1955 stillbirth.) Like my mother, I covet the unconsummated, the never-arrived; as in Delmore Schwartz's story "In Dreams Begin Responsibilities," I pose as Orphean voyeur who wants to turn back time to arrest an unfortunate or desired cataclysm at the instant *before* its fatal commencement.

*

I was ushered into the realm of literature at an early age. When my mother took me to kindergarten the first day, she told the teacher, "Wayne's a reader."

(I've mentioned this incident, a decade ago, in a long poem; repeating the story now is a self-cannibalizing act that leaves an aftertaste of shame.) I knew at the time that my mother was lying, exaggerating, or speaking her own wish. I wasn't a reader, not yet; I could only eavesdrop and fingerpaint. Any good fortune I've had, as someone granted a privileged and seemingly unhindered relation to literacy and to literature, I owe to the stillborn child, for if he'd survived his birth (I recall learning that he'd been strangled by the umbilical cord), I'd be the third son, not the second; in my life-as-fable, only my mother's *second son* is the child destined to have a felicitous and unencumbered relation to literature.

★

Does my relation to literature seem unencumbered? Do I seem a serene-tempered representative of literature's pleasures, rather than its ordeals, curfews, and solitary confinements? Where did you get the idea that anyone's relation to literature could come without fleshly exactions? When I write, I'm on the verge of physically exploding. Hands sweating, I'm hunched over, poised to attack or defend, like a raptor or a cowering dog. Language compels me to sweat, slaver, tremble, squeeze. My body is a bloody washcloth I'm systematically wringing. Sentences demand aviation: adrenaline and anxiety provide horsepower for my freakish, impossible flight. Caught in a schizogenic double-bind, I use language to flee language. To write, I must burn imagination's mansion to the ground, like Rochester's Thornfield in *Jane Eyre*. The guilt and depletion I feel *after* writing is an arsonist's hangover of remorse—an arsonist who knows that he has destroyed the last house on earth, or the last house which his paltry book of matches has the power to destroy.

★

Is masochism the only gate into literature? I'll end on a more cheerful, less self-flagellating note: here, as promised, are six assignments for attempting a practice of asemic writing, the only closure—the only paradise—I can propose.

★

(1) Write a few phrases, without premeditation, on a large surface. Use ink, acrylic paint, tempera, or any other wet medium. Then, take another surface, the same size, and press the two surfaces together, strongly enough to make an imprint. Separate the surfaces; observe the irregular, unscripted patterns that the original phrases imprinted upon the receiving membrane. Reorganize these islets and puddles into new shapes, not necessarily into letters or words. Or else form new words based on the puddles. We'll call this sheet *the puddle surface*.

★

(2) If you are not satisfied with your puddle surface, repeat the process by writing, on a fresh surface, some new phrases, without premeditation, this time using a different color ink or paint than you'd used in the previous experiment. Then, press the newly inscribed surface onto your earlier *puddle surface*. Separate the two surfaces, and examine again your now-transfigured puddle surface. Doctor it, judiciously and quickly, by using a rag, paper towel, or piece of cardboard.

★

(3) Place random strips of non-stick masking tape—known as "artist's tape"—on a large surface, whether paper, canvas, wood, cardboard, or whatever is easily obtained. Then, take a pastel crayon, or any other marker that makes a strong impression, and quickly write some phrases or sentences on the tape. Let your markings exceed the tape's edges and impinge on the surrounding surface. Carefully peel off the masking tape. (You may discard the tape, or you may use it, later, for new experiments.) Observe, on the now untaped surface, what remains of the words you originally wrote. Using a different color marker or crayon, play with the areas formerly covered with tape. Don't feel obliged to reform the asemic traces into words.

★

(4) Using a liquid medium, copy a pre-existing text (for example, a paragraph from the newspaper or from an email) on a spacious surface. Spend no more than five or ten minutes copying. Then, impress this surface onto another surface, of equivalent size. Separate the surfaces; observe the results. (Your focus will be, I imagine, not on the original surface, which functions as a photographic negative, but on the second, imprinted sheet, the so-called "puddle surface.") Now, using any medium, wet or dry, begin to improvise upon this puddle surface.

★

(5) Apply black gesso to a piece of wood. Let dry. Then, with a white pencil, start writing, or scrawling, on the wood. If you are not pleased with the results, cover or circle the parts you don't like with a liquid medium—say, fluorescent yellow tempera paint.

★

(6) In the trash, or on the street, find some refuse elements that seem likely surfaces for your marks. Take these surfaces home, and apply black gesso to them. Let dry. Then, with a strong color—yellow, green, lavender, pink—in whatever liquid medium you like, with finger, brush, popsicle stick, Q-tip, or any implement you desire, begin to write something very unimportant, something so trivial you would

never impose it on a reader. When you lose interest, stop writing words, and let your hand move freely, and with whatever impulse strikes it, across the surface. If you don't like the results of this scrawl, speed up the process, and move your hand more frenetically. If necessary, begin humming, mumbling, singing, cursing, or shouting, while moving your hand.

# 15

# THE SHELLEY JACKSON VOCATIONAL SCHOOL FOR GHOST SPEAKERS AND HEARING-MOUTH CHILDREN

*Shelley Jackson*

A note on point of view to start us off.

Literature is training in doing without oneself. The writer does not write as herself, of herself, or in her own words. The reader hollows herself out in turn, to play host to a host of voices. If she does this, for the most part, fearlessly and with ease, it is because she is, we are, really already hollow. All speech is a speaking *as if*—as if one were a person. As if these were one's own thoughts. They are not; our words, our thoughts, these emphatically included, are not our own, just borrowed for a while. We exist, if you like, but only as fictional characters do. At death, we all fall out of character, and into the world. But some perform this interesting operation before death, and that is the origin of literature.

It is not ordinarily the origin of nonfiction, but then, not knowing its place is literature's place. If it scales its retaining walls, however, it is not to usurp the standard of the factual, but to plant in its place its own equivocal ensign, the bend sinister of the pretender.

So today I speak (not without, no doubt, some recidivist lapses into sincerity), as "Shelley Jackson," headmistress of the fictional school around which my latest novel revolves, the Shelley Jackson Vocational School for Ghost Speakers and Hearing-Mouth Children or SJVSGSHMC (shortened again to SJVS), where we train children with speech impediments to channel the dead. I shall be presenting a white paper on literature, first issued by the SJVS in 1963, revised and expanded in 1996, and updated in 2013, as follows:

The SJVS considers literature a form of amateur necromancy.

This is not particularly remarkable, does not in itself distinguish it: all language is haunted by the dead; all readers have wandered the bush of ghosts. But literature deserves special mention, because of all layman modes of intercourse between the living and the dead, it alone has put its methods to the task of creating a vast if bounded territory—a sort of game preserve or practice arena—where the living may travel among the dead for pleasure and instruction. We regard literature as a collectively authored *Book of the Dead,* and reading and writing as vocational training for future corpses.

A *vocation* is a calling, but who is on the line? Let's hold while we check the dictionary, where etymology offers us a rudimentary caller ID. *Vocare*: the area code suggests ancient Rome, but it is enough to know that the dead are calling.

So, the word *vocation* is itself a vocation, *calling* is a call. The dead call us, and through our own listening mouths.

The SJVS considers that to answer this call is our vocation as human beings. And in fact, we cannot avoid it. We hold the line open as long as we live, though many people never know it, having pocket-dialed the dead, so to speak, in their infancy. They go their whole lives, using up their minutes, oblivious to the intimate eavesdroppers they carry, before they finally take the call. To answer the call is, in the ordinary course of things, to die. We have a vocation for death.

But to answer the call we must first have a vocation for vocation, which is to say, for call and response.

At the vocational school we answer language's call, and respond, thus entering into cordial and instructive relations with the dead.

And literature is this vocational school.

(Let me weaken the rhetorical force of that claim with a parenthesis. Serious students cannot do better than to take up a course of study at the Vocational School proper, which offers distance learning courses through our web annex, but we recommend literature as a low-cost, open-access alternative.)

It offers an experience of death, but literature is not itself "dead." Neither is it, nor was it ever, alive. It is undead. But not because it died (sometime in the last century, say) and was raised again: it came into existence undead, has always been a ghost, an essential or original ghost that knew no prior life. Thus, all fiction is post-apocalyptic; all characters are ghosts and revenants, and we reject as redundant the introduction of zombies into the drawing rooms of *Pride and Prejudice*.

What does this mean for the novel?

For one thing, it means that predictions of its demise are centuries late, and also early. Literature has always been postliterature; the author was never alive in the first place; and as fans of zombie movies know, it is hard to kill something that is already dead. The novel just keeps staggering on, and in hordes.

So, if we are wondering what literature can teach us, perhaps we should ask ourselves, what does a zombie know?

As we have seen from the movies, what a zombie knows best is how to make more zombies. Books make more books; writers make readers who become writers who make books that crawl on though their backs are broken and their signatures coming loose.

If this all seems a bit circular, well, ghosts repeat themselves, telling over their tragedies, and books do too. This is one way we could understand the phrase "re-thinking literature." But let us remove the pejorative tone to the way we repeat ourselves on the topic of the repetitious, considering that the totally new would be a sort of spasm that we would fail not only to understand, but even to experience—like death, rather than a ghost. A ghost comes *back*, that's what it does. It returns to familiar ground, though it is a vector for the strange. Likewise, writing has always been a kind of re-thinking. Re-minding, re-vising, re-hearsing, resurrecting—of living speech, said Socrates, a dead man speaking on through Plato's pen, but speech is not living either. We are all possessed, reciting mnemonics whose burden we've forgotten or never knew. *Thinking* is re-thinking.

But if all language is haunted, if we ourselves have already caught its zombie virus, then literature might seem to be no different from everyday language. Perhaps one difference lies between *is* and *seems*: literature is language that both is and seems to be haunted; everyday language is, but does not seem. (To the objection that some books, too, do not seem to be haunted, the SJVS offers the frankly tautological reply that a book that does not seem to be haunted is not literature. We do not undertake to prove this point.)

Another difference: this haunting is customized. Literature offers a bespoke haunting to those already thronged with ghosts, and a guided tour from the ambiguous safety of an armchair of that land in which all are native, but none feel at home. A creative writing program properly run would be, like the SJVS, a foreign service academy, turning out junior diplomats to look after the welfare of our citizenry abroad. We believe that the purpose of ghosts and literature is not to present the wholly foreign, gibbering in an alien tongue, demanding payment in an unfamiliar currency, but to conduct us over the border, interpret for us, carry the maps, and in short serve as our Virgil as we flatline into the flatland of the page.

Is the goal of literature, then, only to promote a sort of necrotourism? Is there nothing more substantial to be gained through it? Knowledge, for instance, whether of the estate of the dead, or of our own?

We answer that if at the SJVS we stress *vocational* training over pure scholarship, it is because knowledge, understanding, and other specialties of higher education can gain no purchase on our principle subject, death. No Caesar can seize it; we cannot grasp the opening of our hands, nor look upon the closing of our eyes. Yet we have a very near relationship to it. It is even our birthright, and we can learn to comport ourselves fitly toward it, the better to take up our legacy when the time comes. In this project, experience is the only teacher. Literature is vocational training in subsisting *without* knowing—not a bad layman's description of the estate of the dead.

Thinking is re-thinking, so let us go back over some of the ground we have just covered, and examine in more detail the skeletons springing up from its soil.

Language is double and contradictory in its nature: tool of construction and of demolition, world and its undoing. On the one hand, it grounds our reality and makes us masters of it, offering knowledge and the means to knowledge. On the other it subjects us, like everything it names, to a comprehensive wipe and clean-install, erecting a puppet government of ghosts in place of the real world that we have never known. In so far as we dwell in a world shaped by, made of words, we already live in the land of the dead, or rather the undead. Indeed, in so far as we conceive of ourselves, as we do, primarily in words, we too are ghosts.

The layman does not know this. He imagines that his words merely reflect reality, whereas in fact, in so far as we occupy a world of definite subjects and objects, it is granted to us only *by* words, it is only through words that we imagine ourselves to know anything at all, and exactly, if paradoxically, because they are themselves "nothing", chimeras, castles in Spain: ideas are the only things we can understand; thoughts the only things we can think, and knowledge the only thing we can know. It is both our everyday good fortune and our doom to seek truth and find nothing but knowledge.

Generally, knowledge suffices.

However, we encounter a difficulty in speaking of death. We can sense the inadequacy of word to world—no, "I" can't "die", for "I" controverts "die", and vice versa; "I die" is a magnet with two south poles. What other people have said about it comes more readily to mouth than our own thoughts—Walter Shandy downloading the repertoire—because death is what we can't even think, let alone know, not because it is such a mystery (a mystery reserves the possibility of knowing, even if not by us), but because it dismantles the knower. It exists only in the conditional, is possible only in the third person; we may try to imagine the protagonist's experience, but never confuse ourselves with her.

One might therefore say that death is like fiction. Oh, death really happens. But to whom does it happen? Only to other people.

By the same logic, fiction is like death—vicarious, conditional, and unreal.

Reality is unreal too. But literature makes no bones about its make-believe; this is the difference between stories and lies. Thus literature really does mirror the world, just as naïve readers think, but what it reflects is the *unreality* of the world.

Like death, this can be disillusioning. Writing's power to generate fictional worlds is fair circumstantial evidence that our "real" world is just another one. We lose faith in the gold standard of words, that for every "acorn" there is an actual acorn in the vaults, that we can cash in "cash" for cash. And just as "acorn" does not guarantee an acorn, so "I" does not guarantee a self. Writing and reading, we cease to maintain the fiction of ourselves, and we approach the vanishing point of view. Thus when our students ask, "What's the takeaway?" we can only answer, "What isn't?" For literature takes everything away.

You would think that would pose an immediate crisis for knowledge. But does it?

No, because when knowledge discovers its own factitiousness and, learning to scorn itself, seeks to chase away even this knowledge, it finds as a residuum (but a strangely durable one) the seeking itself. This seeking is language still, and though a language in recusal, is quite real enough to support life or at least "life," and impotent to die. In fact the strangest thing about this remainder may be that what the undead lack, and thus what their imperium lacks, as necronauts and readers can attest, is precisely death.

In this residuum, literature, as if through the operation of a double negative, can even seem to restore to us something we never actually had: Fact. For if, avowing its unreality, it slips the tether that binds word to world, withdrawing its mediacy, and offers instead an *im*mediate world of stand-alone words, that might be as close to fact as, living, we can come, since unlike everyday language, it does not lie, but wears its illusiveness like drag—spangled wiggle dress and beard—in a display of essential fakery. It's not a real woman, but then neither is she. And the sequins are real.

It is because sequins, that is words, are as real as anything that the bold necronauts of the SJVS are able on occasion to travel to the land of the dead—an experience that could be compared to that of *Harold and the Purple Crayon,* or to writing a novel: inventing one's way across a void. In fact, this is not just *like* literature, it is literature, which is a language that has run away from home and made itself a squat in the indeterminate. One can live there, after a fashion, or rather dwell in that prolonged undeath that zombies know.

But some writers, some readers go farther. Why? Maybe it's that the desire for something like truth survives the destruction of our faith that words can express it; perhaps we even still believe that language supplies the way to that truth, even if we now see that the way is more tortuous than we thought. Perhaps we seek to patch the breach in our world, or perhaps in a kind of suicidal ecstasy we are instead drawn to pour ourselves out of ourselves through that breach. At the SJVS we find that it is always a mixture of these, and do not demur at taking duplicitous means to our ends—and we do mean ends. (Perhaps all means are duplicitous.) Each student feels in herself both the secret confidence that she, perhaps she alone of all of us, can make herself the master of death, and the lethal allure of the unmasterable. And perhaps the latter impulse only gets so far by cloaking itself in the former.

But should we speak of our*selves* at all, now that we have been drawn to doubt that we are anything but back-formations of the use of the first person? Maybe it's that the zombie horde of language itself, driven to secure its dominion, seeks out every pocket of resistance.

If so, it finds them everywhere; everywhere is practically *made* of the resistance to language—which is strictly nowhere. Perhaps language feels that its very freedom, far from being a display of omnipotence, is proof of its limitations, for it suspects that the world has *weight*, that the word should feel the world dragging behind it. In its vitality it perceives its inability to die, that miracle that happens every day, but not to language, for even dead languages mutter on, complaining that they never really lived.

In any case, whether we desire the truth as the moth desires the flame, longing to kindle even at the cost of going out, or whether, though we know better, we can't help but hold out hope of subjugating it, or whether language itself seeks what it is forbidden by its nature, or for one more reason that encompasses all of these: that it is our vocation—we take the next step. The only one possible, in its acknowledgement of impossibility.

For it is evident that truth can only manifest in the deceitful medium of words as what escapes expression, what can*not* be said. And literature conceives the quixotic, the frankly impossible task of saying the unsayable.

Which is to say that while ordinary fiction is only, enjoyably, undead, we are now approaching death itself, or something we can call by that name exactly because it is the end of names.

Perhaps we thought we had approached it before, saying that death is a fiction, fiction is death. But real death is not fiction any more than it is fact; it is incommensurable with any language in which we speak of it; it is the "force quit" to every Word.

Thus, a writer, despairing of mere fluency, might conceive the futile fantasy of writing, in a language that she does not speak, in an alphabet that she does not recognize, words that because she does not understand them, cannot lie. (And in fact, students at the SJVS are privileged to speak this language in the form of the waxy "mouth objects" they sometimes disgorge during sleep, believed to be words in an obscure language of the dead.)

Or she might conceive herself to be writing for and as another, voiceless and none too human. That *other's* perceptions are the true ones, the ones that are, you might say, on the side of the world rather than on our human side. That *other* is not even afraid of closing her eyes in death, as the writer is, because the world persists and is her. The writer is a stenographer only, and a poor one, whose partisanship makes her fearful and costive, so that what she writes (which is to say transcribes) is a paltry portion of the other's plenitude.

Who is this bosom stranger? We have brushed against her, as children, in the topological and ontological shock of realizing that we cannot watch ourselves sleep; or in fingering our weirdly rubbery lips after an injection of Novocaine at the dentist's; or in the fascination that triptych mirrors hold to this day in affording the opportunity to see oneself *looking away*. The desire to perceive oneself as an other, which would find its extreme expression in a desire to look upon one's own corpse, is thus not a morbid preoccupation of old age but the expression of a very early intuition: I am this stranger.

So now we recognize her: She is the "someone else" we meant when we said, death always happens to someone else. And that someone else is *here*, as, somehow, we are not. This is a truth of our present lives, not only of our future deaths. You could even say that it is *the* truth of life, the truth from which we were exiled when the storyline yanked us into the afterlife we make for ourselves with words.

If the truth of life is that we are already dead, this is not really a paradox. For death is not a departure; it is merely resuming one's place in being. In truth we never left it. Our own bodies come into their own in death, but already enjoy in life the most intimate relations with that material world from which we are barred, relations which they maintain unbroken in death. And so we are, in a manner of speaking, already corpses, haunted by ghosts.

The necrophysicists of the SJVS have produced their own cosmology to account for this conjunction. One of their more speculative theses is that we (that is, our voices) undergo not one but a series of deaths or *de*incarnations, thickening at each instar, until they arrive at solid matter, after which they are generally supposed to thin out again. Thus one aspect under which death as the unsayable appears, or fails to appear, is not absence but something that we would call presence if we were not convinced that it is never actually present to us, that stubborn remainder (though is it right to call a remainder what is, properly speaking, *everything*?) that outlasts the apocalypse that is language—in a word, stuff. At the SJVS, we teach that the entire material world is made up of language in a different state of being; one might equally say that language is made up of *things* in a different state of being. The difference between word and thing is just a matter of degree, or of timing. A person can be understood as a pun or portmanteau made up of words at two different stages of devolution—out of phase, but not antipathetic.

In this image of the circular convergence of opposites (life and death, thing and thought) the age-old fantasy of a legible universe is coupled with the equal and opposite fantasy of a fully thingly, if meaningless, text. And the dream of closing the gap between us and the world, is coupled with the insight that the gap will never close—or that if it will close, if it is already closed, we cannot know it. Indeed, that is what a person is: a part of the world that doesn't know it.

But then isn't literature always in bad faith, futzing around in the antechamber, tucking in its bra strap in ostensible preparation for an encounter that it knows perfectly well it can never have? Isn't it in a way not so much seeking as deferring that encounter, isn't it actually pure procrastination?

Yes, it is. But we must school ourselves to regard procrastination as essential—if I can use that word to designate the essential deferral of essence. Literature seeks. But it does not find. Literature proper *falls short*: the vestibule is its permanent residence. It is K dithering around the castle, the "man from the country" parked at the gates of the law, it is Arthur Gordon Pym carried toward a chasm and Ishmael orbiting the place where the Pequod had been, riding a coffin that is not yet his. The forward momentum of a linear plot may deceive us into projecting a destination, but we will be sucked into the black hole of the final period before we ever get to it.

Stories are in fact *about* not having reached it yet; "it" itself is never the subject of literature. Can we say that, given a form truer to its essence, no book would never end? No, because then we might never give up hope. Or, a subtler error, we would imagine pursuit as a destination in its own right. This is close, very close to true, but wrong, for it robs us of our failure. Our end, seizing us solely and precisely through our failure to seize it.

If we begin writing, and reading, because literature promises something, we keep writing and reading because it doesn't deliver, withdrawing just ahead of our reaching hand, and if some works of literature never stop interesting us, even after we have finished them, we must conclude that they never did deliver. And that this undischarged debt, this possibility preserved for us by impossibility—this failure—is writing's particular attainment.

Even its success. Because it is its way of manifesting the unsayable that it seeks in vain to say.

A proposition: Writers are people who can't write. For if failure is writing's success, then obstruction, inarticulacy, and doubt are a writer's most precious endowments. And this is no doubt the same reason that the SJVS regards stuttering and stammering as signs of an aptitude for mediumship: we yield to possession by the voices of the dead in direct proportion to our *dis*possession of our own.

Thus writing is a form of speech impediment. We are not averse to being taken literally here. Perhaps in childhood some handicap diverted speech from the mouth to the less-traveled path of writing. The stutter of a shy child may become the elective stutter that is writing. The consternation at feeling that your voice is not your own, that you have no authentic voice, may become the *insistence* that your voice is not your own, that no one's is.

But one may also *cultivate* an inability to write. Writing is not natural. Quite the opposite, and so we regard with the utmost suspicion any book commended for its unaffected style. Literature is rarely produced without the psychological equivalent of the "jaw spreading pads, lip holding members, and tongue depressors" that stammerers were counseled to strap on in the innovative 19th century. Writing *is* writer's block.

But there can be no comfort in that thought. We should not, having put aside ordinary egotism, succumb to the subtler hubris of imagining that, if failure can be success, that success at least would be our own, when in truth it would crown with laurels someone who had already left the building, whose career we would no longer care to follow. Failure is the only portion of this speculative venture that we can call our own.

And it must be real failure. We have to try, using all our skill, to grasp what eludes us—just as I have tried, writing this. As if, deaf to my own argument, I imagined that I could overleap the logic that bars me from my goal, like Achilles hurdling a tortoise, or, flipping off Kafka's doorman, hop the turnstiles to the heart of the Law. Of course I couldn't. But my desire to seize answers would not be schooled by the argument that I myself was constructing, and I could not recognize in my frustrations the falling short that is precisely an encounter with death, which is in this room today only because this failed necromancer did not summon it.

The SJVS is not concerned with good writing, since what is good has foreclosed the possibility of exceeding all measures. If writers need a measure, a concept, or a definition of literature, it can only be to show us what we must not write because it is no longer of any uselessness to us.

Or as a ruse, and a lure. Because for those not trained to step out like so many Shackletons across the polar pallor of the page it is well enough to think we know where we are going, for a little way, before the ice of that frozen sea of which Kafka wrote gives way, and we find ourselves in deep water. If the unfamiliar is our end, the familiar is necessarily our means. I said it before: ghosts repeat themselves, repeat themselves. And so, we do not exclude hope of spotting a white whale even in the most landlocked book, for a cold current runs through us all.

This is how we are opened by the very means by which we seek closure. Literature is an empty Trojan Horse, which is not to say that it poses no threat. No. It is the nothing it contains that, boiling out behind your walls, opens the gates.

# 16

# SOME FRAGMENTS

*Maël Renouard*

I have to be done with a text before I can finish it. I'm *done* with it when everything is written. To be done is to set a limit. The limit is the text's frontier, its boundary. Then I can *finish* it: reread it to my heart's content, polish each phrase if I like. To finish is to apply a finish. Finishing can be infinite.

★

The praise that one author sends to another is a courtesy only extended in order to receive praise in return. That's why one so often finds, in the correspondence of great writers, wild accolades addressed to scribblers whose names no one can remember. Critics who take them at their word are grade-school pedants who do not have the slightest notion of the conventions of society.

★

Most people base their judgments on etiquette. Many, nevertheless, can recognize when something is good. Some can speak of it fairly well. Rarer are those who can explain exactly for what reasons something good is good. Even rarer are those who, at the moment of choosing what is good, don't abandon themselves to wild intuitions, unworthy of their understanding. Only a few are capable of making something good. This holds for both wine and literature.

★

There are writers whose lives hinder our recognition of their work, and then there are writers whose books we only read because they managed to make their lives interesting. For certain rigorous readers, those of the second category can also belong to the first.

★

The initial idea has to be simple. Complexity comes soon enough in the execution.

★

To hand in a work early is to waste precious time that could have been used to approach perfection.

★

Books of aphorisms or fragments: no one ever finishes them; that's why they are always such a pleasure to reread.

Bad writers rarely publish aphorisms or fragments: it would be clear at once just how much is wanting in their sense of phrase.

★

People think that writing fragments is stingy, as if it could only come from an impoverished mind, barren and short-winded—as if fragments remained always unfinished, nostalgic for an elusive whole, as if they were the ruins of a text that never took shape. My own experience has been just the opposite: not only is the writing of fragments generous, as each written fragment affords the idea and the inclination for another or for several others—like cells multiplying of their own initiative—but it also creates a heady sensation of completion and closure, like finishing a drawing over the course of an afternoon.

★

Writers are dry; authors are dazzling. Authors write to appear on television, to become celebrities. Writers are incapable of talking about their books. They have put everything they had to say in them. If they had had anything else to say, they would have put it in there. They haven't kept any spare phrases in reserve. As for repeating what they have written, the very thought of it is torture, for they know from the outset that this spoken paraphrase could only fall short of the finish they have given to the text itself.

★

The distribution of roles between the author and the writer establishes itself in each person according to various proportions.

★

Plato intuited the intimate link between writing and death. For him, this was cause for wariness: the written word is dead as a painting or a statue; it cannot respond to our questions anymore. Nevertheless, Plato himself wrote, and his work is rich with a great many enigmas whose key he did not pass on to his successors. This too is one of these enigmas.

★

The writer knows that the author's life gets in the way of reading his text. The author's body interposes itself. To become painfully aware of this interference, simply read a text written by someone you know and try not to hear the sound of his voice.

★

If the author reveals the answer to the enigma, he eviscerates his text. If he says the enigma doesn't have an answer—that it was just a general sense of enigma—he also obliterates the interest of his text. If he steadfastly refuses to give the answer to the enigma, we end up believing he is awkwardly hiding the fact that really there is no answer at all and he is just toying with us.

★

Only a text whose author is dead can ever be praised for its unfathomable depth, its inexhaustible richness. As long as the author is alive, we ascribe to the text the same limits we ascribe to the author. The author's death makes the text infinite.

★

From a living author, we demand clarity. From a dead author, we appreciate obscurity.

★

Flaubert: the more I reread *Sentimental Education*, the more comical I find this often-misunderstood book; the more I reread *Madame Bovary*, the more pornographic I find this book which people were perhaps not entirely wrong to want to censor; the more I try and reread *Salammbô*, the more I find this book, so highly acclaimed during the Second Empire, to be botched.

★

Some time ago, I happened to reopen *Roland Barthes by Roland Barthes*. I had always felt that in making this strangely exasperating book, where on several occasions it is impossible to resist flying into a rage or bursting out laughing, Barthes had lost control of his talent—as if intoxicated by his own power as a writer—and that he had unwisely left himself vulnerable to his detractors. For Burnier and Rambaud's satire published two or three years later, it was an incredible godsend.

But this time I saw it with new eyes. It suddenly became clear to me that this book—a truly strange object from the perspective of the history of publishing—had been a kind of singular premonition, forty years ahead of its time and startlingly precise, of the form that we would one day give to our Facebook profiles. Barthes, for that matter, even speaks of himself in the third person, as was customary in the Facebook posts of a few years ago—an appalling craze, encouraged back then by the website's layout but now thankfully on the decline.

As a book, *Roland Barthes by Roland Barthes* is maddening; as a Facebook profile, it's first rate. Yet another sign that our values have already shifted, imperceptibly.

★

*Hotel books*. I often wonder whether the books left out for travelers in hotel rooms or lobbies have been abandoned there for no particular reason by previous tourists, or whether, on the contrary, they have been scrupulously selected by hotel management according to some mysterious plan. Probably in most cases the truth lies somewhere between these two surmises and, as order goes hand in hand with disorder, abandoned books intermingle with chosen books.

Believing them to have been abandoned encourages you to carry them off again without a scruple; believing them to have been chosen argues against this same impulse and gives it a sudden tinge of sacrilege.

The difference between these two alternatives lives principally in their moral implications—for whether you attribute the presence of these books to chance or secret foresight, at root this hardly changes the fleeting impression they sometimes give you of coming face to face with your destiny. One of these books perched nonchalantly on a sparsely lined shelf might be the one that holds my entire life written out beforehand, allegorically or literally; or the one in which I first encounter the problem to which I must later devote long years of study; or else it might be the book I have been wanting to write and that, here in this distant room, I will discover has already been written by someone else before me, at the other end of the world, without my knowledge.

In the summer of 2012 we spent several days on Cap Corse. I would reserve hotel rooms at the last minute and often they were only available for a short stay. One night, we slept in the village of Ersa, at the peninsula's northern tip, halfway between the eastern and western coasts. The hotel proudly overlooked the sea: from the window, you could make out the Giraglia Lighthouse.

Four or five books—no more—lay on a shelf. The entire room was arranged with a kind of luxurious simplicity. I only remember one of them, published by

Plon at the end of the 1990s and entitled *A King's Son*. The cover was blue. The author was a certain Robert Casanova. There was a black-and-white photograph of him on the back cover: he was an old man with a bony face, emaciated beneath large steel-framed glasses. At least that's how I remember him, falsely perhaps. A short biographical note accompanied the portrait; it said that Robert Casanova was a Corsican professor of literature, born in the 1920s, who had taught for many years in Marseille. Flipping through the book, I understood that it was probably a slightly fictionalized autobiography. Toward the beginning there were long, beautiful descriptions of the crossing between Corsica and the mainland that the narrator regularly made in his youth.

The further I carried on with my fragmentary reading, the more I had the impression of hearing a familiar melody. This feeling reached its peak when I turned to the following page, which I quickly transcribed onto my computer:

> The Mail (as we always called the ship) could just as well pass through the harbor channel here, and if I followed it further out to sea, I might feel that mist which bathed the deck and even drenched it at times in twilight with a streaming evening dew. Of all the hours of the crossing, I loved this one best, when you could still make out the color of the waves alongside the hull without being quite sure whether their sea foam shone in a last trace of day or already glimmered in the lights of the promenade deck.
>
> I would like to think that passing suddenly from the coolness of the deck to the warmth of the curtains and carpets stunned us—that we yielded ourselves to the brilliance of the bronze, to the soft luster of the mahogany panels, but it was only later, on other ships, that I was to experience such luxury; our cabins here were made entirely of steel and no matter how far we found ourselves from the engines their enameled sheet metal still vibrated incessantly.

And on my computer, I went and reread the opening pages of *Ocean Kingdom*, a novel I had started writing in 2003, put aside in 2009 and finally resolved to abandon definitively only a short time earlier in that very year, 2012. In particular, I came across this set of lines that seemed to me strangely reminiscent of what Robert Casanova had written. I recognized in them not only the theme of the indeterminateness of sensations felt at sea, but also a way of dividing up and pacing the phrases—not to mention a certain lyrical use of "if" and a touch of preciousness that comes from slightly too studied a search for musicality (I believe I write differently now). Rarely have I had such a distinct feeling that I could have written someone else's text or that he, reciprocally, could have written mine:

> I used to call by the name of "grace wind" a magnificent and fair breeze lying at an angle between a close reach and a broad reach, leading straight to harbor at a brisk pace without imposing a wearisome series of tacks, never raising a hideous sea, never jostling the boat with the slightest rocking and always blowing under a clear sky.

When the grace wind blew, if I stretched myself out on a side deck—its wood scalding to the touch under a noonday sun—it was only to give my back that sensation of heat mingled with the newly deposited coolness of a fine mist of sea spray, at that precious moment when the moisture has already lost its coolness but tempers still the deck's burning surface.

Of course, I badly wanted to carry off that twin book when we left in the morning. But we were in Corsica. On the Cap, the roads are few and far between and particularly narrow. I barely knew them: it would have been easy to ambush the stranger who had dared make off with the book written by that country's native son.

★

Over the course of the past fifteen years—and others have spoken to me of having had the same experience—I have dreamt on several occasions that I was reading dazzling pages, written in a style I judged perfect. I would not dream that I had written these pages myself; I would attribute them to a friend, to one of my professors or to an author I had studied. One night, I read the magnificent first page of a novel by Gilles Deleuze.

In waking, alas, nothing remained—not a single phrase, not even a word, nor the slightest notion of what it was about. Sometimes, I would realize I was dreaming: I would see myself in the midst of my dream, and I would do all I could to catch a few fragments of these sublime texts before waking. But they always slipped through my fingers, like a powder too fine to hold, a substance from another world that couldn't be borne across from dream to waking without dissolving entirely. At times, I would doubt their existence: I would tell myself that these texts didn't exist even in the dream itself, and that there was nothing more than an illusion of reading, incited by the dream.

But the last time I had this kind of a dream I finally managed to recover a fragment of text.

It was in November 2015, shortly before the Paris attacks. We were spending a few days in Turin, where we had rented a little apartment on Via 20 Settembre, right behind the vast Piazza San Carlo. It was on the top floor of a building that must have been built near the end of the nineteenth or the beginning of the twentieth century. At any rate, it was built around the time of the first electric elevators, for the one that proudly presided at the center of the stairwell here—with its singularly vast dimensions, its sliding gate which you had to close by hand and its ivory buttons that took long moments to transmit the signal you had given them—did not seem to have been installed after the fact, as you so often see in Paris even in the most sumptuous buildings. Rather, the elevator seemed to have been conceived from the very beginning as one of the building's centerpieces, perhaps even as a token of luxury rare at the time. The building's main entrance was monumentally high; in the entrance hall immense golden plates with "ATTORNEY" written in huge letters welcomed and intimidated the visitor. It was a décor straight out of

*The Trial* by Orson Welles. Nothing had changed since the days in which this place had been the very model of luxury and modernity—nothing except that it had lost all trace of both luxury and modernity. During the few days we spent there, the building stayed somber and deserted; not a single contrite citizen caught in the machine of tedious legal proceedings sat in the antechambers waiting for his short-tempered attorney to condescend to give him a hearing.

Since you had to close the sliding gate yourself, you didn't have a precise sense of the moment at which you would rise, a sense which comes in modern elevators precisely from the automatic closing of the folding doors. Two or three times the mechanism took so long to engage that—thinking it was perhaps temporarily out of order and afraid of getting stuck in this antique carcass—we started to reach out to open the gate before thinking better of this, for exactly at that moment the first jolts made themselves felt and it would have been even riskier to interrupt this laborious onset at the wrong moment. Often, as a precaution, we took the stairs. I don't think I'd ever set foot in such an old elevator.

All the way at the top, the studio in which we were staying looked like a museum dedicated to the 1990s: we had the use of a television set dating back to before the introduction of flat screens, with a VCR and a line of VHS cassettes. Aside from the invisible Wifi connection, no equipment seemed to have been added to the room in at least twenty years, as if a cultural heritage officer were scrupulously watching over the place. We realized fairly quickly that each time a tramway passed below a hellish noise shook the room as the whole building trembled.

On the second evening, we had dinner at a trattoria on the Piazza Carlo Alberto. We liked the place and came back again the next evening. But this time it soon became obvious that the weakness I had felt over the course of the afternoon was the early symptom of a nasty infection. My stomach turned at the sight of the pizza's thick, soft crust, almost raw; I could hardly swallow a bite. The next day, I was quite a pitiful walking companion: I came back early and went to bed in the afternoon. I fell into one of those feverish states in which you can no longer distinguish very clearly between night and day, waking and sleeping, dream and reality. When I'm like this I often have dreams that I call hyperrealist—dreams whose plot holds nothing extravagant, in which I'm in the same room, at the same time, and the only thing that I'm dreaming is that I'm awake, that I'm getting up at night to quench my thirst. These hyperrealist dreams are the ones that obliterate in the most disturbing way the frontier between dream and reality: the awareness of dreaming has no reason to recognize the dreams as dreams and therefore lets them easily pass—until the sensation of actual thirst wakes me up and informs me that it was only in dream that I feverishly arose to go pour myself a glass of water in the middle of the night.

Around ten o'clock in the evening I had the urge to reread on my smartphone some sonnets sent to me a few days earlier by G.M., a poet, translator, and scholar who specializes in Voltaire and Nietzsche and the relation between them, on which he wrote his thesis. That night, I dreamt that he had sent me more sonnets, and they had, of course, the aura of texts that exist only in dreams. A moment arrived in which, all while dreaming, I became aware of what was happening: I gathered my mental strength, determined to return to the surface of day with a fragment, with a piece of the perfect text. I knew from experience that it was futile to try to come back with the entire text; I decided to focus immediately on a few lines and hold on as tightly as I could. I hoped that the feverish state in which I found myself, in which the boundary between waking and dreaming was blurred, might finally allow the precious merchandise to pass from one realm to another.

The surfacing began. I could feel the golden text crumbling between my fingers, faster and faster. And yet a little remained, a little still remained. And when I awoke—a miracle—I still had two lines in my head ripped from a sonnet which had otherwise vanished, two lines which I didn't have to jot down on a piece of paper as I kept repeating them to myself and gazing inwardly on them as on a trophy. I had done something I had sought to do for many years. I had proven the existence of texts read in dreams, that the dreaming mind isn't subject to an illusion of reading, but reads real phrases. I had broken through the dream wall.

Here are the two lines:

> Have you known, O Mary, Virgin,
> That night of Hellenic rutting?

> *La connais-tu, Vierge Marie,*
> *Cette nuit des ruts helléniques?*

Certainly, I was very glad to have ripped a fragment of text from the realm of dreams for the first time; but I couldn't conceal from myself a certain disappointment.

First of all, they were short verses, eight-syllable lines and not alexandrines. I like octosyllabic poems: they have something lively about them, enchanted, musical; I find those of Mallarmé very pleasing for example, and when I wrote a pastiche of Mallarmé in 1997 it was a sonnet in octosyllables. Nevertheless, I would have been more impressed with the literary output of my dreams if they had known how to compose alexandrines—beautiful and noble alexandrines, like those of Gérard de Nerval that had evidently inspired my fragment:

> Do you know, Daphne, that song of the ancient days
> At sycamore's foot, or under the white laurel. . .

> *La connais-tu, Daphné, cette ancienne romance,*
> *Au pied du sycomore, ou sous les lauriers blancs...*

Also, my two verses weren't rhymed. Of course, one could suppose that in the totality of the lost sonnet (a form in which the rhymes traditionally interlock with each other) these two verses would have rhymed with others, but I would have liked to have had slightly firmer evidence of the lost poem's ineffable virtuosity. It was plain, for that matter, that the classical rule of the alternation of masculine and feminine rhymes had not been respected.

Finally, it had to be admitted that this strange anticlerical squib wasn't particularly sublime. It was fairly easy to interpret it as an allusion to the sarcastic wit of

Voltaire and Nietzsche, the two thinkers on whom G. was a recognized authority. It wasn't impossible to pad the interpretation a little: this was Dionysus mocking the mother of "the Crucified"; it was the prideful last cry of paganism, before the Great God Pan died and Christianity won out. It was the uproarious laughter of the ancient days, when orgies were mystical and sensuality was innocent. It was the mirth of Julian the Apostate… But none of this was enough to redeem the fragment from its trivial prosody and impoverished imagery.

When a few days later I told G. about this experience of which he had been the protagonist, he made an amused but dubious face and clearly gave me to understand that he too was disappointed by the verses of which I had dreamt he was the author. We were at the Petit Suisse, a café next to the Théâtre de l'Odéon. I did my best to hold forth on the fragment's Voltairean or Nietzschean character, to which I would have thought him more receptive. He said to me with a knowing look: "And what about Turin…" "Turin?" I said, without emphasizing the question mark, as I could feel there was perhaps something here that I couldn't admit being ignorant of. "Turin," he said again, hardly able to believe that I hadn't grasped his allusion. "Yes, Turin…" I said, pretending not to have forgotten that Turin was the town in which Nietzsche had gone insane upon seeing a poor horse whipped by a driver on the Piazza Carlo Alberto.

# 17

# FICTIONAL HABITATION

## Camille de Toledo

★

It is quite surprising for me – if I may say this as an introduction – to question the relation between literature and power, since, as a writer, I tend to prevent myself from thinking of literature in terms of power: be it a quest for power over reality (writing to create one's own rule), or a fiction-writing responding to the fictional power of media stories (writing to create a counter-fiction, or a minor narrative). This is an attitude I might have had at first, as a young writer, but, as years pass by, I tend to be more attracted to the autonomy of fiction, the silent and discrete sphere in which literature happens and the way through which by chance literature finally hits, displaces, or reveals what is our contemporary. This accident by which novels gradually reveal the relation we have to our time, as it can never be the result of a conscious strategy (what did Kafka know about how his work, about how his *kleine Literatur* would actually echo modernity?), has really driven me to be more indifferent to the context, and ignore the lexicon in which the contemporary is presented to us. This growing indifference can be seen as an endeavour to extract myself out of what has been the ironical age – i.e. the never-ending quotation of forms, of references, and a fictional irony coined as "postmodernity". Of course, media, soft powers such as Hollywood, gaming, entertainment, TV series, all part of what I call the story-taylorisation of reality, are like rain. They pour down from whatever cloud there is, a *tech-cloud* pouring rain – fiction – onto us, a cloud under which we do get wet, no matter what shelter or refuge we find. This rain of fictions puts us – and I think any modern writer – in a new position. What was rare – fictional production – has become overall abundant. What was happening on the side or the margins of reality, has become the very heart of a reality in the making. What was separated between fictional instances of enunciation – the authors – and non-fictional instances of enunciation – institutions, scientific authors, the press, the media – is now in the course of fusioning. The *fictional cloud* is everywhere, overshadowing our life experiences, with added emotions, added sensations.

## Into the fictional cloud

I was saying that I would try, as a writer, to ignore the cloud; one reaction to this cloud would normally lead us to consider literature as a shelter, a place where *we don't get wet,* where one can happily disregard the fictional flood, the *fictional cloud.* But we do know that this would be pure illusion, as there are no shelters, as rain drops and finally reaches us. Therefore, writing in the 21st century has become the story of an attempt: trying and failing to escape from the rain of stories that are told and sold and imposed on us without our consent. Walking in this fictional rain, to get wet, and then going back to writing, trying to maintain in one's work a *fictional singularity*, a *decontaminated authorship*, where *influences* would be chosen and not imposed. In order to write this essay, "Fictional habitation", I have been voluntarily submitting myself to the *fictional cloud.* I have been, for that matter, consuming in the past few months quite an amount of TV series. I have consumed enough – series like *Breaking Bad* – to feel that fictional imported experiences have reached a new stage at the beginning of the 21st century. With *Breaking Bad*, we have a perfect symptom, a *turning signifier,* where the subject of the series meets the process of *fictionalisation*, the way *fiction* is becoming a complete habitat. What is really happening in *Breaking Bad* is the fact that the story intends to get you addicted to a plot that tells you a story of addiction. In other words, a professor becomes a major drug dealer, and thus, becomes addicted to making the world addicted. This fictional loop or addictive feedback of the series onto the viewers is the sign that we have reached an age when fiction becomes a chemical habitat, when fiction-writing, and, in this particular case, script-writing, compete with drugs – the chemical habitat which the modern subject has built. An age when the art of narration becomes a chemistry in order to keep us emotionally busy. So, in that new context – fiction as habitat – what can literature do? What kind of habitat is literature proposing, in the general settings of this fictional habitation? Should it surrender to this new *economics of fiction*? As literature has neither sound, nor image, nor music to increase addiction, nor post-production effects to enhance sensations, should it be seen as a handicapped art form? What is the role and the place of literature, when the demand for such addictive forms of fiction is so strong? Should it accept its faith and be considered as a *slow culture*, just as *slow food* responded in the last 20 years to *fast food*? On the contrary, should it try to accelerate? How can we measure the power of addiction of literature and distinguish it from other fictional habitats? Would Proust's *In Search of Lost Time* be the acme, the eternal testimony of a *slow culture*, demanding us to extract ourselves from the acceleration of time, when the "moderns", since Rimbaud, up to the *beat generation*, would represent the stream of acceleration? What is exactly *speed* in literature? The speed of style, of the phrase, of the grammatical pulsation? The speed of the narrative structure? The speed of *flow*, that of Virginia Woolf's *flow of consciousness* or the *flow of life* in Kerouac?

There is indeed a modified fictional exosystem for contemporary scholars and writers in the fact that forms of fictions have diversified considerably; it obliges us to reconsider the position of literature within a general *economics of fiction*. Haven't we all experienced this everyday choice: Should I read or should I play? Should I run a movie or download the last season of such a series? The 1970s were the time when drug addiction was democratised, both through legal and illegal drug consumption. Before that time, drugs – illegal – were for the elite, the artistic elite in the avant-garde movements, searching the *modern* forms through the *Rimbaldian* credo, "le dérèglement des sens". At this very moment – in the 1970s – when drug consumption was democratised, there was coincidentally the fast development of popular cultures, within and beyond literary culture. This first collective *acceleration* in the *economics of fiction* broke the traditional "high" and "low" division of cultures. Then, the 1980s and the 1990s of the last century have been amplifying this move- ment – fictional production and consumption – through tech innovation, making it possible to shift from a collective consumption – concerts, movie, theatres – to individual modes of consumption – walkman, VHS, CD, DVDs, MP3, and personal computers. In the first years of the 21st century, those modes of consumption had synthetised into one global cloud of content, acting the fusion of all *narratives* into only one mode of storage. Drug consumption, during that time, consistently and massively developed, in such a way that it allows, now, a real-time monitoring of our emotions. The *tox* of the 1970s has led to a wave of *detox*, making the oscilla- tion from *tox* to *detox* an everyday choice. We get plugged, then unplugged. During that time, one type of consumption – drug – has merged with the other – fiction. In fact, what we have been witnessing is the fusion of two fields of experience, the *drug experience* and the *fictional experience* into one unique form of habitat. And it is within this cultural merge that one has to rethink the position, the role of literature.

## What is exactly "in decline"?

I will here quote a vision that I have kept in mind, as I was traveling through the different literary scenes of Europe: literature as an old melancholic Western *habitus* – here, the figure of Michel Houellebecq might help readers figure out what I am talking about. A heterosexual male, persuaded that *he is the End,* the *last man,* writ- ing for melancholic European readers, delivering a diagnosis of decline and exhaus- tion. That is the on-going "myth" of the end of the literary culture. This, of course, is a caricature, but there is a point in starting with this percept of decline, the way this percept is supported, I would say, quasi ideologically, by what one could call a "literary endism", as there has been an *art endism* in the 1980s (Arthur Danto) and a *historical endism* in the 1990s (Francis Fukuyama). This *endist* perspective – the end of the book, the end of literature – reveals an actual fact. Literature is no longer alone. It is one form of narrative art among many others. It certainly is not, in our age, the most powerful. What author could argue to have as many *players* – i.e. *readers* – as the 75 million Pokemon Go augmented reality addicts? If we look just a couple of decades ago, in the time of Faulkner or Joyce, there was indeed a domination of literature – on other *narrative art forms* that were, at the time, still in the age of experimentation and collected to a mode of consumption that implied to "go out", in a movie or a theatre. Within this domination of literature – a solitary mode of *consuming fiction* – there was a traditional domination of male subjects. Those entitled to write and publish – those with authority – the *authors*, were massively males; white males, coming out of the best colleges and universities. Thus, the perceived decline of literature, even if it is connected to a real fact – a strong competition between the different *regimes of fictionalities* – is biased. If we look at the narratives coming from subaltern subjects – women, post-colonial, and minor narratives, in other languages than the dominant English, French, German and Spanish domain – the picture is totally different. The perceived decline of literature – from a white educated male perspective – is counterbalanced by a prosperous subaltern subject. Even though literary culture is under hard competition from other forms of fictions, it is expanding, if we take a subaltern perspective. Thus the question, for the 21st century, is not at all that of *the end of literature*; but that of the competition between different *regimes of fictionalities*. How, in this competition, can we qualify the literary habitat? Where does literature's power lie in the 21st century, with regards to other forms of fiction?

## Fictional habitations

I would define the *contemporary* as a relation to our epoch that is mainly the result of "fictional habitations". Be it through entertainment, story-tourism, story-warfare, narrative-gaming, series or augmented reality, the ecosystem of fictions in which we now live is so dense that one can describe it as a "habitat". How does the Cambridge dictionary define it? A "habitat" is "the natural environment in which an animal or a plant usually lives and grows". In other words, *fictional habitations* are now the "natural" environment in which humans and non-humans in the 21st century, live and grow. Indeed, we live in houses of fictions, encapsulated in them. In these houses, we are stimulated. Our minds are filled with fears and plots and dangers and laughters and sadness, with joy and thrill, with excitement and hope, with expectations and despair, thus maintaining, within our homes, a high degree of brain activity. The "habitat" designed by all those layers of fictions is one that is expected to fill us with "more life", "more experience". And certainly, one of the most important assessments of 20th century philosophy is to have understood that modernity is dragged by this search for experience, this quest for intensity. In this "habitat of fictions", we have been wanting to live *more*. We have built this architecture and we have acquired the technical means to encapsulate ourselves into it. We have willingly destroyed silence, *Ruhe,* calm, and traded our Montaigne's interior – the home of our cultivated *libre-arbitre* – to a never-ending home *inquiétude.* The central dilemma identified by Pascal in his time (the choice between "l'ennui" and "le divertissement") has become an everyday mind case: a struggle, if we may put it this way, to maintain a *literary habitat* against the permanent assault of other fictional homes. Within those *moving homes*, there is no more room for boredom, no space and no time for boredom, *l'ennui*. Every bit of our subjective mindspace is occupied.

The term "surround" used to qualify the way sound systems are designed, is an interesting qualifier of our condition. The modern subject, indeed, is *surrounded*, a subject *assiégé*. And within this siege – fictions surrounding us – what is literature doing? Is it simply one layer among others, a layer of *low intensity* when gaming and TV series would offer a layer of *high intensity*? The irony of this "house of fictions" – literally, our *home cinemas* – is that, in the name of a higher intensity – more life – we have opened our doors, our windows, to a flux of narrations that are exhausting us. Fiction stimulates us, it is intended to thrill us. Thus, our minds are over solicited. The very "habitat" that was conceived, in the first place, to offer a shelter, a home, is now filled with content that is putting us at stake, throwing us in the inside-outside flow of fiction. We are at home, and yet, besieged, surrounded by a never-ending possibility to enhance our experience, to augment our reality with imported narratives. The production, through fiction consumption, of extra adrenalin, extra endorphin – which we get also, by drug consumption – creates psychological dependencies of a new kind. It influences our physiological capacity to reach satisfaction – pleasure – without these "added lives", these "added experiences". Beyond the pleasure that we have as entertained viewers, readers, a neuronal chemistry happens, in connection with the fictions that we consume.

## The search for "more life"

The individual quest of modern subjects – the search for more life, more experience – is being, in a way, captured and used to fulfil the objectives of the entertainment industry. We know that it is a well-established strategy of the advertising industry: occupying the mind. But this strategy, which also massively expanded in the 1960s (*The Mad Men* series is another good example where "addiction" is a central theme, in a fictional loop involving the *authors* of the story, the *actors* and the *viewers*) was eventually extended to the narrative industry. What is *now* the goal of a film, a game, a TV series but to *occupy our minds*?

This new economics of fiction – which grammar is addiction – is changing the way we inhabit our "homes". The competition to capture our attention has grown fiercer, and our Montaigne's interiors have been gradually destroyed. If the "experience" of life has grown in intensity, our "habitat" has become *too* intense. We are tired. Our subjectivities are exhausted, just like our ecosystems, our natural resources. The objectivity – the outer world – and the subjectivity – the inner self – have reached an equal state of exhaustion, obliging us to unplug, to invent new tactics to resist to further intoxication, to find *defictionalised* habitats. *Jaws*, by Steven Spielberg, was quite visionary in that perspective, as it was showing, on a metaphorical level, the predatory face of fiction. *Jaws* – the images of those jaws – eating our flesh and brain. One could consider that this was the "latent meaning" hidden behind the manifest content of the film. In the age of television, when children, in the 1980s – my childhood – were spending more and more time on ads and TV series, when image was becoming the first element in the process of civilisation – the *Bildung*, the imitation, the process of fictionalisation becoming the structuring common ground in the process of civilisation – the film *Jaws* was telling us something that was beyond the movie, that was the devouring of our minds by the story. We were being eaten, and we didn't know it. We believed we were choosing our narratives – designing our fictional habitats – but we were actually consumed by them. It was not only taking our time, structuring our feelings, taking our attention. It was influencing our deep neuronal chemistry; an influence that should be measured in order to understand, now, from a neuronal perspective, what fiction is doing to us, and as a consequence, how it is influencing the way we inhabit the world.

## The neuronal perspective

The first serious progress in the understanding of the human brain – and the electro-chemical reactions in the neuronal network – were made at the end of the 19th century, at a time when Freud was studying the effects of cocaine and hypnosis. In less than two centuries, one has shifted from an *anatomic perspective* – first half of the 19th century – to a *psychological one* – second half of the 19th century and first half of the 20th century – to an *electro-chemical perspective* – second half of the century, up to now. The result of this shift is a crucial change in the apprehension of the mind. What we would call "emotion" – what we still call "emotions" in the traditional approach to our fictional consumptions – is now observed, and has been for more than 40 years, in the scientific field, as electrical impulses causing chemical reactions in our neuronal cortex. The fact is that what we name "emotions" and "feelings" remains, as perceptions, as experience. There is no replacement of psychological understanding by the electro-chemical one, but an accumulation of these two forms of knowledge. As we know from the everlasting conflict between *science* and *poetry* – the truth of the law *vs* the truth of the heart, those changes in the modes of investigation into our brains do not make literature obsolete. Stendhal and his triangulation of desire, or Zweig and his understanding of the mechanics of sentiment, are not condemned by the neuronal approach. On the contrary, what we witness is the accumulation of *all cultures* – the scientific and the literary – an accumulation of knowledges that extends, in a dialectical way, how we perceive reality. Yet, this shift from the psychological to the neuronal paradigm modifies what we are now, as writers. What powers do we have, as writers, in the general economics of fiction, when neuroscience becomes the ally of fictional producers?

The progress in neuroscience tends to aggravate the asymmetry of powers through which fiction is conceived, produced, distributed and consumed.

At the time of Balzac up to the generation of Zweig, fiction writers were princes in the field of sentiment – i. e., in the making of stories that eventually went to structure our emotions. But, as the mechanisms of the human brain have been apprehended through this electro-chemical perspective, writers have become the "poors" – *les prolétaires* – the ones who have only the tools of subjective experience, when the industry – the entertainment complex – has the financial means to integrate the latest scientific data in order to shape fiction. Since the functioning of the mind is understood in this electro-chemical perspective, the industry – those who have an interest in keeping us busy in our fictional habitats – can design their stories with greater technicity. This could be described as a passage from an age of *story-tellers* to an age of *story-taylorism*: a fictional industry in which the specialisation – the taylorisation – is comparable to that of other industries. Monitoring of audiences, testing of stories, matching plot with targeted audiences, integrating product and story into one unique story-selling continuum. The merging of the two legacies of the 1970s – that of drug and fictional consumption – is being re-appropriated by those who have the means to integrate the scientific updates. In this "neuronal turn", the two legacies that were the keys to emancipation – free access to culture, the exploration of desire and imagination through fiction writing, viewing and reading, the freeing of the individual from social conventions through drug consumption – have been used by the entertainment industry, in order to control, saturate and occupy the minds of individuals.

## Towards a general economics of addiction

In the age of Netflix, are we, as writers, just obsolete craftspeople, writing in the discrete literary sphere, keeping the "fiction of the author" alive, and through this fiction, sustaining the heroic fiction of an individual, in a time where the neuronal paradigm allows the industry to understand us, our collectives, our receptions, as electro-chemical reactions, and our social bodies – audiences – as particular "targets" that can be easily reached? To put it in a more prospective way: in order to contribute to *new ways of thinking literature in the 21st century*, shouldn't our contribution – "Fictional habitations" – be understood as an appeal to comparative literature departments, as well as cultural studies departments, and neuroscience departments, to open up to new fields of investigation. This is how we could try to fix our new *axes de recherche:*

A new approach to literature in the 21st century should be *neuronal*, in the sense that the fiction produced by literature must be observed in a *general economics of fiction*, along with other forms of *fictional habitats*, be it series, video games, augmented realities, films, in a continuum linking the producers of fiction to the consumers of fiction. This new approach, by looking at fiction as a biopolitical tool, would thus lead to describe literature as just a part – an important part as it was, traditionally, the mother of all fictions – of a fictional economy. In that wider comparative perspective, the differences between literatures – according to genders, languages, cultures – would no longer be central to our research, but the different *regimes of fictionality*.

The comparison of the different *regimes of fictionality* would have to apply to the multiple stages of this economics of fiction: 1. Production: how is a *regime of fictionality* organised? What kind of *story-taylorism* does it rely on? What level of specialisation is requested to produce the story? How are the electro-chemical reactions to the story integrated in the production process? Is the act of creation monitored by marketing?

What kind of fictional addiction – what intensity – is aimed at by producers? 2. Distribution: how is the distribution organised in the different *regimes of fictionality*? Are the viewers or readers or gamers monitored as the consumption, the *downloading* happens? Is the private data of the audience – the fictional consumer – collected through the distribution process? And as a consequence, what is the ethics of such and such *regime of fictionality* with regards to private life? What are the financial means dedicated to support a "story", and thus, through which power structure are the different *regimes of fictionality* imposed upon us? 3. Consumption: with the help of neuroscience, can we measure the effects the different *regimes of fictionality* have on consumers? What kind of fictional addiction does each different *regime* achieve?

How can we conceive and structure a *neuronal approach* to fiction in order to describe those different *regimes of fictionality*, and what would be the criteria to measure the intensity of fictional addiction? What would be the ways to qualify and typologise a fictional habitat? Time spent per story, per regime of fictionality? Estimated subjective dependence? Scientific measures of the brain activity of the consumer during fictional consumption? Localisation of the brain activity and level of chemical interactions – on serotonin, endorphin, adrenaline? Comparison of the intensity of brain activity during a fictional experience?

Opening those fields of research, those "territories", implies though that we face, in new terms, the myth that has established, until today, "the neutrality of fiction".

## Bovary and the myth of fictional neutrality

One of the key concept in neuroscience is "neuronal plasticity". This plasticity refers to the neuronal network's endless changes under the impulse of electric stimulations. The multiple forms taken by this chemical plasticity have been brought down to a group of neuronal "behaviours": 1. Habituation. The neuronal complex, through the repetition of a stimulus, gets used to a pattern. 2. Sensibilisation. The way the mind perceives variations in the outer context, and how, after a period of habituation, it can reach a state of desensitivation. 3. The potentialisation. The way the neuronal network responds to a stimulation in terms of projection. 4. Depression: the "gripping" of neuronal reaction, caused by the decline of our neuronal capacity to overcome new stimulations. This "neuroplasticity" depends on the connections between the context – electric impulses produced by a change in the surrounding context of the subject – and the neuronal network. Thus, if fiction means building, around us, different forms of "fictional habitats" – each with their intensity – if "fiction" is a key element of our life experience – our added lives, our added emotions – at the beginning of the 21st century, how can we measure the level of mind activity – the electro-chemical reactions – caused by this "more" life? And in that perspective, how can we distinguish, in terms of electro-chemical effects, the impact of the different *regimes of fictionality*?

Asking those questions – studying what fictions do to us, to our "fictional habitats" – obliges us to relaunch the interpretation of one of the founding myth of fictional neutrality.

We all have in mind how literature has acquired its autonomy – has been "emancipated" from the real – and by the way, how we, as writers, have acquired our "rights to fiction". It was in the time when Flaubert published *Madame Bovary*. The novel of Flaubert was put on trial as being immoral. One of the arguments of the prosecutors – who wanted to ban the book – was that direct speech, rendered into indirect form by the author, meant that the author was guilty for thinking what the character was thinking. Those "immoral thoughts" of Madame Bovary were that of Flaubert, they argued, because of this formal innovation: making direct speech indirect. Despite the arguments of the prosecutors, the novel was authorised, though being held as a highly immoral piece of prose. This was the starting point, in modern writing, of those "rights to fiction", that can always be invoked – and are indeed – each time a novelist is accused for what he has written.

This founding legal case of *Madame Bovary* has been the basis for a legal principle, whereby "fiction" cannot be put on trial for what the "consumers" of this fiction have done as a consequence of this consumption. The impressive extension of "fictional productions" in the 20th century would not have been possible without those "rights", and this legally acknowledged "neutrality". The Bovary case serves, since the 19th century, as a shield of protection, against all legal attacks. And one can easily imagine what kind of world we would live in if the producers of fiction would be held responsible for what the readers, the viewers, or the gamers do, as a consequence of getting into their stories. We would witness a quick process of "de-fictionalisation" of the world, and see the rapid collapse of the entertainment industry. It would not be the "State" as in China or as in other authoritarian regimes restricting, from the top, the "rights to fiction", but the consumers themselves, through a series of trials, who would bring fictional producers to bankruptcy.

And yet, what happens to this shield of protection – the rights to fiction – when we enter a new stage in the fictionalisation of the real, when the *electro-chemical* action of fiction onto our minds becomes the object of scientific investigation?

In a *speculative mode*, we could ask: what if a killer follows André Breton's *acte gratuit* by going into the street to shoot people at random? What if the young mass murderers of the Columbine massacre leave a testimony where they ask themselves who will be the director of the film shooting their "story"? What if the drone pilots in the American army have psychological troubles in distinguishing the *real* and the *game* on which they are trained to target their enemies? What if Anders Beiring Breivik, the extreme-right Norwegian killer, responsible of the Utoya shooting, says in his trial that he has exercised himself by playing with such and such video game?

Are we still *in the age of Bovary,* in which the authors and the producers of fiction should not be held responsible for any of their formal innovation? Shouldn't we accept the fact that both our knowledge has changed – neuroscience – and the intensity of exposure to fiction has increased in such a way that we should rewrite the *Bovary case,* reconsider the "myth" of the neutrality of fiction? The interactions, in the 21st century, are so numerous, between the *stories* that we are brought to consume and *actions* that we are exposed to. Shouldn't we rethink the Bovary settlement with new eyes? And yet, how? How could we guarantee the freedom of creation, of writing, in this *economics of fiction* where fiction *is the real*?

The *fictional habitation* approach is certainly not advocating to change the legal principle of the Bovary case; a change that would lead to the end of fictional freedom, and consequently, of our right to write stories.

What it proposes, on the contrary, is to extend the legal rights to fiction – to democratise those rights so as to enable every individual, every entity, to fictionalise his or her life, to change his or her biography, to transform his or her gender, to modify the facts that establishes his or her identity, to access to the status of a *creative writer* – and yet to face, in a new way, as scholars, as scientists, as writers, as fiction producers, the role of fiction. The Bovary case, in that context, is extremely interesting to re-open for interpretation.

What is Flaubert's *Bovary* story about? A woman reads love stories and is being intoxicated by her readings to the point when she finally betrays her husband and commits an *adultère*. The core of the story is that of a woman *intoxicated* by her readings. In the structure of the novel – and this is one of the reason why *Bovary* is so crucial to our modern understanding of fiction – literature appears as an *addictive fictional agent,* causing a change in the behaviour of the main character. The *toxicity* of fiction, and in other words, the conditioning of our life, through fictional habitats, is at the heart of Flaubert's novel. In that context, how does Madame Bovary die? Again: intoxicated. The life and death of Madame Bovary are the prefiguration of our *regime of fictionality,* the regime in which we now live, when *fictions do become a life and death matter,* where *fiction is life and death in the making.* What is at the basis of the novel is the gradual contamination of the real (the real life of Madame Bovary) by fiction consumption (her readings). The paradox of the legal settlement that eventually put an end to the Bovary case is that, despite the plot that is, from beginning to end, a story of intoxication, from fiction into the "real", it concluded, on the contrary, that the novel and the author could not be found guilty; thus, developing the arguments for the "neutrality of fiction" for the years to come. Instead of the interdependence – between life and fiction – the judges acted the independence of the two domains.

It is this paradoxical settlement that our approach to fiction in the 21st century would propose to aggravate: on one side, reinforcing the rights to fiction, as being a right to life itself, a right to rewrite one's life, from beginning to end, from gender, to identity, to culture, to nationality, in order to allow a general migration of oneself, of one's meaning – a constituent right of all humans following the famous quote of Flaubert, *Madame Bovary, c'est moi,* understood as a right of each individual to fantasise one's life, to the extent that this fantasy supersedes reality – and, on the other side, the full right to investigate, scientifically, into the interactions between fictional experiences and our neuronal reactions.

Berlin, September 2016

# 18

# ACT TWO

## Why I am a destiny

*Vanessa Place*

The literary is not literature. Literature can be dismissed straightaway as a matter of opinion, whereas the literary is a matter of style. From Stein to Rimbaud, Kafka to Hurston, Proust to Perec, the literary is redolent of style ages before it's churned to literature. And I am concerned only with style, for style is what changes thought. Thought will follow style, by way of explanation; the coupling of thought and opinion, hearts and minds, is what makes literary history—brought to you by its three obligatory apparitions: the Ghosts of Literature Past, Literature Present, and Literature Yet to Come. Like the spirits in the story, they can appear over the course of a long weekend, but sponge the writing from the stone as nourishment, not negation. Like Dickens's specters, they rise to be rewritten.

Simply put, the literary is a feast and feat of production; literature once again can be kicked curbside as a matter of consumption, though this will soon prove to be today's taxonomical puzzle. If we are to reconsider the literary, and all art *is*, like philosophy, the happiness of constant remastication, then we must first recognize that the literary is how writing writes itself: stupidly forward, like cartoon characters building a bridge across the abyss they are in the middle of crossing. Don't look down, and if you do, don't worry too much. Do chew the scenery during the abyssal plunge. Remember that death is just the beginning. In other words, I'm very much looking forward to my post-mortem collection.

So it is from this plummy post-mortem position that I can properly decide what is properly literary in the time we are properly in. As a matter of structure, we are no longer a dialectical society, not in the manner of either the moderns, with their frozen snowglobes of meaning, sealed with something like a good student's bad kiss, or the postmoderns, with their particulate significances more loosely enveloped, designed to litter the carpet and confetti the lap, both depending on perpetual play within a set cosmos. These are mere games of abstraction and figuralism, *i.e.*, patterns and their obligatory recognition. We are now more quantum than that, and it is understood that in our trilectical today, the third term is always context. Context is always contingent and somewhat chaotic: what makes context will come up later. The point now is that contingency must also be written, in current retrospect.

But this seems to be a paradox: how to write forward while being written behind, and this calls for Echo, the smarter of the couple, and who knows, maybe the cuter as well. The one who was a figure with no face, a sound with no voice, an *I* with no self, Echo persisted in playing it forward while feeding it back, and this is where I, artist and advocate, come in, along with the difficulty of producing what is consumed and consuming what is produced, for I am the very image of Echo, writing in art and law, two practices that are famous for their contrapuntal play of making and taking and shifting POVs, or a point of voice that passes for a view, in which space and time have themselves become categorical, and there's no categorical difference between them. I said difficulty, but that's wrong. Production is terribly easy—literature depends on writing rolling out with industrial regularity, awarding prizes and granting grants on those who meet industry standards. Is there any book more boring than a Booker, any poet more perfumed than the Guggenheimed? No, the hard part is refusing to produce while casting a style.

I use to be an artist. Use this or that or the other, borrowed or poached, or, in pinch, handmade. But it makes no difference whether I make or take, thing as writing or writing as thing, for the point is that it is all citation as style, a call for and of authority which is the failure of authority's call. If I were to refer, I would call to confess my lack of real authorship, relying on the honk of the *guillemet* to signal that I mean something, *et hoc genus omne*. If I refuse to refer, letting my plagiarisms rip, that is understood as a refusal, and to refuse a call is always understood as another kind of answer, *et id genus omne*. Of course, the smarter money is on providing the reference, as the reference reflexively confers authority. This is why literature keeps one hand broken, set in the ideological cast of its ideological histories. This is the difference between style and temperament: temperament mocks style, but hedges its bets. Didi-Huberman said that Godard lays claim to the right to cite and the right of citation: this is his cinematic success. But I say the failure of authority's call is even better, and I'm right again, because my success lies in this failure: I confound the right to cite with the fact of being cited. Prisons and workhouses, all one and the same, for I am speaking now of law and art as common language: in each, we rely on our precedents, which promise the continuity of history. This promise is, naturally, meant to be broken, as history sees fit, which is another example of the tolling of something. As lawyer and artist, I purposefully move language through various spaces, to varying effects. Like sound, language makes and breaks walls, and, like speech, is often sounded.

Law is the speech that acts foremost, that is to say, constitutionally, as *I* and *them*, and presents as the sound of *us*. This is different from the speech act, though the speech act is perhaps its most elegant symptom. Rather, this is more stupidly and brilliantly reductive: law is language (pace Constitution), language is law (pace Lacan). It sets itself in place, as do I, through its own say-so. Law is the regulation of language that is law. The First Amendment of the United States Constitution is a great feint in this regard: by proscribing the prohibition of speech, the law enacts a double *jeu* that demonstrates its constituent elements: it writes itself into being, *i.e.*, as authority, by stating what may not be, what is unauthorized. What is il-legal. Il-legal has much in common with il-literate as both invoke a kind of illegibility, a failure to read or be rightly read. And while those opposed to the appellation "illegal alien" say that the law cannot make a human illegal, this precisely misses the point: the law is the device or process by which we agree to recognize ourselves and formalize the others. American slaves were prohibited from literacy by way of keeping them both illiterate and illegible. *Sans papiers ou avec papiers*, it's written all over your face. Recognition, *i.e.*, cognition as predicate, like trauma, is set retroactively in fact.

Law is thus not a fiction but a kind of primary censorship, for its speech are acts and its acts enactments, of the most efficacious, that is to say, the best and flattest speech. All gesture is symbolic, as murder in the name of some higher authority (god, country, tribe, clan, any biggish group with standardized outfits) is a cleaner murder than murder that passes as simple predilection. Death is better if broadly, if not rightly, cited. And also censorial in the sense of what may not be said, or said as yet, remembering that citation is a call for and as authority. In times of tragedy, *i.e.*, death to scale, it is quite popular to say: "words fail." You understand this well, those of you in the business of typing thought, but it's not chez Wittgenstein, for to complain about the failure of language in language is happy enough. Words fail because they are not to scale: the attacks of September 11, 2001 came from the sky. Heaven-sent, as long as one remembers that god is not always pleased, and not always for the home team. But they were attacks of a theistic order, *i.e.,* cinematic attacks, meant to impress the omniscient with a *ciel*-eye's view. The attacks of November 13, 2015 came from the ground, made by men and women, meant to impress other men and women, that is to say shot on iPhones, like Godard's latest. The attacks of tomorrow, yesterday's today, will come from inside the house, and will be caught on the next generation of wearables, like smartwatches and (who knows?) tracker wedding rings. That is to say, they will be as meaningful and meaningless as any given marriage or other civil war, meant to impress only our selves.

When we say that "words fail," what we mean is that they evaporate, that they transmit temporarily something we would imprint permanent. What we ask is that words last. Like laws are imagined to be. Like the last words of executed American inmates, which are, in the state of Texas, recorded for someone's posterity. But in the last words of the condemned, and the state of Texas is in the business of producing the condemned, first by way of the text or death sentences encoded in the law, second in their reception, in the individual sentence of death, and third, in the context, in the death sentences uttered by the dying. In these last words, and we should be so lucky as to have a heads up on our own, there is not the failure of language, but imagination. The prisoners lapse into genres: loving, forgiving, sorrowing, righteous, reformed, religious, virtuous, vengeful. At best the damned shut up, refusing to answer the call to call themselves into being while dying—although how many of us would forgo swanning our innocence or experience, or would not otherwise feel the need to cast our *I* out in a final bon mot of transcendence that is the closest we might get to enlightenment. The best legal speech is just this, murder sweetened with its own propriety, but the best ethical speech may be unsounded.

To put this in the language of art, is it that Gertrude Stein was a great literary artist in 1911 or that she became a great literary artist in 1911 sometime in the late 1970s when enough literary critics recognized Stein as a great literary artist in 1911? Here, words don't fail, they flutter, waiting to be caught by a wind. Literature being the university gate they get stuck in. For the artist thinks il-legally, il-legibly, imagining the landscape within which we people our portraits. All literary portraits are self-portraits, a fact Stein well knew, just as she knew something about composition and the preaching of history. So let's assume that the *I* that is currently *us* is subject to the same pressures and perspectives as our other contemporary selves, and let's note how our contemporary selves are increasingly papped, like mother's milk, into and through our various material and domestic intermediaries, such as online platforms and supplementary texts. And that there is also via these very platforms a counter demand for an essential self, a kernel of an *I* that can be caught in a tiny box suitable for snap judgments or shots. And that this essential self, not without coincidence, is cast in the forms that the law likes best to recognize: race, sex, and national origin. And that perhaps we can begin to see that to rethink the literary today is to rethink notions of what makes the self that writes itself forward.

For the law, like the literary, is always a contingency that passes for a permanence. I have said that I am Echo, by which I mean to say that I make language move in space, but also that my language is often recycled, not mine, or at least not mine by way of instigation, though we all know—do we?—that construction doesn't just construct itself, and that the symbolic order of what passes through, in, and by, me needs my voice in order to be heard through, in, and by, me. Which also means you. The law is understood as an affirmative progressive recycling, that is how the law of *stare decisis* works: a decision is announced, "published," officially, and the rule kernelled in that decision is taken as a nugget of prospective authority, to be applied and amplified or, as the judicial chamber changes, muted (mooted) in subsequent decisions which will in turn serve as further precedent. Precedent, from *pracedentum*, a thing or person that goes before another, precedent itself a partial definition of *example*, taken from the old French *essemple*, and described in the late fourteenth century (here I echo selectively, for Echo is always selective, some online entomological dictionary) as a model, *either good or bad*, an *object of imitation, punishment as a warning*. Model, finally, being a mannequin, taken from *manikin*, or *little man*, but resonant of something missing, another dummy. I've followed a thread that leads, not to the Minotaur, with his promise of a hero's death, but Ariadne, who helps in and out, and who then goes on to be wined and dined by the best of the lesser, and to come to some immortality herself, if only in the spinning of the tale.

For the ear is a labyrinth, and things often get lost within. Easily entered, always open—with juries, we say that you can't unring a bell, and once rung, you have three choices: pretend you did not hear, implying there is nothing to see—ear will translate to eye, somewhat easily; seize the clapper, *i.e.*, object, and ask that the sound be stricken, going for censorial muteness; or ring more bells. This roughly corresponds to the feat of the literary: don't write about the past, do write rules for writing about the present, and always write blindly, for the yet to come.

Text and context: Anonymous takes down thousands of Islamic State Twitter feeds and someone on Facebook writes, "Okay, so censorship IS sometimes acceptable." Eliding the censorial nature of social media itself, both in its official guidelines of what may/not be said, and in its deeper truth which is that it is an advertising platform that depends upon constant and accurate reportage of the sobjectified self, that amalgam of subject|object that we all are, as we are all widgets of semiotic significance sold by the head (heads, like last words, come in sets, suitable for posting) to advertisers. We collaborate in this because it is convenient and because we now see speech as never free, but always situated conditionally: we write what we know to write and what we know to like. If you say something, see something. For if you don't say something, you will not be seen as seeing. As it turns out, we are the police.

Text: While film always moves materially forward even as it flashes back, the literary has heretofore been in a state of contextual stasis, bound by the page and book. A stasis mirrored in the law, likewise framed in a book. The literary is also a state of stasis as described by Agamben: what the ancient Greeks called a state of civil war, or war within the family, in which one was obligated to publicly state one's allegiance. Stasis is etymologically linked to standing, as in up, for, and on one's ground. Stasis is linked to standstill as well as sedition, it is the basis for *state* as in condition, and is the root of all articulation, and may signal disease, as in the unnatural stoppage of normal bodily function. Inertia is abnormal, although homeostasis is the state of the well-ordered hive. Like *collaboration*, *hive mind* is now thought of as a positive, and is actively sought on social media, which imagines itself sufficiently free thinking whilst everywhere in cookies, if not chains. The story of Hansel and Gretel, which is another tale of being left in the wood, abandoned by father, teaches us what happens to those who follow those who follow breadcrumbs, and the value of well-timed stupidity. The relationship between hive and mob, and the abandonment of the law of the father, are imprecisely considered as yet, as are the connections between the platform's marketing of the widget of the singular snowflake self and the literary as singular expression of singularity communally cast—it's practically medieval in its topologies. The current aesthetic condemnation of individuality as an artifact of Enlightenment rationalism, as well as rationalism itself, in favor of the elevation of affect, imagined somehow purged of sentimentality by way of demonstrably good intent, but still crammed in a sack of skin, simply plays to the dumb luck and self-satisfactions of the well-meaning. It wants to be assigned reading. And there is nothing literary about being someone's homework. There is a midcentury joke, background provided upon request, in which one widget says to another, *Et si demain on tuait tous les juifs et tous les coiffeurs?* And the other widget responds, *Oui, mais pourquoi les coiffeurs?*

Civil war is a time for killing, and, famously, killing kin. The aim of the literary as I practice it also involves premeditated murder. Murder because it is only after the war is won and all the laws rewritten that any death is deemed either legit or il-, and premeditated because what will become illegal in retrospect is never so at the moment the trigger is pulled. The literary is a style, and styles are always suspect until they've been turned into just another voice. I don't have a voice, that thing earnestly cultivated by youth, pimped by profs, prized by paying periodicals, greased by the status quo with the "literature." I have a style. One must kill the hairdressers because they set the style.

Context: Form and content in the contemporary literary are not merely the bits between shape and sonnet or what makes "a novel" meaning some saggy argument about what news is fit to print, but also the contextual (*con* here tucks in gestation, like the ancients believed she-bears licked their cubs into being), which is also to say material, form of the content. We must think through our context as the third element in our trilectic: object, receiver, context. Each of these things is more or less contingent, and that's the thing constant, the accounting for the fact that all art is contingent, or site-specific, including the literary. This contingency means an awareness of materiality in the medieval way, which is to say, in the way of under-standing the teleological implications of medium and material as well as message. The literary can no longer ignore the insistent materiality, the thingness, of its rep-resentation as part of the aboutness it represents. Just as a printed photograph must today be considered sculpturally because photographs may also be kept digitally in 2D, today's literary is not necessarily made manifest via page or book, its type is no longer set, and scroll is to skim, not a skin. To put text on social media as a material medium is a way of expressing something of ephemerality and simultaneity, the immorality of any moment, to set something in print on paper says something of sculpture and sequence, the immortality of the already dead. The representation of representation: is this text-object a piece of paper, bound with its kin, is it a social media engagement, and of what point is its chosen platform, is it streaming online or stuck in a space? How thick is the book of it, how long its reading? When, and for that matter, where? Who, as it turns out, was there? Was the language received with the soft grunts of satisfaction of a thing said just so, just in the way one ought say it, with all the lowing pleasures of a host pressed to the fat tongue of the faith-ful, or was it spat back out because the flavor was unrecognizable and the texture, unpleasant. Con-text, as Echo knows, can be a killjoy: always remember the law only appears to work in proscription, *i.e.*, tell me what not to do and I'll be certain what's been done.

I have said before that all poetry is is that which is not *not* poetry. We must rethink all the values that have heretofore shoveled the literary, with its glitter of hot blood and ambition into the thick compost of literature. Let literature bake. The literary should ruthlessly spew, contradicting what has passed for beauty as philoso-phy contradicts its prior truths, abolishing all beneficent gesture in favor of better malediction, knowing that even the boldest lie does not fail to tell a truth. The literary should not partake intentionally of morality, for morality as intentionality is simply a lack of real faith. Refuse to see good, that's my first literary thought. If it's moral, it's already infused with the rot of its own immorality. Absolutely refuse to speak pap is my second, for the speaking of pap is what they regularly prize, so they can rope you into writing mere literature. In other words, what we do not need is yet another B=i=b=l=e, another odious tribute to our kind. For my third thought is to forego all forms of fundamentalism save my own. I asked a famous artist what the crime of American art was. She said art is not a crime, which was very disappointing. If art cannot be a crime, then it's nothing but another kind of copper. In other words, what could happen if there was a law that mandated that no other law was to be obeyed? Who then would be the criminal?

There's the fat paradox of the First Amendment, the necessary silencing of someone, echoed in the killing of killers that characterizes certain punishment as Capital. Observe that the last words of the condemned are also when somebody finally shut that guy up, after first making him talk. Confession and condemnation, there's a narrative loop for you—as La Fontaine noted, every lamb has its wolf. For myself, I won't say what is to be gained from any of my work, and this has made people demand that I stop, or walk out on the work, or otherwise call for my silence. That's my secret: the punishment is also the crime.

I use to be an artist. I don't speak as myself very often, though I very much echo the speech around me. Speaking and spoken through like the ventriloquist's dummy, the one that serves, typically, as the desublimated side of the couple, the nihilistic mouthpiece, the defense attorney par excellence, the one who represents you in all your lies and guises, besotted and beguiling, the one to whom you confess in your hottest breath that you are not as it were your very best, and who does not care about the stick on your hands and the crust about your mouth because this is the point, isn't it, for the muck of the real is a sublime reality, and that there is no thought that is not literary and we will write ourselves into being no matter what, which is only to say that the matter of fact is a matter of capital adjudication. You really should get a lawyer.

There's nothing beautiful about it, except the refusal to speak, by which I mean the refusal of all interpretation. Let it be, dumbly, in the face of dumb accusation, including that of literature. *Nitimur in veitum*, let the figs fall where they may. If you must glean some sort of possibility in this, it will be found to the degree that words fail. They will fail you, and they will fail me. But their failure is tied to their degree of retinality, of legibility. If we instead go forth blindly, madly, like Oedipus at the end, then we will at least have seen what we were looking at. Repeat, after me. I've taken Nietzsche's title because we are now *echo homo*, and I am Echo supreme, my amoral truths gleaned from our collective moralities, as sick as we want and need me to be, and this is pleasurable to each of us, in the way of free expression, freely served and served freely. This is why *I* am a destiny.

# CONCLUSION

## Ay yay! The cry of literature

*Hélène Cixous*

### Ever-Rêve

Ever, that's her name, still here, always here at the end, as soon as there is end, abyss, she will always have been here, Ever, literature, at the end, bringing about, coming about, giving place and taking place – for re-beginnings when the life-vessel sinks, when in 12 verses and 10 minutes *all is lost*, we are lost, it's done, quick, clear off, next scene! In two words as the crew of HMS Shakespeare do, cast into the Tempest.

> BOATSWAIN – Lay her a-hold, a-hold! Set her two courses! Off to sea …
> Lay her off!
> *[Enter Mariners, wet]*
> MARINERS – All lost! To prayers! All lost! Pray her off!
> *[Exeunt Mariners]*
> BOATSWAIN – What, must our mouths be cold?
> GONZALO – The King and Prince at prayers! Let's assist them,
> For our case is theirs.
>
> *Shakespeare,* The Tempest, *I.1*

*Die Welt ist fort/ich muss dich tragen*, that's her this *ich* who says these words *I must carry you* in Paul Celan's language, that do not console, that save and carry, *all lost*, and one second later we awake a survivor – at the shore of an island Shakespeare never had to name because it's literature herself, lifeboat-theatre, emergency-theatre. *Enter Prospero and his quill-staff. Enter Prospero (in his magic cloak, with a staff) and Miranda*: writing and reading.

*Prosopopoeia*:
– I, literature, lift the world with eight words.

*Fort, die Welt, ist, ich, dich, tragen, muss.* With eight words a tiny poem, a few syllables, a world-group.

With the word *Los* last spring I sowed a book. *Los* is a grain of life and of death. *Los* is a word full of words and spirits. *Los!* Give up! Go on!

Warning! Have we lost the world? Quickly, to prayers, raise the call, launch two words overboard, stretch literature over the abyss.

- *All lost!*
- *To prayers!*
- *"He war!"*
- Two words!

Do you remember? How Jacques Derrida knew that for literature (whom I call *la Toute-Puissance autre*, the other-All-Powerfulness) *two words* suffice to manifest her power. Two words to saturate the abyss. But what words! Nutshell-words, genius-words, dried grains of sleeping time, that a bit of humidity will suffice to resuscitate. There he was, one New Year's day, immobile at the edge Nothingness' muzzle, leaning towards the entrance to Hades, two steps from Dante, returned in the exhausted features of Celan. And there was psalm and resurrection, and meagre immortal roses, kept since the beginning of time, to be transmitted from poet to poet.

There must be hundreds of murmuring volumes on the soul's shelves in order to obtain, by condensation and displacement, quintessential words. Inexhaustible alchemy. In 1907, Sophocles' atoms return to be sprinkled on one of Proust's notebooks.

How does this transmigration function?

At the beginning of the beginning, there was the first note of our pain, and it rose from the diaphragm to the sky, like this:

> AY YAY!
>> The universal word, the Call. My cats also cry Ayai! Myayai! Roland's horn as well.
>> And thereafter comes the Response.

Nine times in the last nine years I have been at the last end of the world. Death attacks. Each time the end was coming, with its slow lightning, the end lasts, rises to collect the living like an inexorable tide. During the slow tempest first one cries [*crie*] adieu! then one writes [*écrit*] verse 59.

The terrible Thursday of the cruelest month when fate tore my father from me from one instant to the next and at the same time half my heart, and the entire ground of the earth, when there were only wounds and fright, I was ten years old, the February violets were about to bloom, I clutched onto a notebook and literature began its work caulking, plugging up the abyss. I was annihilated, all is lost save the word and its polyphoenix polyphony. In my father's garden that Thursday the gods were performing *The Phoenix and the Turtle*.

*Néant*, nothingness, *née en*, born in, dead in, *néant*, nothingness! Néant! In French what a fabulous word, a volley of words fell on the flowerbeds and the mimosas, everything was cries and music, I cried out: Live on! I cried: Papa! Papa! When a life is taken from us, you will have noticed, we cry out the name of the cherished being, we conjure it, we repeat it, in place of all language's words we name and call, we endlessly ring out: Grandma! Papa!, we stab the void with the unique name, we stitch it back, we multiply it infinitely to change the nothingness into music, we hammer the anvil of silence with our chanted names: Eurydice! Mama!, we cry out for the being who does not respond, we shout in her place: calling chases away the silence, contradicts death's sentence. We call the being who is not here, we hold her back by the fringes of her being, by the letters of her name, we pray we cry Dieu! We cryate God! Dieu, Nothingness. And the prayer answers itself. The cryayer [*la crière*]. The invention of literature, like the invention of drawing by Butades or the invention of writing, is an urgent defense against pillaging, massacre, forgetting. Against our own auto-immunity. Our terrible system of adaptation, our awful submission to reality. Our detestable spiritual economy. You are dead. I snatch the world from you. I take your breath away. It's over. Done for. Finished. Says mortality.

– No! I cry.

I do not capitulate. What is finished is not finished. What is done and cannot be undone can be undone. I take the word Néant, Nothingness, and I turn it into its opposite. Né en: born in.

– Ah! you'll say to me, you, my English-speaking friend, but my language does not know this word Néant. My English knows only Nothingness. It's not the same.

– But you, musicians of the English language, have the extraordinary luck of the word *Done*. And it occurs to me that the great English symphony must have begun with a blow of *done*. From Beowulf to John Donne, from Shakespeare to Joyce, the memory of English rings with those claps of *Glas* whose infinite litters of meaning in French Derrida brought to our ears. *Done*.

*Done*, in English, the past participle of the verb *to do*: it's done. Its: it's done, it's finished. *I am done*, I am cooked. Done-for. Finished. *Done* is the toll, the mental alarm bell in *Macbeth*. *What is done is done, it cannot be undone*. Can one undo what has been done, can one un-die, un-finish, un-undo? No. But yes. Literature can redo life with ashes. Other-life. Life afterlife. Lived-on life.

*Done* dies and resuscitates in *Donne's done*. Just as the *fichu* in Walter Benjamin's dream is transformed by the magic of French into *fichu*, and as the scarf changes into a poem, and subsequently a dream of immortality for Derrida.

In the land of lost lands where texts germinate – where all is lost, all is *fichu*, a *fichu* is also *fichu* otherwise, a text is always *fichu*, more or less, and better or worse, in this land where ruins dream, dreaming of the one who will revive them – lives the genie of metamorphosis.

Literature is that sublime Divinity of Transformation that always busies itself around the same tombs, the same secrets. Anatole's tomb (Mallarmé). Morella's tomb (Poe). Julien Sorel's head's tomb. Cleopatra's tomb. Benjamin's tomb-*fichu* (Derrida).

I was dreaming.

- Rise up, dead ones, and live otherwise!
- Dead ones, rise and tell me of your death.

No sooner had I sent out this call on this paper than I heard Agamemnon's voice giving Ulysses this poignant testimony (In my dream, Agamemnon spoke Greek in English):

> As I lay dying I tried to raise my hands, the woman with the dog's eyes would not close my eyes as I descended into Hades.

How we forget! I had forgotten the voice choked with sobs of the first of returning ghosts, I had forgotten the pain-stricken ancestor of the semi-dead who cannot reach the other side, deprived as they are of the attributes of a death well executed. I had forgotten that before Addie Bundren (the agonist, the soul of *As I Lay Dying*, whose posthumous thoughts are collected by Faulkner) and before disconsolate Hamlet, there was the first king of literature's assassinated tribe. A grain of *The Odyssey* (Book XI) germinated in the genus of the American South. In Addie Bundren moans king Agamemnon, king of kings. And this is the fate of the badly dead, those with botched deaths: they wander in a perpetual dying, and their voices which depict their pain wait on Lethe's quay for a poetic ear to receive their plea: Forget me not! Add not a death to my elimination, write my name, do not erase me from the book! You who live later on, imagine the unimaginable, write my story, be the guardians and the cantors of the breath that was stolen from me. Signed: Agamemnon, Hamlet father, Hamlet son, Addie Bundren, J. Derrida.

It has been 40 years since I heard the bitter words of Addie, since I completely forgot the wild cries of the black geese that are words for her. And now the bitter cries tear the green cloth of forgetting, shatter the window that stops me hearing the last words of my dying father.

> And then he died. He did not know he was dead. I would lie by him in the dark, hearing the dark land talking of God's love and His beauty and His sin; hearing the dark voicelessness in which the words are the deeds, and the other words that are not deeds, that are just the gaps in peoples' lacks, coming down like the cries of the geese out of the wild darkness in the old terrible nights, fumbling at the deeds like orphans to whom are pointed out in a crowd two faces and told, That is your father, your mother.

We go dying through life.

Sometimes we die-already long before death. Sometimes we can't finish dying. One dies of more than one death. Sometimes, like Elpenor, one suffers terribly for having lost life without having been able to gain death. One dies.

One lives without life. That's life.

- Mother I shall pierce your heart with killer words, says the furious son.
- Come, come! says the queen
- What did you say? says the son, unhappy to be so

- Go, go. Enough! Enough! says the queen, Gertrude
- Mother, don't go leaving! Come back, father!

What a mystery! There are chains of words that possess a power of resurrection. Words, perhaps names, that have gentle fingers, that touch the eyelids of our soul, with lips closed, and in an instant we awake, just in time to answer the telephone and hear my father, my mother, my beloved, feeling abandoned, erased.

- List list o list! Hallo! It's me! Can you hear me? I am thy father's spirit. I am the wandering voice of your mother. Have you paper? Write quickly! I have 59 things to tell you.
- 59, you say?

## 59

Fifty-nine, verses, strophes, chapters. Fifty-nine is the number of chapters of the voices of *As I Lay Dying*. Derrida's *Circonfession* is exhaled in 59 periods. While his mother is dying. In 59 verses all the horror of the world is poured by the *Ghost* into Hamlet junior's ear. *Brief let me be. Adieu, adieu, Hamlet. Remember me* (Act I, Sc. 5).

Fifty-nine? One day I will write a book with 59 pages and on the 59th page, I will say .............................................................................................

Is 59 literature's secret number? Fifty-nine has the charm of an apocalyptic password. From Homer to Joyce to Mandelstam perhaps, from Dante to Beckett, have the poets been whispering the password to each other? Is this recurrence a cipher or a marvelous coincidence?

It occurs to me that what enchants me in literature is the insistence, the returning, across centuries and languages, of a heart's beating, that death does not extinguish, we die and our wonder will survive, and it's this melody, this rhythm, this sentence of 59 words that makes us feel there is something stronger than nothingness, less vain than our short life; and what enchants us is that this rhythm of our fear, of our suffering, this stubbornness of the dead to write and describe their death, is always exactly the same; it is life's heartbeat that means to live, that hears itself living and that, passing from one author's work to the next, transmits, perpetuates, never dies forever.

Everything is destroyed. Nothing is lost. I thought you were dead, my love, but you had only passed into another life.

> Death be not proud
> When one man dies, one chapter
> is not torn out of the book, but
> translated into a better language.

All those that I love, that I love to hear writing, had their experience of revelation. We die. We lose our life. We find it again. What joy, what lightheartedness! This is what happened to Montaigne, Rousseau, Dostoyevsky, Blanchot. They were all pardoned at the last minute.

I must ask Stendhal, I think to myself, I must ask Melville, Celan, what 59 means to them. This permanence makes us dizzy as the 13th subjugates Nerval by returning, always the same, always the first.

In the meantime I ask my son, the mathematician: — What is 59?

And he immediately responds: — 59? It's— ...

If I had the time, I'd tell you how 59 is *one less*, one less than 60, and what is hidden in the fateful difference between these numbers.

But I don't have time to tell you here. Because the law says: this meditation must not last more than 60 minutes.

## "To air out the chamber of the crime"

this is my *dream*. Says Proust. I say.

Like Proust, and Sophocles or Milton before him, we also want to air out the chamber of the crime.

There is a bedroom for the crime. In the first chapter, which serves as the first scene, there will always have been a bedroom and a crime. A bedroom for the crime. A haunted bedroom. Suffocating. Too many curtains, too many wardrobes filled with too many black velvet coats with pink satin linings, too many armchairs with outstretched arms and curved backs. Where literature germinates.

Whether I consider the bed, the body, of starets Zosima, the hieromonk saint with the stinking corpse, or Ligeia's body, whether I lean over my disappeared son's bed or the lovers' bed where Beaudelaire is rotting, whether it is Stephen Dedalus' mother who is passing on or the dying, the dead woman of *l'Arrêt de Mort*, or whether I meditate on love in Père Goriot's miserable bedroom, the heart of the scene is always the same, the same kernel of the poem and it's always *the bedroom* where Socrates lives his death like a long monologue of Hamlet. Literature plays its scene, happens, behind thought, on the other side, which is accessed by going through a broken window partially patched with a piece of green percale.

Here we are in the bedroom of the crime. It is always in the same place, on the floor above the family dining room. The same passions, the same thoughts fill it, the same furies. – You killed me. I'll kill you! says the subject. "You are imbeciles!" cries young Santeuil.

Enter: *Anger*! It whispers the unbearable Truths with great liberty. In the literature-world, it is sovereign, whereas in the ordinary world it is disciplined and punished. At last, it cries, here I can spew forth my lavas and pour out my insults. It is I who causes. It is I who dares. I am the furious captain of literature. I attack. I direct the *Iliad*. I destroy everything. And I am adored. All human beings, beginning with my readers, are joyously thankful to me. I incarnate their death drives. To kill one's father, one's mother, the king, the child: this is my work and my mission. I am there to represent massacres and frights that jostle each other in the enclosure of dreams. I make you enjoy your throat-slittings. I am the irritated spirit of Yaweh in the Bible, it is I who suggests to Job his imprecations, to

Moses his bad thoughts. What a pleasure when Jean Santeuil yells "You are two imbeciles" at Monsieur and Madame in the middle of a literary luncheon. When Stendhal is transported by bloody hatreds, it's my doing. Father Cherubin and Aunt Seraphie, you'll be strung up. I am responsible for all the madnesses that Shakespeare sings. I am the cold and sadistic law that condemns young Kafka, each time he desires. Dostoevsky's storms, that's me. Don Quixote's 120 furies, very me. Literature storms, it falls upon us, sword lunging, it offers us *hostipitality*, baptized by Derrida. It is a problem. *Problema*. Shield. It protects and attacks. Here, in the psychic space where Anger is acknowledged, where Polyphemus roars, and Ulysses laughs at the mutilations he inflicts, where everything is Ahab's dark overintensity and hate for the white whale, the roars pierce the air. Here we are frightful. In the chamber of the crime, we are cruel, we are wounded animals, urges to tear to pieces tear us to pieces. No use denying it. A young girl of 19 surrounded by poets is the only one to *take Polyphemus's side*. Her name: Mary Shelley. Never has so much hatred and anger coursed through the universe as in Frankenstein's book. No! Rage is entirely me!, grumbles Heathcliff.

Yes, literature sings the praises of Anger, it celebrates the divine fury to which it owes its existence.

Anger is always the same unchained chained, whether it yells in Greek or Russian, it is always the same tragedy. The only difference is the furnishings of the chamber, depending on whether the crime with punishment, the double suffering, takes place at Wuthering Heights or on the Pequod or in a squalid Piter slum.

Cruelty, the dirty attribute proper to mankind, needs a chamber, a furnished scene. It wants to *take place*. It wants to be seen. See itself commit the worst. "There's everything in Piter," writes Dostoevsky to himself in his notebooks. But it lacks father and mother." This is because literature is "parricide," as the Greeks say, using this word for the mother-killers as well.

Literature is Anger transformed into hymn, rhythms, sentences.

Because we insist on safeguarding this force that is stronger than we are, on finding pleasure in our suffering. On keeping what we have lost. On tasting the bitter-herbs-taste of the kiss drying on our separated lips. On accusing ourselves of having "given" death to our mother.

My mother no longer speaks. One week ago she said two words. "*Trop vieux*," she muttered. Too old. Unsexed. Too late. The last poem. Naturally untranslatable. Now I pose my lips on her temple hollow like the beginning of a tomb and with these miserable remains of provisions I still have enough to write.

We have withdrawn to *Grenzland*, the border-zone between solitude and life in common, *dieses Grenzland Zwischen Einsamkeit und Gemeinschaft* (Kafka's *Journal*, 25 October 1921). That is where I write. I am beneath the volcano. And yet I tremble with cold.

I would put a chapter here on the border and its words, on the border between languages' borders, on the untranslatables that congregate at the edges of languages, on the word *frontière* in French, on the guardian word at the border of nothingness

if I had the time

It was in September 2001. The world was collapsing. *Die Welt war fort.* You will remember that autumn and those ruins. So Derrida invoked the great *fichu* destinies of Benjamin and Adorno. He already felt he himself was *fichu*, that he was *fichu* and *fichu*, and *fichu* like an arrow in the flesh of a dream of literature. Dreaming of going further than philosophy. And already hearing the bell toll for him. Done! Done! Ding! Done! Ah! Donne! Ay! Literature is lived in haste, o the fear of dying before finishing one's knell, Proust's fear and Kafka's fear, quickly, before being Done. Better yet: *s'envoyer vivre mort*: send oneself off to live dead.

Is he calling me? wonders the pupil Abraham, in the class where the master calls the name of the one elected for the crown of laurels, and the master, we know this with Celan, the master is death. Or is it another Abraham, the one Kafka conceives for himself alone, a certain Abraham Kafka, a shopkeeper, a literary salesman.

Is it for me that the bell tolls?

Death's letter has departed. It is searching for its addressee. And my life is a flight, too long according to some, not long enough for others, in the face of the letter. While fleeing I have just the time to write *The Verdict. Das Urteil.* The whole time I am running before the letter, before the Law, I contest the address – is it me?, I don't recognize myself with that homonymic name, get lost!, and during the entire time of *my* destinerrance, because it is I who misleads the message and not the message that gets lost, I know and do not want to know I do not know and fear knowing, that in the end I will avow what I deny, that I am the *thee* for whom the bell tolls, then I will throw myself from the bridge from which long ago I threw – crime against life – the most beautiful love letters in the world. I confess that I had wanted to be done with literature as a prophet of posthumous life, but in the end I hear it murmur in my ear: why send a messenger to ask if my monotonous cry is really addressed to you? You very well know that *each time* I toll, at each unique end, as you would say, it is you who is struck, each knell celebrates you, you die in each death. Towards the end you fall more and more frequently.

One by one your friends descend to Hades, your I's are more numerous on the other side than on this side.

You just did a pastiche of my *meditation XVII*: I wrote the first version for you. Already in 1624 you were destined to receive in your turn the mission of translating the cry of the knell in one of Babel's languages.

On Thursday, 12 February 1948, the first messenger to bring news of the death of the emperor of life, my father, was my brother Fips the dog, he shouted in dog language: Dead! Dead! Daddy dead! And I translated his 59 cries into French, first text, 1948.

It was in December 1964 in Manhattan, I had just died in Central Park, I had just read Celan's poems, and in the night abandoned by the world, I blindly scribbled the first orders dictated by literature. I no longer knew who I was, god no longer had a name. The squirrels were half dead. Their mouths full of earth they said *Nevermore*. Perhaps they were *ravensquirrels*. I no longer remember in which language I wrote. Perhaps it was English. Yet when Derrida – the first, the only and the last reader – received these shreds from Manhattan, they were soiled in French.

Maybe they were translated or converted during the crossing of the Acheron. Or else in German? In any case no one could say exactly who had written it. The author is legion, as they say; I was one of them, that's all.

- Doubt not that the bell tolls for you
- Doubt that it is for you, you there, yes you, to sign this thing. This creature.

As soon as we "write," i.e. "believe we are writing," we are gripped with doubt, we lose ourselves, we are no longer ourselves, *ourselves we do not owe*, we are as criminals who are always innocent of their actions. We regain our lost spirits sitting broken before a sea of sheets of paper, of insane confessions, of traces of tears and of blood, we cast an eye over this chaos (we have only one eye left, like Henri van Blarenberghe), over this carnage – and we are stupefied. Did I cause that? No! And we are overcome with a mixture of horror and admiration. Which proves that it isn't me, but another me, a crazy person, a nightmare, a terrible mare who gallops us in we-know-not-where at night, who are unleashed in the back of my mind, in the sleeping house, and who have committed such violent and naked extravagances, without reserve, without shame. – Henri!, cries the mother in me! Henri! What have you done! (and all the poet criminals, upon awaking, are called Henri, or Charles, or Edgar, it's all the same, it's me, it's you, *it is thee*).

You killed your mother, you were dreaming, it's just the same thing, in the other reality you killed the herd of rams with white hooves, unfortunate Ajax, Julien, you killed a great deer and your father, you killed Monique, Augustine, it's the same thing and it's worse, you killed the awful Chérubin and the cruel Séraphie, Henry, Henry.

Henri? you say. What a name! Yes indeed! Enough to make you laugh, no? Oh! The things that are in a name! No, it is not only Stephen Dedalus who says that, in the first place it was Juliet Capulet. Capulet, what a name! And Montague as well! What a poem a name can be! And what damage it can do! What a name does with what simmers in the secret of its letters: this is the part of literature that makes us laugh in the middle of the tragedy.

Two years, ten years, at five o'clock, as soon as I leave my kingdom my lightless deathless kingdom, as soon as the daylight reality ravens toll the somber world's knell, pull me from the rowboat of my bed, throw me into the emptiness whose chasm's mouth has no lips, while repeating their three-note tune *Nevermore* – because death has never finished biting our ears, its hunger cannot be appeased – right away already literature *responds*. It defies the end, it slips away evasively, like Eve my mother evading the end with her 102 years in her back-pack. Here is how it happens: take the day Derrida's last mobile phone breaks down,

J.D.'s words: We'll find another way of phoning each other dead

Eve's words, hailing me from the quay where her last boat is waiting: – Hélène! What are we doing? – We're sleeping, Eve, I say, and we're dreaming. Eve ève rêve.

*Literature:*

– Since 13 January, I have passed the months between the edges of life and death in that zone, that band – moor – border, that land where one would so like to go if one was sure the voyager could return, that cage where one is sometimes condemned to stay, too long, not long enough. One can visit as a foreigner between life and death in a halted time. During this visit, I read.

Literature is the antideath telephone, the magic that establishes the link between us, the orphaned Orpheuses, and our apparently invisible, but present, cherished beings, but present "according to the wish we express." For the miracle of resurrection to happen, we only have to move our fingers towards the magic rectangular parallelepiped we call by the equally magic name of *Book*.

*The sound that comes from close up very far*

> And we are like the character in the fairy-tale to whom a sorceress, on his uttering the wish, makes appear with supernatural clearness his beloved mother or his betrothed in the act of turning over a book, of shedding tears, of gathering flowers, quite close to the spectator and yet ever so remote (...). We need only, so that the miracle may be accomplished, apply our lips to the magic orifice and invoke the Vigilant Virgins to whose voices we listen every day (...), and who are our Guardian Angels in the dizzy realm of darkness whose portals they so jealously keep; the All Powerful by whose intervention the absent rise up at our side, (...): the Danaides of the invisible who constantly empty, fill, transmit urns of sound; (...) the forever irritated servants of the Mystery, the shadowy priestesses of the Invisible, the Damsels of the telephone!

### First we cry into the Theolephone

- Hello!
- Cry!
- Ay Ay!
- Ai!

The cry [*cri*] is torn from me! Who tears the cry from me? I take it back!

Then we write [*écrit*]: we translate into the ultrasilence of writing the sharp and short cries of reality. Literature is for yelling at length, pushing cries all the way to music. The right to literature or the right to cries that reality or the community forbid us. In the family, we are full of muffled cries, we are muzzled wolves, we are sitting at the table where our parents are playing cards, why don't you play cards, my son, why do you refuse to be a *Mitspieler*

> My parents were playing cards, I sat there alone, totally alien; my father said that I ought to play or at least watch the game; I talked myself out somehow. What was the meaning of this refusal repeated so many times since childhood? What was offered to me in this invitation to play was community, social life, to a certain extent; I could have brought myself to participate as I was asked, not well, but ably enough; the games would probably not even have bored me too much – yet I refused.

CLAUDIUS – How is it that the clouds still hang on you? Come, play with us.
GERTRUDE – Good Hamlet, cast thy nightly colour off, come, watch the game.
And let thine eye look like a friend on Denmark.
Do not for ever with thy veiled lids
Seek for thy noble father in the dust.
Thou know'st 'tis common – all that lives must die,
Passing through nature to eternity.

Why do you sit there, my son, like a stranger perturbing the family circle?

CLAUDIUS – How is it that the clouds still hang on you?
[…]
GERTRUDE – Good Hamlet, cast thy nighted colour off,
Come play with us
And let thine eye look like a friend on Denmark.
Do not for ever with thy vailed lids
Seek for thy noble father in the dust:
Thou know'st 'tis common; all that lives must die,
Passing through nature to eternity.
HAMLET
Ay, madam, it is common.
QUEEN GERTRUDE
If it be,
Why seems it so particular with thee?

Why don't you play cards with us, Hamlet?

We cannot respond, we would vomit a volcano's worth of cries of pain and horror. We write [*écrit*] in our journal. We read the book of ourselves.

As soon as I pass to the other side, as soon as I find myself in the literature-world, I hear (as at dawn the birds sharing the acoustic territory – have you heard the orchestra of the indecisive hour? They pass the cry between them), I hear literature's *mole cry*.

One of my treasures is a fabulous text that sits in my hand like a magic parrot: it is a nanotragedy. It contains the keys to all of Proust's work. His *Filial Feelings of a Parricide* [*Sentiments filiaux d'un parricide*]. This brief and terrible text appeared in 1907 in the *Figaro* newspaper and summarizes, in the guise of a tabloid news item, all of Sophocles and all of Dostoevsky.

(Add here The Mystery of the *Fait Divers*. This is an idiomatic French expression with no equivalent. A wily character, a vice one enjoys in the morning with a coffee. Secret necrophiliacs.)

I take the keys; they open all the texts. We have all killed and cried, and we have felt in us the flames of the tender and burning filial sentiments of a parricide.

With what did Proust feed the book he was dreaming of? With cries, cries, and cries. He recognized literature by the *melody* of its lamentation. He loved

Chateaubriand for the monotony of his owl's cry. Madame de Sévigné for her mother hen letters with Niobe's cackle.

Ajax, Aias, do you remember, the one of whom Sophocles, his most avid confident, says that his name is his destiny,

> Aiai! Who ever would have thought my name
> Would chime so well with my condition!
> Time for me to cry 'aiai' again,
> And a third time, so deep are my troubles.

Alas! what terrible powers, in a secret name, Aiai, Ayas! the unfortunate one whose unfortunate name calls him to respond: – It's me, the misfortunate one, named for misfortune, I was designated by fate to be the example of the unjust destiny attributed to men,

Sophocles sings the troubled non–justice that inspires destiny.

It's as if at his birth, his death knell had rung out, Ayas! Ayas!

And what if the son of Telamon had received another name? What if Romeo was not named Montague?

Aïas, Alas, Ajax is us, no, you don't remember, Alas! we have forgotten Ajax: he cries, he vomits blood and sound for hundreds of verses, he complains to himself that his unequalled velour has been forgotten. He who is, since Achilles has died, the first, the greatest, the strongest of heroes, his hostile and mediocre companions treat him as a second, dishonor him, prefer the wily Ulysses to him, castrate him. From then on he will be eternally debased and forgotten. And we forget him as well, 3,000 years later, we diminish him. He cries his name of pain. Ay Ay! Who remembers Ajax? The man disappears. The pain remains. We register his bitterness. Thereafter his cries are heard and reignited by Samson Agonistes, by Dostoevsky, by Proust. Cries travel. The boat makes land on many foreign coasts. And immediately the hymn to desire and regret is raised. You have killed me. How short life will have been. Forget me not. Two months! You have already forgotten me! Death goes fast! Not only did I suffer from dying of death. But in addition I suffer death by dying of forgetfulness.

I had found in Proust's notebook 59 an injunction that I took for myself: "Find the rhythm of the double suffering."

That's it, to write one's threne. One woe for me, one woe for you. I suffer from your suffering at my suffering. *Je me souffre à toi.*

Now, the other day, sitting next to the electric bed that has replaced her normal bed and where my mother lived this year laid out like in a boat rented from the hunter Gracchus, which makes an electronic wheeze at regular intervals, I read – having received a telepathic injunction – I reread *Ajax*. That was when I had the surprise of discovering the *double suffering*.

> TECMESSA – If given a choice, which would you prefer?
> To grieve your friends, but feel pleasure yourself,

Or to share the pain together with them?
CHORUS – The double pain seems the greater evil.

The idea that the first groan against the double suffering was formulated and questioned in 440 BC transports me. I add that this double suffering makes its way to me by the electric force of writing-that-keeps, by all-powerful literature our mother memory-forgetting, and transmits the music of the cry by architelephony.

What?! A thought that wounded a soul 2,500 years ago is here, perceptibly, in my office, in my papers, in my little memory? Yes. No. However yes. It was about this evil, circling around it, that J.D. wrote *Psychoanalysis Searches the States of its Soul.* He had not reread *Ajax.* And yet Ajax's complaints screamed in him all night long, by means of some secret telepathy.

Ajax is no longer. Nothing more. Today 2014, Jacques Derrida is no longer J.D. 2000. You are no longer H.C. 2000, says my son. There is not a single atom of your body that was part of your body 15 years ago. And yet there is a you that is you. Memory is stronger than death. Materially inscribed in you there lives a text that was telegraphed to you from Homer c/o Sophocles. Memory outlives the matter in which it is inscribed. Atoms of the genius of Shakespeare and of Freud, musics, you are here, and mixed with Philia's and Aletheia's purring, you surround me in an organization that we do not know how to think today...

## Neither night nor day

Between − 440 and + 2014

It is 4 a.m. With my cats at my side, I place my hand on this paper and Montaigne's tower, my beloved mother, awakes, takes off the veil covering her, and comes forward naked, out of abolition. And almost simultaneously here I am under the cold wind that lashes the terrace of Elsinore and pulls tears from my eyes, not of sadness but of black anger: the literary dream that I just received from my brother still rants its cries of murder in the stairwell. Every one of me is in a state of alert, we are an army and we are all the characters in the cast of *Ajax*, including the chorus, including the herd of lambs and cows frightened by the knife, and in me Tecmessa, love herself, speaks to the madman with the calculated tenderness, the analyst's patience that a sister invents to halt the death that screams in her brother, and that the young Proust (he is 35) dispenses on Henri van Blarenberghe, unfortunate mother-killing Oedipus, his double, his shemblable. From Sophocles to Shakespeare, from Ulysses to Macbeth, from Samson to Dimitri Karamazov, from Rousseau to Ingeborg Bachmann,

lady Literature archives our suicides and our bereavements, grants asylum to our dark forces, to the violences that cannot be avowed except to her. Literature acquits us. She is mobilized against the death penalty. And for good reason: literature is the scene and the confidante of our assassinations, the patience for our madnesses. The proof that we passionately love the life that we curse and to which we address cries of horror by return mail.

Every poet discovers rather quickly the severe, rigorous truth that there is salvation in loss, happiness in misfortune. My impotence is the secret of my power, whispers to me the most powerful of thinkers. My weakness and my faults are the secrets of my genius. Writing is this gift of discovering a deep link between two ideas that embrace and overturn each other. It is when I am most poorly, when I have no strength or ideas in my head, when I can barely be distinguished from the dead, senses Proust, when I no longer play on the ruins, ruin that I am, that this I whom I sometimes recognize living inside me perceives it, just as it is often in the autumn, when there are no more flowers or leaves, that one can smell the deepest harmonies in the landscape. The moment this I in me says he is annihilated, he escapes. Ah! Old Chateaubriand, our likeness, our neighbour, how he fills Proust with emotion: he too slips away when he is annihilated.

What an ecstatic horror to discover that one can live without life. Wonderful horror of life that desires still when it desires no more.

> Pain does not kill in an instant, since he did not die upon seeing his assassinated mother before him, since he did not die upon hearing his dying mother say to him like the princess Andrée in Tolstoi 'Henri what have you done with me! What have you done to me!'

Each time it is the same wrenching surprise: we do not die from pain. Your death which kills me engenders a me in me that is stronger than I am. Your whole bedroom kills me (as a Marcel de Sévigné would say), but I remain attached to it, clutching your ghost that flees me and that I retain, I want to burn there, I want to taste the pain all the way to ashes, I want it to end, I want to escape, the pain cries and bites me to the marrow, I cry Stop! No! Continue! It wasn't I who cried Stop!, it was the little fearful I inside me, the one that Marcel calls the Instinct of Conservation as he is being tortured by the sentence '*Mademoiselle Albertine est partie*' [Mademoiselle Albertine is gone]. Ah! that Instinct, that troll, that imp, that animal guided by the need to live, simply to live, simply to remain, to be: it is he who searches at full speed for the first tranquilizers to apply to my burns. And these first-aid bandages are sheets of paper on which bewitching sentences are displayed, chants that hypnotize and charm the suffering. And keep it alive, as life.

Threne, complaint, is a poet. Right where the sun has been silenced, the heart-rending hymn of darkness arises.

Are there any more beautiful melodies than those nocturnes where the voices of those whose daylight has been stolen, whose eyes have been gouged out, whose light has been confiscated palpitate? The atrocious and adorable cry of Samson the Agonist (v. 59).

> O dark dark dark, amid the blaze of noon
> Irrecoverably dark, total eclipse
> Without all hope of day!
> [...]

The sun to me is dark
And silent as the moon.

Ajax – Lo! Darkness, my sole light!
Death's shadows, so clear to me!
Take me! Take me
To live with you!

Homer was blind. It helped him scrutinize the darkness of the heart. Shakespeare was also blind, on Thursdays and Saturdays and when the wind was North-North-West, Joyce nourished his glaucoma, all poets are blind, so as better to see in the great depths of the soul, and if they are not blind then they are "Jews," as Tsvetaeva reminds us, they are separated otherwise, deprived of the common sunlight and condemned to invent another freedom.

## El que te dije

When I read

> I cannot, for my soul, remember how, when, or even precisely where, I first became acquainted with the lady Ligeia. Long years have since elapsed, and my memory is feeble through much suffering. Or, perhaps, I cannot now bring these points to mind, because, in truth, the character of my beloved, her rare learning, her singular yet placid cast of beauty, and the thrilling and enthralling eloquence of her low musical language, made their way into my heart by paces so steadily and stealthily progressive that they have been unnoticed and unknown. Yet I believe that I met her first and most frequently in some large, old, decaying city near the Rhine. Of her family — I have surely heard her speak. That it is of a remotely ancient date cannot be doubted. Ligeia! Ligeia! [...] And now, while I write, a recollection flashes upon me that I have never known the paternal name of her who was my friend and my betrothed, and who became the partner of my studies, and finally the wife of my bosom. Was it a playful charge on the part of my Ligeia? or was it a test of my strength of affection, that I should institute no inquiries upon this point? or was it rather a caprice of my own — a wildly romantic offering on the shrine of the most passionate devotion? I but indistinctly recall the fact itself — what wonder that I have utterly forgotten the circumstances which originated or attended it?

I know that Literature has begun. Indeed I already don't know who is writing. Who writes while trembling, who writes in the place of whom. Who in me writes to whom? Is it you? Or my father? Or my children? In Kafka is it the other Kafka, or Kafka Senior? In Rousseau the young mother-deprived Jean-Jacques vituperates. After Maman's death, Proust writes letters that his parents would have written, Derrida writes letters his parents would never have written, in Montaigne La Boétie sews the soul edge to edge.

When I read these texts, these textaments, whose referents slip away while advancing, it *seems* to me that I recognize them, it seems to me. As if I wanted and didn't want to read what I am reading. As if I didn't want and wanted to say what I am saying, and that is literature, the uncertain that does not lie, the scene that gives the undecidable its due. Who never knows, or only confusedly, who doesn't know who it is?

Who is speaking? "*Qui parle de vivre?*" "Who is talking about living?" asks Jacques Derrida's voice, rising to a high pitch to hold back an indignation.

*The Response responds*: 'The-one-I-told-you-about'. *El que te dije.*

– Who? You say. – You know who! It's You-know-who! – Ah! Him! How we forget! There he is! The ghost! To insert here. Or perchance elsewhere.

It occurs to me that in *The Book of Manuel* (you remember *Libro de Manuel* – the manual of how-to-make-everyday-life-become-literary, written by my old accomplice Julio Cortázar), El, "he" was called, or was hidden, through antonomasia or pseudonym, by the name of *El que te dije*, and he was always there, a crucial, main and *self-effacing* character. The witness *in person*.

This essential "Add-on" is all the more delicate in that by inscribing him one forgets him because by function, he-she is the doorman to the infernal paradise, the guardian of the Law of Literature, the threshold of space, the Moses who conducts the people of books to publication, the one who argues on the mountain with god and below with the herd, the one who receives the messages from above, transcribes them onto tablets, transmits them to the readers, expecting that the forever exasperated tribe will treat the magic tables like illegible rags.

I am speaking here (since the word "add-on"), as you will have noticed, of this being who knows not what he does, El, whom I call *the Purloined Author*, *L'Auteur Volé*, the stolen author, *volé* like the letter that he writes, in the folds of which he writes himself a letter that he reads, as Hamlet reads in the book of himself, desperately trying to understand why, how, not to be what he is, why it seems I always do the opposite of what I think I want to be obliged to do, how I set out in the direction opposite to my direction, how I take the side I disapprove of, why I am the one I am not, I is not me, I take the road to my own ruin, that's not what I wanted to say, that's not the one I wanted to kill, I am not in my place, it's you, madman, who move me and act something out that then I sign *I*.

To write, thus, to go off in search of the young me who sings and cries in me, to distance oneself from oneself, and thus voluptuousness and terror of sensing oneself, with the distance, becoming forest, desert, characters of another century, of another book, becoming a bedroom on the walls of which, under the ceiling, live subjects, people or creatures who are the actors of one's work.

Add here Proust's love letter to Musset, the marvelous mirror page where Marcel looks at himself and, surprise, surprise, it is Musset who reflects him on this day of January 1910. The last time, I was Senancour, another time we would have been Antony and Cleopatra, both of them, we would have been all the inseparable *tous-les-deux*, both of us and all the twos, all–two–of–us, the same ones who repel each other to attract each other, we could be Genet Stilitano. We all share something of Oedipusjocasta.

> One senses in his life, in his letters, as in a mineral ore where it is barely recognisable, a few lineaments of his oeuvre, which is the only raison d'être of his life, his loves, that only exist in so far as they are the materials of his oeuvre, that are oriented towards it and will survive only in it. In his letters, which are like the stage wings of his oeuvre, I can see the little purse from *Un Caprice*, and waiting in a corner the wig that will cross the stage at the end of a hook in *Fantasio*. He was in love and when that was the case he was delirious, and related his feverish state to God.

We play amongst ruins and in cemeteries. It smells of God. What are you doing here, what have you done, who will you have been? *Alas, poor Oedipus*, when one writes, without knowing it, one is an *écriminel*, a writer-criminal, but what does *Oedipus* mean? Did you mean to say *Orpheus*? I don't know. We say Oedipus to say Ajax to not say Othello to say Julien, I mean Julien l'Hospitalier, but there is the other Julien as well, Julien Sorel, to say Marcel alias Swann, to say the one, he or she, who writes the letter he steals from himself, that steals from him, that flies, that blinds him, that he tries desperately to recover, it's a question of life or death. There was an assassination. The body is here. Death is here. The dead woman is here. Morella. Someone has (been) killed. Who? Who killed whom? Who killed me? Who put the pen in my hand? Who struck me, who blinded me? Who was killed in my night?

One writes while advancing, under a rain of questions with poisoned tips, needled by the first and last questions that the human being hurls into the empty space of destiny. I hear them resonate in my mother's last bedroom, when she again opens her eyes, another day split open in the wood of the 103rd year and croaks: – Who am I? – Where am I?

– Hélène! *Was ist los?* What are they doing to me What are you doing to me? My child!

– Henri! What have you done to me? cries Madame van Blarenberghe.

It is our Great Astonishment, the ghastly secret of life. How life gives us death. Executes us. How it brings us to give death.

The purloined author comes staggering out of this horrified astonishment, singing the praises of mystery and fright. There is only one crime, everyone comes to confess it differently. But from Sophocles to Poe from whom Baudelaire receives the letter that Blanchot countersigns, it is the same tragedy and the same distraction, because the terrible subject always surpasses its sayer.

I did what I could not do, it wasn't me, it was Notme who did it.

Who wrote this? Stendhal? Perchance Derrida? Or perchance Rousseau? If it wasn't Shem Joyce, it was Shaunjoyce. My shemblable, my freer, my fear, my worse, my more than me.

Was it you, J.D., who said that literature begins where we no longer know who is writing, or was it Virginia Woolf? Was it the virgin or the wolf, is it the lion or the python, was it Montaigne or La Boétie, or was it me or Eve my mother? For whom the bell tolls.

## Envoi

AJAX – The executioner is set where it can cut
Most cleanly, if there is time for such thoughts.
The gift of Hector, whom I loathed so much,
Whose sight I hated most of all my enemies,
Is planted in this hostile Trojan soil,
The blade just sharpened on a grinding stone.
I have embedded it with care so that it may
Oblige me kindly with an instant death.
[…]
Helios, when you spy my native land,
Check your reins, all laden with gold,
And tell my aged father and poor mother
Who raised me of my disastrous downfall.
Unhappy woman, when she hears the news
She will send a great cry throughout the city.
[…]
Death, Death, come gaze upon me now –
Wait, I will speak to you later below.
But you, light of this radiant day,
And Helios, in your chariot, I salute you
One last time and never again!
[…]
And glorious Athens, kindred race to mine,
You springs and rivers, and you plains of Troy,
You who have nursed me, I bid you farewell!
These are the last words Ajax has to say.
The rest I'll tell in Hades to the dead.

*(Ajax falls on his sword. Enter Hamlet)*

HAMLET – I am dead, Horatio. […]
You that look pale and tremble at this chance,
That are but mutes or audience to this act,
Had I but time – as this fell sergeant Death
Is strict in his arrest – O, I could tell you –
But let it be. Horatio, I am dead,
Thou liv'st. Report me and my cause aright
To the unsatisfied.

O God, Horatio, what a wounded name,
Things standing thus unknown, shall live behind me!
[...]
Absent thee from felicity a while,
And in this harsh world draw thy breath in pain
To tell my story.
[...]
O, I die, Horatio!
[...]
I cannot live to hear the news from England,
But I do prophesy th'election lights
On Fortinbras. He has my dying voice.
So tell him, with th'occurrents, more and less,
Which have solicited. The rest is silence.

Hamlet dies. Ajax dies. Likewise.
*(Enter Celan. Or Akhmatova. Or Vesaas. A poet to dig the text.)*

We work and work,
and that brings on more work.
Where have I not walked? Where?
No place where I have searched
has revealed to me where that man is.

*(Tecmessa's voice)*
Here is Ajax, now dead.
Such is his destiny. We may cry: Aiai!
Silence!
*(Cries)*

# INDEX